SANTA CRUZ
The Early Years

SANTA CRUZ
The Early Years

The collected historical
writings of

Leon Rowland

— including —

OLD SANTA CRUZ MISSION
VILLA DE BRANCIFORTE
THE STORY OF OLD SOQUEL
THE ANNALS OF SANTA CRUZ
LOS FUNDADORES

PAPER VISION PRESS
Santa Cruz, California
1980

LOS FUNDADORES was originally published by
the Academy of California Church History and is
reprinted with their permission.

Cover and text design by Michael Banta
Leon Rowland's portrait courtesy Alan Wheatley Rowland

Published by

PAPER VISION PRESS
1111 Pacific Avenue
Santa Cruz, California

Printed in the United States of America

◄≣►

Copyright © 1980 by PAPER VISION PRESS

Library of Congress Card Catalog Number: 80-81418
ISBN: 0-934136-04-1

To Jeannette

Leon Rowland

✒️ DEDICATION

I T IS SAID THAT ALLEN NEVINS was motivated by a feeling
of responsibility to record history before the event, per-
sonage or phenomenon passed from the scene and memory
and be forever lost.

It was, I believe, in this same spirit that my father did his
research and writing. His compulsion to record accurately genealogies and history had him both translating early-California
mission and civil records and interviewing surviving descendants of early pioneers.

His familiarity with Spanish was largely self-taught and
acquired so that he might work directly from records in that
language. In addition to the acknowledgments listed in the
foreward to *Los Fundadores*, research for that book took him to
Hermosillo and several other sources in the state of Sonora,
Mexico.

Initially, much of his work was researched for and written in
the "Circuit Rider," his weekly column in the Santa Cruz
Evening News and later, when he was also city editor for that
newspaper, the *Sentinel*. The "Circuit Rider" was a happy marriage of his wanting to record local history and do so in a
palatable journalistic way.

The impetus to republish these small works in one volume
came from my friend Patricia Jones and from Al Schadel of the
Santa Cruz County Historical Museum, both of whom are
stewards to the perpetuation of accurate Santa Cruz history.

— Alan Wheatley Rowland

◄■► CONTENTS

◄╡╞► INTRODUCTION

I FIRST CAME ACROSS Leon Rowland's five slim books ten years ago while looking for secondary material on the history of Santa Cruz County. The books occupied less than three inches of my bookshelf, and several of them had rust spots where their bindings had been stapled. The absence of footnotes and bibliographies combined with the fact that all but one had been privately published led me to conclude that the books were vanity publications by a local antiquarian. I set them aside and continued my search for reliable source books on the history of Santa Cruz.

When Margaret Koch's *Santa Cruz County: Parade of the Past* was first published in 1973, I was delighted to have a history of the County with footnotes. But, when following Margaret's citations back into her bibliography, I found that often her source was one of those five skinny books by Leon Rowland which I had put in an unfrequented corner of my bookshelf. My skepticism spread and I dutifully continued my own research, reading nineteenth-century Santa Cruz County newspapers and searching through County records. The staples in the Rowland books rusted further.

I refused to look at Rowland's *The Story of Old Soquel* when Carolyn Swift and I were working on *From Soquel Landing to Capitola-by-the-Sea* for fear that I would be influenced by questionable material. After our book was completed, however, I sneaked a peak at Rowland's Soquel book — my heart sank. Much of the factual material and many of the dates and names had a familiar ring, and I matched newspaper references with Leon time and again. He had been through all the archival material too, but had failed to leave a map of his footprints in the form of footnotes.

I reread each of the five volumes with increasing respect, but my training in historiography was difficult to overcome. Obviously, Leon Rowland had done a great deal of research, but there was much information in his books that was beyond the archives and the newspapers. Where did he get his material, I pondered.

Then, in the fall of 1979, a pile of musty cardboard boxes at the Special Collections Library at the University of California, Santa Cruz were made available to the public. Leon Rowland's wife Jeannette had willed all of Leon's files and scrapbooks about Santa Cruz to the University Library, and as my hands ran through the cross-indexed card files that Leon had kept, much of my skepticism fell away. Leon had used not only the local newspapers but also court records, deeds and Spanish- and Mexican-period documents. The files were the base of the iceberg; Leon Rowland had put forth for public scrutiny only the facts about which he was certain. If he had any doubts, the information stayed in his files with notations about the conflicting reports. What was finally published was the end result of an elaborate distilling process — no analysis, no speculation, just the straight, pure truth as Leon saw it.

Who was this compulsive researcher who devised the masterful filing system and wrote sentences as spare as telegrams? Born in Sac City, Iowa, in 1884, Leon was by training and profession a newspaperman. After jobs with several newspapers in the Pacific Northwest and a few years with the Associated Press in San Francisco, Leon and Jeannette moved to Santa Cruz in 1929 where he worked as a newspaperman until his death in 1952. For the first decade he worked with the Santa Cruz *Evening News* (see pg. 205), going to the *Santa Cruz Sentinel* when it absorbed the *Evening News* in 1941. He was city editor at the *Sentinel* when he died at age sixty-seven. His collected historical writings are best understood against this background, for though historical and genealogical research occupied his spare time, his professional training influenced everything he wrote.

Leon Rowland's writing style is terse — staccato. The abbreviated line of thought sometimes broadens into descriptive narrative, but more often the dates, names and places line up like fence posts. Some of those who knew him say that Leon had a life-long desire to write novels, to expand his writing style, but was unable to do so. What he finally published was a set of books filled with vignettes—little pieces carefully measured and drawn but presented without interpretation and analysis. The ingredients for richer characterizations and broad analysis are in his files, but apparently his newspaper training would not permit him to venture beyond the Who, What, When and Where. Nor did he inject his personal opinion into his writing. There are few clues in his books about his own feelings, and he rarely took sides in the controversies he described. Leon Rowland always tried to be objective and down-the-middle. His primary purpose was to write as best he could the facts of Santa Cruz's early development.

This objectivity made Leon Rowland one of the first local historicans to write about Santa Cruz County's past without an ulterior motive. All the histories of the County published before 1940 had purposes beyond the historical, from the sale of real estate to the fabrication of reputations. The first accounts of the area were published in the 1860's and consisted mainly of personal accounts of early pioneers. Thomas Farnham's journals, for example, promoted the Yankee settlers of the 1840's and belittled their Spanish-speaking precursors. While Issac Graham was eulogized by Farnham, the Mexicans were portrayed as shiftless and untrustworthy.

In 1879 and 1892 two subscription histories were published about Santa Cruz County, the first by the Wallace W. Elliot Company *(History of Santa Cruz County, California),* and the second compiled by Edward S. Harrison *(History of Santa Cruz County).* The biographies included in both books most often reflected the number of pre-publication subscriptions bought by the subjects rather than their actual accomplishments. Since the Spanish-speaking and their descendents did not generally subscribe to these publications, they were mentioned infrequently. In the later 1890's, history-by-subscription gave way to history-to-sell-real-estate when the Southern California land boom caught hold in Santa Cruz County, resulting in the publication of Phil Francis' *Beautiful Santa Cruz County* in 1896.

After World War II, when Santa Cruz readers were a generation removed from the pioneers, local newspapers began to
print historical articles about the area's settlement. Curiosity
about local origins, place names, community histories and pioneer biographies was satisfied by F. W. Atkinson in Watsonville
and Ernest Otto, Preston Sawyer and Rowland in Santa Cruz.
By 1932 this curiousity grew into a modest boom in interest
about the Spanish period, a boom represented in Santa Cruz by
the erection of the scaled-down Mission Santa Cruz replica and
the publication of *Story of the Mission Santa Cruz* by Henry
Albert Van Coenen Torchiana a year later.

Not content with the tantalizing but sparse references to
Santa Cruz in the journals of the Spanish explorers which were
being translated by historian Herbert Bolton, Leon taught himself to read Spanish, and his search for Spanish-language sources
became an obsession. He spent his vacations roaming through
archives in Mexico, Santa Barbara, Monterey and Berkeley
seeking documents pertaining to the star-crossed Mission Santa
Cruz and neighboring Villa de Branciforte. His personal files
are replete with not only Spanish-language documents but also
lengthy genealogies of the early Spanish and Mexican pioneers.
Not surprisingly, the Spanish and Mexican periods are the most
fully developed in both Leon Rowland's files and his published
works.

Leon broke a century-old pattern of neglect when he wrote
extensively and respectfully about the Spanish-speaking pioneers in Santa Cruz County. He continued another tradition,
however, when he excluded the story of the poor relations that
existed between Yankee pioneers and Spanish-speaking residents of the County. The racism and animosity that accompanied
the ethnic diversity of Santa Cruz were unpleasant facts not to
be mentioned. Leon does mention the 1877 double lynching in
Santa Cruz (see pg. 189), but does not place it in the tradition of
Mexican-Yankee conflict where it belongs. He reports the
lynching in his facts-only style (failing to note that both men
were Spanish-speaking) and closes the paragraph as if in a hurry
to be done with the unfortunate event. That Santa Cruz mob
action was a signal event in the history of Mexican-Yankee

relations, however, as it marked the end of twenty-five years of mob violence against the Spanish-speaking in California; to see it in isolation is to miss its significance for both Santa Cruz and California.

At times Leon's tendency to slide over unpleasantness intruded into his genealogical work. Still in his card file is the fascinating account of Soledad Castro and her husband Rafael battling in and out of court until their eventual divorce in 1872. That story helps explain Rafael's taciturn character as well as his willingness to sell most of his property to Claus Spreckels in 1872. Although the entire divorce account was in his notes, Leon chose not to speak ill of the pioneer California family of Aptos. Certainly this reluctance to speak directly of divorce is as much a reflection of the 1940's as it is of Leon Rowland.

And, as did most local historians writing in the 1940's (Ernest Otto is a delightful exception), Leon Rowland paid scant attention to the stories of pioneer communities whose members came from Asia. The Chinese, Japanese and Filipinos are not mentioned in Leon's work, and few of his notes deal with them. For example, in his treatment of the 1894 Santa Cruz fire (see pg. 186) he failed to mention that Chinatown was destroyed along with the county court house, the Leonard building and the People's Bank. Perhaps had his research continued, he might have come to spend more time on the Asian immigrants, but it is clear that he was just getting into the 1890's period when he died in 1952.

Leon Rowland's work did not stop completely with his death. Leon's wife, Jeannette, kept the spirit of his work alive with her leadership in the Santa Cruz Historical Society and her painstaking index of Leon's bulging scrapbooks of newspaper clippings. Now and then her handwriting appears at the bottom of one of Leon's file cards, revealing her efforts to keep them up to date by noting the demise of historic buildings and people. To Jeannette must go credit both for the forebearance it must have taken to live with a compulsive researcher like Leon as well as for her contribution in making his files useful and available to local historians to follow. (Rowland's research materials not relating to Santa Cruz are at the Bancroft Library).

And, follow they will, for the Santa Cruz County of 1940 (population 45,000), which could not support the commercial publication of Leon Rowland's work, now has a population nearing 200,000 in 1980. Both natives and newcomers once again express a healthy curiosity about local history. Cabrillo College offers courses in local history and the University of California at Santa Cruz maintains a regional history project.

This collection of Leon Rowland's five books should not be seen as a comprehensive analytical history of Santa Cruz County — that history still needs to be written. Rather, it is a valuable research tool for both those fascinated by the area's history and those who research, analyze, and write local and regional history. We all should give Leon Rowland's fence posts a good shake before building on them. However, I believe that when the dust settles we will find Leon's work as sound as two decades of patience and devotion to the County's history could make them.

Recently, a student working on the Spanish-language document inventory at the University came to me to share his excitement in finding Marcelino Bravo living in Soquel thirty years before Martina Castro received the Soquel grant. Leon Rowland wrote of Marcelino in his *Story of Old Soquel* forty years ago! With an inward smile I informed the student that he might supplement his research by reading Leon Rowland's works. An excellent place to begin, I said. Good advice for us all.

Sandy Lydon
Department of History
Cabrillo College

Leon Rowland's writings have been arranged chronologically by subject rather than publication date. *The Story of Old Soquel* was printed in 1940 at the Soquel Print Shop. It was followed in 1941 by *Old Santa Cruz Mission* and *Villa de Branciforte.* *Annals of Santa Cruz* was printed in 1947 by Branson Publishing Company, 342 Pacific. It also carries the imprint of the Seven Seas Book Shop in the Palomar Arcade. All were privately published. *Los Fundadores* was published in 1951 by the *Academy of California Church History,* which has graciously permitted its reprinting.

I have edited the books with a light hand. Obvious typographical errors have been corrected, and I have attempted to standardize the punctuation. With the exception of the index to *Los Fundadores,* the books originally appeared without Spanish accents, and they have not been added to this edition.

Rowland refers frequently to contemporary buildings in order to specify historic sites. Many of his landmarks have since disappeared. In most cases, a check of John Chase's *Sidewalk Companion to Santa Cruz Architecture* or Sandy Lydon and Carolyn Swift's *Soquel Landing to Capitola-by-the-Sea* will locate them. For sites not covered in these books, I have provided brief notes in the appendix. In addition, a few problems in the text have been noted. For ease in research, the index for *Los Fundadores* has been kept separate from the general index, which is based on the original for the *Annals* with additional entries for the early books.

I would like to thank the following people for their kind assistance in preparation of this book: Alan Wheatley Rowland, Pat Jones, Sandy Lydon, Carolyn Swift, Al Schadel of the Santa Cruz County Historical Museum, Sherry Davis, Michael Banta, Phyllis Grossman, Peter Hanff, Ceedola Parrish Duff and Rita Bottoms, Paul Stubbs and Carol Champion at the UCSC Special Collections Library.

— Michael S. Gant

Old Santa Cruz Mission

1941

Mission Santa Cruz

‹∃E›

MISSION ESTABLISHMENT
WAS LARGE ONE

THE ADOBE BUILDINGS of the Santa Cruz mission, as it existed in the first half of the last century, comprised much more than the chapel which is usually thought of as "the mission."

The structures, if placed end-to-end, would have measured almost 900 feet.

They were built on three sides of a nearly rectangular plaza. Unlike the missions in parts of California where the Indians were more warlike, Santa Cruz had no wall enclosing its plaza. Roads entered it from three sides and the longest row of buildings stretched away at right angles to one side of the plaza to a distance of 300 feet. Two of these adobes, on what is now School street, are still standing, 130 feet long and 23 feet wide.

A map of Santa Cruz's first real estate subdivision, filed by Elihu Anthony with the county supervisors in 1854, shows in outline the buildings of the mission establishment.

On this map the mission church is outlined $1\frac{3}{8}$ inches long and a little less than $\frac{1}{2}$ inch wide. From other records it is known that this chapel was $112\frac{1}{2}$ feet long and 29 feet wide. Establishing from this a scale of approximately 1 inch to 70 feet, the dimension of the other buildings can be worked out.

Back of the chapel and adjoining it end-to-end was another structure about three-fourths its width, which was the blacksmith shop and housed similar industries.

At right angles to the church and joining it on the west was a wing 156 feet long, which housed the priests' quarters and offices. It had an open passageway, along the front, with wooden posts supporting a tiled roof.

Another row of adjoining adobes about 185 feet long faced the west side of the plaza, on a line with what is now Sylvar street.

Across the plaza and down what is now School street was a ditch of flowing water, diverted from one of the "ojos de agua" on the hills to the west, which was the domestic water supply and irrigation source.

Across this ditch from the two adobes still standing, one of which has a low second-story room and was the home of the corporal of the escolta, were two buildings which were probably the quarters for the "neofites," the converted Indians, or at least for the unmarried women and girls, who were securely locked in each night.

THE FIRST CORPORAL

Luis Peralta, first corporal of the Santa Cruz mission guard, who held that post nearly a year, obtained in 1820 grant to San Antonio Rancho, which included the sites of the present cities of Oakland and Alameda.

➤➤

PALOU LIKED SITE

THE SITE near the mouth of the San Lorenzo river was selected in 1774 for a mission by Fr. Francisco Palou, chaplain of an expedition with Governor Rivera, who entered in his diary:

"Early in the morning before daylight I said mass, which was attended by every one as it was the third Sunday in Advent." (The morning was December 9, as the party had left the Golden Gate on December 4 and reached Monterey on December 11.)

⊣⊨⊦

MISSION DATES

1769   The Portola party gave the name Santa Cruz to a confluent of the San Lorenzo river.

1773   Viceroy Bucarelli in Mexico City ordered more missions in Alta California.

1774   Fr. Palou, in a party headed by Governor Rivera, picked the mission location.

1787   Viceroy Count Revilla Gigedo in Mexico ordered a mission established at "the place called Santa Cruz."

1791   On August 28 Fr. Lasuen planted a cross to mark the site.

1791   On September 25 Alferez Sal brought two priests, members of a guard and Indian servants, with supplies, to start work.

1793   Cornerstone laid for rock and adobe chapel.

1794   Chapel completed.

1820   Mission establishment at its height in number of converts, herds and crops.

1834   Mission secularized.

1840   Tower shaken down by quake.

1844   Padre Antonio Real, last Franciscan, withdrawn.

1853   Archbishop Alemany restored Santa Cruz as mission church.

1857   Another quake crumbled front walls.

1886   Last of old adobe chapel razed.

"At half past seven we set out from camp, approaching the seacoast by the bank of a lagoon, where, on the sand of the beach, we crossed the little stream, which enters the sea with a good flow of water.

"We continued in sight of the beach, over a wide plain which skirts the range of hills, all good arable land with fine pasture.

"In half an hour we crossed a little stream of more than two bueys of water which flows with the slope of the land. From it it would be easy to irrigate the plain, more than a half a league wide, over which we passed, as well as another which reaches from the hills to the cliff at the beach. When the first expedition (the Portola party of 1769) came this stream was called the Arroyo of Santa Cruz.

"We crossed this and, traveling a short distance, came to the San Lorenzo river, which is quite large and has a wide bed, the water reaching to the stirrups. The banks are well covered with cottonwoods, willows, alders, little poplars and other trees, and near the ford, close to the hills it has much timber and groves of redwoods.

"This site is fitted not merely for a town but for a city. Nothing is lacking to it. It has good land, water, pasture, firewood and timber, all at hand and in abundance. It could be established a quarter of a league from the beach with all these advantages."

The stream "called Santa Cruz" is the Laurel street brook of present days. The ford of the San Lorenzo was either the Water street or Cooper street ford, both of which were used until after American occupation of California.

The expedition was one primarily to find new mission sites. It started from Monterey, crossed the Salinas river and went on over the hills into the Santa Clara valley, which it descended, past where San Jose is today, and went on to the Golden Gate.

The slowness of communication of those days is shown by the fact that it was January 14, 1775, when Fr. Palou found opportunity to forward a report of the trip to Viceroy Bucarelli and May 24 when Bucarelli wrote a letter acknowledging its receipt and adding that he was directing Governor Rivera not to delay the erection of new missions.

Rivera was busy with administrative affairs, and Bucarelli had been succeeded as viceroy by Antonio Flores, and the latter by Don Juan Vicente de Guemes Pacheco de Padilla, Conde de Revilla Gigedo, before the matter was again taken up, in 1787.

◄≡►

VICEROY ORDERED MISSION

THE FOUNDING of Santa Cruz mission was ordered by Don Juan Vicente de Guemes Pacheco de Padilla, Conde de Revilla Gigedo, viceroy of Mexico, on August 30, 1787.

The order was issued at the instigation of Fr. Matias de Noriega, temporary head of the college of Fernando, the Franciscan establishment in Mexico City.

The order by the viceroy, translated, was:

"Agreeing to the proposition which your reverence makes in your report of last September I have resolved that two missions should be established in Upper California, one in the valley called Soledad, close to the Rio de Monterey (Salinas river) between the mission of San Antonio and that of San Carlos; and the other between the mission of San Carlos and that of Santa Clara, about twenty-five leagues from the former, at the place called Santa Cruz.

"That this decision, to be so greatly beneficial to the gentiles, may be carried out as quickly as possible, I beg and charge your reverence to name four religious who shall found and serve these missions."

The news of this order reached Monterey on August 2, 1790, on the same schooner from San Blas which brought the four priests, Antonio Danti, Jose de Miguel, Mariano Rubi and Estevan Tapis.

⟿

STONE AND ADOBE CHAPEL

THE CHAPEL of Santa Cruz mission, which was completed after fourteen months work and dedicated on May 10, 1794, two years and seven months after the mission was established, was a building of the native limestone rock and adobe.

It was $112\frac{1}{2}$ feet long, 29 feet wide and $25\frac{1}{2}$ feet to the eaves, with walls nearly 5 feet thick.

When the structure was first erected, to replace the temporary church of split redwood palings, its roof was described by the padres as "vaulted and made of tule"; it was later covered with tile made by the Indians, who shaped them by laying them over their leg, from the thigh to the knee.

The whole front of the chapel was of limestone and the side walls were of rock six feet up, with adobe above.

COWHIDE BOUND RECORDS

Ink of the entries in the books of baptisms, matrimonies and deaths at Santa Cruz mission is as legible today as when Frs. Lopez and Salazar first wrote them in 1791.

The books, of heavy rag-content paper, were brought from Spain, unbound, and at the mission given a covering of tanned cowhide, with knotted thongs to hold them closed. Ink came in hard tablets which were pulverized and dissolved. Pens were made on the spot from quills, and fine sand was their equivalent of a blotter.

The records, carefully preserved by the parish priests of Holy Cross church, are one of few complete sets of mission documents in California.

The present Holy Cross mission is a reproduction of the limestone and adobe chapel of old Santa Cruz mission. It has the architectural lines and proportions of the original, but is about half its size. It was erected in 1932 with funds given to the church by Mrs. Gladys Sullivan Doyle. Its site, at School and Emmett streets, near that of the original chapel, was the location of the first court house of Santa Cruz county, a story-and-a-half wooden residence and saddlery for which Thomas Fallon in 1852 received $5000.

◄╢►

THE PORTOLA PARTY
AND EL CAMINO REAL

THE PRESENT HIGHWAY from Watsonville to Santa Cruz and up the coast to New Year Point follows approximately the Portola trail of 1769 and the Camino Real of mission days.

The Portola party, worried and sick, with food almost exhausted after the three months march from San Diego, had, when it reached the Pajaro river on the evening of Sunday, October 8, failed to recognize an arroyo almost dry at that time of the year as Vizcaino's Carmelo river of 1602.

A day of rest there was followed by a day's march "across level land" to the Corralitos region, where a four-day camp was ordered while Sergeant Jose Francisco Ortega with eight men, each taking three mules as remounts, scouted ahead.

The excellence of the route-finding ability of Sergeant Ortega is evidenced in the diaries of Michael Costanso, the military engineer; Fr. Crespi, the chaplain; and of Don Gaspar de Portola himself.

Ortega and his scouts were the first white men to see the San Lorenzo river. Their reconnaissance took them up the coast well past Laguna creek before they turned back to rejoin Portola at Corralitos after an absence of four days.

A three days march took the main party to the river which Portola named after St. Lawrence, paralleling the coast a league inland, and making camps at Valencia valley and Soquel. Another three days saw Portola and his men up the coast at what is now Waddell creek, which they named Canada del Salud because a day's rest there relieved so many of the sick of their pains.

In mission days the military expeditions and padres making their way from Monterey to Santa Cruz followed the same route, which was again found the best when American road building began in the fifties.

To ease the grade for the caretas, the Camino Real at Aptos and Soquel canyons turned south from the present highway and angled back up the other side of the little valley to regain the course.

The padres occasionally used the route up the coast to San Francisco and at one time planned a mission at what is now Pescadero, but their travels were afoot with pack mules and there was no need for road making.

BOUCHARD THE PIRATE

When Hypolito Bouchard, the Buenos Aires privateer, with his two vessels and their crews of 360 men appeared off Monterey on November 20, 1818, Fr. Olbes, obeying Governor Sola's orders, departed for Santa Clara, turning the mission over to Comisionado Joaquin Buelna of Villa de Branciforte, across the river.

Olbes' return, when he found the pirates had not landed on the north shore of Monterey bay, was followed by accusations of theft by the Brancifortians, including charges that one or two casks of aguardiente had been destroyed. Fr. Olbes was so angered that he wrote to Sola that he would favor abandoning the mission rather than go back to submit longer to the inhuman outrages on the part of the people of Branciforte.

◄═══►

INDIAN RANCHERIAS

PORTOLA'S PARTY brought into California the designation "rancheria" for a group or community of Indians. They were not in any sense tribes, as the number in Santa Cruz county shows; nevertheless, so low was the civilization of California's aborigines that it was said those of a rancheria could hardly understand the speech of those in another only a score of miles away.

When the Franciscan missionaries of Santa Cruz began baptising and burying the Indians, they carefully recorded the name of their rancherias, at the same time bestowing the name of a saint upon the community. The Indian name, as recorded, was of course a phonetic spelling in Spanish.

Soquel, Aptos and Zayante were the only rancherias in Santa Cruz county whose Indian names have survived. Soquel rancheria was of sufficient importance or size that the baptism of its chief as "Balthazar" was recorded.

Rancheria names recorded by the padres were:

Achila (Achil)	Linguamenit
Achistaca	Locobo
Alutca	Luchasme
Asam	Mallin
Aptos (Abtos, Avtos)	Mutchas
Ausentaca	Notuals
Cajastaca	Osocalis
Cajastac (Cajasta, –aca)	Partascsi
Chaloctaca	Pitac (Pitaca)
Chanech	Sachuen
Chichutac	Sagiianacu
Chiputac	Sayanta
Chitactac	Sipieyesi
Chruistaca	Somentac
Chuchumis (Chumistaca)	Soquel
Conoch	Suchesum
Coochi (Coot)	Sumus
Copcha	Tejey
Cotoni	Tomoi (Tomoy)
Cucurum	Vypu
Huachi	Yamayan
Huocom (Huocon)	Yasmil
Hupnis	Yeurata

That the rancheria names were used by the Spanish as place names is shown by documents in the old Branciforte archives. In one, dated in 1811, Lieutenant Jose Maria Estudillo, comandante at the Presidio at Monterey, rebukes Comisionado Jose Antonio Rodriguez of Branciforte:

"That which you should have done immediately it was reported to you that the Russian Indians who left here had stolen the cayuco during the night was to have sent two or three invalidos or militiamen who could most easily have followed their trail and compelled their return; now to capture the malefactors will be most difficult.

"It is necessary that with the greatest haste and caution you make inquiry among the Indians of Soquel, who gave the information to the holy padres, and do the same among the Indians who were with the cayuco. Inform me promptly."

The "Rusos Indios" were Aleutians who had come with the Russians from Sitka. Their mention is of interest, for only two years before had Alexander Kuskoff made his voyage of exploration south from Alaska to Bodega bay, and only in 1811 did he make his second trip.

For twenty years and more the Californians resisted the efforts of the Aleutians to hunt otter along this coast. In 1817 Estudillo won from Governor Sola recommendation for promotion to a captaincy for having commanded a party of thirteen which prevented seven Russian fishing canoes from landing on Monterey bay, killing one of the occupants and wounding several.

⊲⊟⊳

FOUNDED BY MILITARY

SANTA CRUZ MISSION, twelfth in Alta California, was, like the others, actually established by the military authorities under orders from viceroy and governor and turned over to the missionary priests.

After Padre Fermin Lasuen, accompanied by Corporal Luis Peralta and five soldiers, marked the location with a cross on August 28, 1791, Alferez Hermenegildo Sal, commander at San Francisco presidio, sent a mule train of supplies and equipment on September 17 and five days later started out himself, guided by Corporal Peralta.

At Santa Clara they picked up Padres Baldomero Lopez and Alonzo Isidro Salazar and more supplies and livestock, with which they arrived at the mission site on September 24.

The next morning mass and the Te Deum by the priests and firing of guns by the soldiers constituted the formal ceremony.

The personnel of the mission establishment in its first months is best given by the list of godfathers for the Indians, whom the priests immediately began baptising. The first baptism was of an Indian girl, on October 9.

Godfathers named in the first month were:

Alferez Sal, Cabo Peralta and Soldados de Cuera Pablo Azebes, Jose Vicente Aguila, Francisco Tapia, Ramon Linares, Bartholomo Pacheco, Joaquin Bernal, Ignacio Alviso.

Sirvientes Maximo Estrada, Francisco Nisifort, Francisco Gonzales, Anastasio de la Cruz, Salvador Rubio, Manuel Villanueva and Pablo Vejar.

Twenty-five fanegas of wheat, given by Santa Clara mission, were planted on the flat land to the north still known as the Potrero.

The first building was a temporary chapel of palisades, slabs of split redwood thrust upright in the ground. It was on a location lower than that eventually picked; perhaps the same where tile were being made when it was overflowed, a few years later.

As each Indian was baptised careful entry was made of his rancheria, which brought into the mission books the names of Soquel (or Osocales), Aptos and Zayante, as well as of a score of other rancherias whose names are no longer extant.

On February 27, 1793, the cornerstone for a permanent chapel was laid. It was completed on May 10, 1794, an adobe and stone building 112 feet long.

The autumn of 1794 saw a harvest of 1200 fanegas of wheat, 600 of corn, 60 of beans and some lentils. By the end of 1795 priests' offices, homes for the escolta and store rooms had been erected.

By 1800 a total of 949 persons had been baptised, almost all of them Indians; 272 couples had been married and 477 buried. There were more than 4000 head of livestock, large and small, and crops were good.

An 1880's view of the mission plaza from Highland looking southeast. The Holy Cross church of 1858 is to the left, the old juzgado is in the center. Behind it to the right is the Sisters of Charity school building.

UCSC SPECIAL COLLECTIONS

Father Lasuen paid an official visit in 1793. Lopez was succeeded by Padre Manuel Fernandez in 1795. Padre Jose de la Luz Espi relieved Salazar in 1796, staying until Padre Francisco Gonzales came the next May. Padre Domingo Carranza came in 1798 to replace Fernandez, who, discouraged and resentful, reported to his superiors that the mission was in a bad way; the neophytes were deserting and high water washing out the fields.

In 1805 Padre Andres Quintana took Gonzales' place, to serve until he was murdered by Indians in 1812.

In the first decades of the nineteenth century Padres Carranza and Quintana were given an assistant, Jose Antonio Uria, and building was pushed. Houses were erected for the Indian women and girls. A better building for the soldiers of the escolta and their families was constructed.

Rains hurt the crops and Indian scares on the Pajaro brought Sergeant Pedro Amador and a few soldiers from San Francisco, but the mission prospered. By 1820 its herds were grazing as far north as Punto Ano Nuevo and as far south as Corralitos.

With the secularization of the mission in 1834 Governor
Jose Figueroa made a short-lived effort to constitute the mission
establishment and its converted Indians into Villa Figueroa.

Administration of Santa Cruz was given over to the authorities of Villa Branciforte across the river and the two communities were merged until American days.

FIRST BAZAAR

Undoubtedly the first annual bazaar of Holy Cross parish
was in the summer of 1838 when Fr. Antonio Real wrote to
Juez de Paz Joaquin Buelna across the river that the church
roof needed some new tiles and its tower needed timber re-
inforcing. F. Real urged donations of articles to be sold, himself
offering to give two fat steers.

⇒⊨·

PARCELLING OUT WATER

THE DITCH which the padres who came in 1791 had dug
across the plaza, to bring water from one of the springs
on the higher land to the west, not only furnished water
for domestic purposes but for irrigation.

On May 11, 1844, Alcade Manuel Rodriguez issued regu-
lations:

"So that all may benefit by the usage of water, I have judged
it wise to observe the following:

"On Monday, in the morning, there may take the water for
irrigating, from 6 in the morning until 12 of the day, Don
Nicolas Dodero, and after that until 6 in the evening, Don
Rafael Castro.

"On Tuesday, in the morning, Don Juan Gonzales, and for
the afternoon, Donna Gracia Rodriguez.

"On Wednesday, in the morning, Don Antonio Rodriguez,
and in the afternoon, Don Juan Perez.

"On Thursday, in the morning, Don Guillermo Vocle, and in the afternoon, Don Roman Rodriguez.

"On Friday, all day, the gardener of the mission garden may take the water.

"Those individuals of whom the preceding articles speak shall under no pretext take the water more hours than those designated, and those contravening this order shall be fined that which the first or second alcade may hold it proper to impose."

The same stream was the supply for Santa Cruz's first water system, a reservoir at the end of School street and hollowed wooden logs as pipe line to "the flat," which was installed in 1859 by F. A. Hihn and Elihu Anthony.

THE OLD JUZGADO

The largest building of the mission stood at what is now School and Emmett street. It was granted by Governor Juan Alvarado in 1839 to Job Francis Dye, who sold it in 1848 to William Blackburn. The latter operated in it the Eagle Hotel. The building in mission days served as hospice. After 1834 it was the juzgado, the city hall and jail, of combined Santa Cruz ex-mission and Villa de Branciforte. In it in 1862 the sisters of charity founded Holy Cross School. The building was torn down about 1880.

⟨✦⟩

QUAKES DESTROYED MISSION

EARTHQUAKES destroyed the limestone and adobe chapel of Santa Cruz mission, which stood for sixty-three years on approximately the site of the present Holy Cross church.

Earlier quakes may have weakened it but the first recorded destruction was in 1840, when the tower at one front corner fell.

The next quake came in 1857. On the morning of January 9, in the midst of a cold snap which records state formed ice half an inch thick, two shocks occurred which were felt from the northern Sacramento valley to San Diego. Eleven days later was another, less severe.

Thirty-eight days after the shock of January 9 the south-western corner of the old edifice fell, at 3 o'clock in the morning, with a crash which wakened residents about the plaza.

Father Benito Capdevilla launched plans for another building and on July 5 Bishop Thaddeus Amat came over from Monterey to lay the cornerstone, preaching a sermon first in halting English and then one in Spanish.

A year later, on July 4, 1858, he returned to dedicate the frame structure, accompanied by Fr. J. B. Comelies of Monterey and Fr. F. Mora of San Juan Bautista.

The building was 110 feet long, 36 feet wide and 27 feet to the eaves. Waters and Beck, Santa Cruz carpenters, were not only the builders but the architects. They provided it with four gothic windows on each side and two in front, one on each side of the door. The interior was plastered by George Stevens and painted by Robert Lampee, both Santa Cruz artisans.

It stood until the present brick church was erected in 1889, when Father Hugh McNamee was the parish priest.

⬛

NEIGHBORLY GIFTS

ELDER MISSIONS of northern California helped the new Santa Cruz establishment out when it was founded in the fall of 1791.

Livestock and supplies were donated and vestments and altar ornaments were loaned.

In April of 1790 Sindico Fr. Geronimo de Semelaya, the business agent in Mexico of the Franciscan missions in Cali-

On a shady back street which runs east from Santa Cruz' "upper plaza," which was that surrounded by the mission buildings, stand two adobe residences, all that is left of the establishment started in 1791. Two buildings, 23 feet wide and, combined, measuring 130 feet long, are separated by a 5-feet-thick common wall. The buildings on School street were erected probably sometime in the first decade of the nineteenth century. In one, believed the residence of the cabo de escolta, is a low second-floor room, in which the Santa Cruz Masonic Lodge was organized in 1853.

fornia, forwarded tools and provisions for the proposed Santa
Cruz establishment to a value of 1,020 pesos. On January 20,
1791, the viceroy wrote an assurance that the necessary sacred
utensils would be sent. The latter, however, had not arrived
at Monterey by autumn and the new mission borrowed chalices
and vestments from San Carlos and Santa Clara.

Santa Clara, in addition to loaning the services of converted
Indians to help with the building, furnished Santa Cruz with
twenty-six fanegas of wheat for planting and twenty-six loaves
of bread, thirty cows, five yoke of oxen, fourteen bulls, twenty
steers and twenty-two horses.

Carmel sent over seven mules and eight horses, concerning
which Fr. Lopez reported later that one mule was so weak
that it died in three days.

San Francisco sent five yoke of oxen, seventy sheep and two
bushels of barley. Two of the oxen, Fr. Lopez reported, were
so unruly they had to be killed.

The military establishment, through Corporal Peralta of the
escolta, supplied the two missionaries with foodstuffs for
immediate consumption to a value of forty-two and a half
pesos, which the priests were to pay back later.

‑‑

FLAG RAISED IN 1842

FOUR YEARS BEFORE California became part of the United
States the American flag was raised at the mission plaza.
Commodore Thomas A. Catesby Jones had received at
Callao word from the east coast indicating that the United
States and Mexico were at war. He sailed for the north and on
October 19 sent word to Governor Juan Alvarado at Monterey
that he would land forces the next morning, whereupon the
Mexican official formally surrendered.

Two men in a small sailing vessel departed hastily across the
bay to Santa Cruz where Josiah Belden was running a branch
of Thomas O. Larkin's Monterey store. Belden produced a flag

from his possessions and climbed the pole in front of his place of business.

On October 21 Commodore Jones, convinced he was in error, turned Monterey back to Alvarado and a day later word was taken to Santa Cruz that the appearance of the Stars and Stripes was premature.

FIRST BAPTISM

The first baptism in Santa Cruz mission was of an eight-year-old Indian girl.

The entry of the event, as written in 1791 by Fr. Lopez, is still to be read in the carefully preserved mission records:

"On the ninth day of the month of October, of the year 1791, in the church of this mission of Santa Cruz, a girl, about eight years old, daughter of gentile parents (her father called Ynoc and her mother Frocsen), was baptised and solemnly annointed with the holy oils, called in her gentile tongue Moslon, born in the rancheria known by the natives as Achistaca and by us of reason as San Dionisio; given the name Micaela; her god-father being Luis Maria Peralta of the mission guard."

VEGETABLES FOR BRITISH NAVY

CAPTAIN GEORGE VANCOUVER of the British navy had spent thirty months exploring the California coast when, just before sailing on December 2, 1794, from Monterey on his ten months voyage home, he sent three small boats across the bay to buy vegetables from three-year-old Santa Cruz mission.

Vancouver, in the *Discovery*, with its companion vessel, the *Chatham*, under Captain Puget, was at Monterey for the third time and suspicious California authorities doubted the desirability of continued courtesies.

So, when Vancouver sent his small boats under a petty
officer named Swain, to Mission Santa Cruz, Governor Diego
Borica hurried a mounted messenger around the bay to notify
Padres Lopez and Salazar that they might have Indian servants
deliver vegetables to the Englishmen but should not visit the
boats themselves.

The same courier took an order to Corporal Jose Antonio
Sanchez of the escolta to see that the conditions were fulfilled.

The English boats left Monterey on November 24 and were
back on the 28th. On November 29 Corporal Sanchez wrote
Governor Borica that none of the sailors had visited the mission
nor had the priests gone down to the beach.

Sanchez had also sent a courier to Comandante Hermenegildo Sal, in San Francisco, when he saw the small boats
approaching; that officer, misunderstanding the message,
rushed five soldiers down to augment the mission guard.

Despite the documents still in existence showing Borica's
efforts to prevent contact between the Britons and the priests,
communication must have been established. Padre Salazar, who
returned to Mexico the following autumn, wrote there a report,
"Condiciones Actual de California," in which he said that
Vancouver had presented to Santa Cruz mission iron work for a
grist mill, of a value of 1000 pesos.

In 1796 Governor Borica sent to Santa Cruz artisans to erect
a mill, which undoubtedly was that which the English explorer
had donated. It was installed and operated for many years at
the foot of what is now known as the Laurel street hill in
Santa Cruz.

FIRST TEMPORARY BUILDINGS

Padres Lopez and Salazar, with their soldados and sirvientes
and some baptised Indians from Santa Clara who had been
taught the art of tree felling, speeded construction of temporary
buildings after their arrival in the autumn of 1791.

At the end of the year Padre Lopez wrote a report to his
superior, the presidente of the missions:

"We have erected a house twenty-six varas long by six wide, with the rooms necessary for the priests and offices.

"The church is twenty-one varas long and six wide, with a vestry four varas wide by six long.

"Both of these buildings are formed of palisades.

"We have enclosed a corral for the cattle, sheep and horses; we have brought water to the mission and have enclosed ground for an orchard and garden."

✦

ORDERS TO ESCOLTA

A FTER ALFEREZ SAL, comandante of the presidio at San Francisco, had made his trip down to "the place called Santa Cruz" in the autumn of 1791 and settled the two priests and Corporal Luis Peralta and his escolta of five men, he went back to the Golden Gate and drew up a set of instructions which he sent down to Peralta:

"Excess rations are not to be allowed. Exact amounts of maize, beans, tallow, cigarritos, soap and chocolate are to be apportioned weekly to each of the soldiers and to the six servants of the mission.

"The Indians are not to be permitted to taste beef, lest evil consequences result.

"The soldiers are to obey orders of the missionaries, either oral or written.

"An armed sentinel with musket and sword will be maintained day and night.

"The Indians must not be allowed to consort with the guards.

"The Indians will not be permitted in the mission except when disarmed; strictest precautions are to be taken against surprises or uprisings.

"Horses and cattle are to be watched constantly; if they stray they must be sought; if stolen the thief is to be informed of the magnitude of his crime and punished with fifteen lashes; if a theft is repeated or an animal killed, word should be sent this presidio.

"Two horses should be kept saddled by day and four at night, picketed close by, to meet emergencies.

"The grass fires set by the Indians each autumn must be carefully watched to prevent damage.

"If one of the padres leaves the mission on foot he must be accompanied by a soldier with a musket; if he leaves mounted he must be asked his destination and should be accompanied by two or three armed soldiers, according to the distance.

"The soldiers will not be permitted to gamble, either among themselves or with anyone else.

"The soldiers are to have no communication with the Indian men, and particularly not with the women, under penalty of extreme punishment.

"The soldiers and sirvientes must attend prayers regularly.

"On the last week of each month a report on the condition of affairs shall be sent to San Francisco by way of Santa Clara.

"Because of the lateness of the season and the approach of the rains, the Indians are to be asked to help in constructing the buildings immediately needed, to be paid for their labor with maize and blankets."

FIVE YEARS PROGRESS

At the end of five years, by 1796, Santa Cruz mission had 523 neophytes, converted Indians receiving food in return for labor. The number of yearly conversions did not hold to that average, and by 1800 the mission priests had baptised a total of only 949.

During the first decade of the new century baptisms were 668; the second decade saw 393 baptisms of Indians; and the period of 1820–30 saw a further decline.

Villa de Branciforte

The Village That Vanished

1941

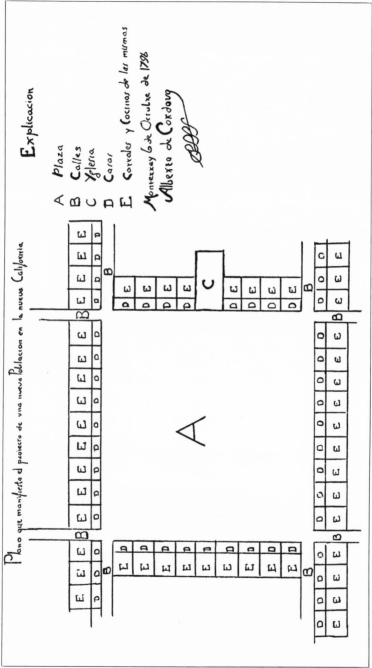

Cordova's Plat

⇥

VILLA DE BRANCIFORTE

ILLA DE BRANCIFORTE, under its own municipal government, grew from a compact little village on the east bank of the San Lorenzo river into an area of huge estates which spread forty miles along the California coast. When American days came it lapsed into a rural community under county rule.

The site of Branciforte was picked by a lieutenant of engineers in the Spanish army, California's first city planner, who drew a plat, which was never followed, based on the "Plan of Pitic." Pitic is now Hermosillo, Mexico.

Madrid, in 1795, with an eye on Russia's Alaskan colony or possible aggression by France or England, ordered three pueblos in California, independent of religious or military.

El Pueblo de Nuestra Senora de los Angeles, by political influence, and el Pueblo de San Jose de Guadelupe, just established to the north, were designated.

For the third the site just across the river from Santa Cruz mission was selected by Lieutenant Alberto de Cordova of the engineering corps of the army of Spain as having everything for a center of population, rich soil, water, timber, stone, lime, summer anchorage and favorable climate.

Cordova and Governor Diego de Borica spent several weeks at Santa Cruz mission in the early summer of 1796 confirming their selection. Cordova made visits both before and after the arrival of eight settlers from Guadalajara in July, 1797, preparing reports and making plans.

Dated Monterey, October 6, 1796, he prepared a plan for a projected center of population in new California, indicating plaza, streets, church, houses and "yards and kitchens of the same."

Cordova's estimates of building costs ran to 23,400 pesos, a prodigious sum for that time, which was never forthcoming from the viceregal treasury.

To Corporal Gabriel Moraga, one of the most capable of the soldiers of Spain in California, then comisionado at San Jose, went the selection by Governor Borica to administer the new pueblo, named after Viceroy Marques de Branciforte in Mexico.

On the opposite page is a reproduction of the original letter written on May 26, 1797, by Borica to Moraga directing him to go to Santa Cruz and begin home building.

The coming of the first families of Branciforte is told on page 32. By 1802, with their number augmented by eight or ten retired soldiers who had come with their families, they elected Vicente Moxica alcade, although Ignacio Vallejo, who in 1801 had succeeded Moraga as comisionado, continued in that capacity. Regidores were Fermin Cordero of the Guadalajara settlers and Tomas Prado, probably a retired soldier.

Moxica died October 5 of the same year and the villa worried along without an alcalde until 1805 when Felipe Hernandez, convict settler of 1798, granted privileges of a poblador in 1803, was elected, with Cristobal Cimentel and Jose Antonio Robles as his regidores.

A population of 120 gente de razon, living in adobe houses scattered for a mile along what is now North Branciforte avenue in the city of Santa Cruz, was in 1822 rudely told that, lacking sufficient number to have their own ayuntamiento, they would be subject to San Jose, which would name a juez de paz.

The change meant little. Branciforte pobladores received the appointments as jueces de paz but were called alcades just the same. Six years later Monterey began naming the jueces, but to Brancifortians they still were alcaldes.

When the mission was secularized in 1834 Juan Gonzales was made its mayordomo and the two communities were merged, with Alferez Ignacio del Valle, juez of Branciforte, as comisionado of the mission, which Governor Figueroa attempted futilely to convert into a pueblo named after himself. The two communities continued in this status until American days.

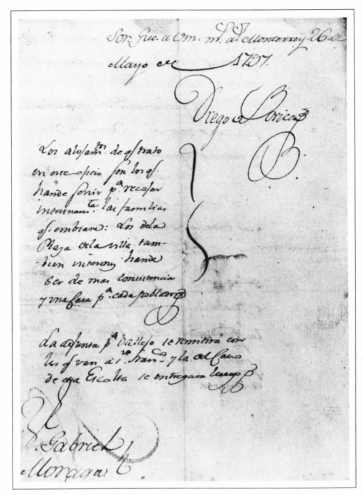

Borca's letter to Moraga. UCSC SPECIAL COLLECTIONS

Santa Cruz, west of the river, granted a charter by the legislature in 1866, incorporated in 1876. An election in 1907 brought Branciforte into Santa Cruz again.

The compact little Branciforte laid out by Cordova had its center about where Branciforte school stands today, but as the invalidos obtained grants spreading twenty miles to the north and south the Branciforte government kept them in its folds. The yearly padrones counted residents from the Pajaro to

Point Ano Nuevo, virtually the territory comprised in the present Santa Cruz county.

The visitor who today seeks vestige of the villa can do no better than find North Branciforte avenue and drive the length of the mile long track laid out by Cordova in 1797 for the villagers to race their horses, or drop to the flat between Branciforte creek and the San Lorenzo and make mental note that on that level the Brancifortians of a century and more ago held their bull and bear fights.

THEY DROPPED THEIR H'S

Ability to write was rare among the residents of Branciforte. Those who could were only too likely to do their spelling phonetically.

Records of Villa de Branciforte indicate that they dropped their H's. When Felipe Hernandez recorded his cattle brand, the juez de campo entered his name 'Ernandez; and 'Iguera passed for Higuera in the alcalde books.

⊪

TRANSLATION OF LETTER FROM GOVERNOR BORICA, IN MONTEREY, TO CORPORAL GABRIEL MORAGA, DIRECTING ESTABLISHMENT OF VILLA DE BRANCIFORTE

BY YOUR COMMUNICATION of the twenty-second of this month I am informed that in consequence of my orders the commission which puts him in charge of the Pueblo of San Jose has been delivered to Corporal Ignacio Vallejo; and by the accounts signed by both of you it is shown that Vallejo has received to his satisfaction the archives, stores of munitions and other effects.

As soon as there is erected at Santa Cruz a building for temporary occupancy you can send for your family. To the end that the construction may progress you will, with the aid of the mission guard there, have erected near their houses a general shelter large enough for fifteen or twenty families, even though all together, so that they may be sheltered until they can be better accommodated.

If the new pobladores arrive before the general shelter is finished you will put them to work on it. In the meantime they will find accommodations for themselves with the families of the soldiers of the escolta, or the latter can occupy one or two less houses, giving them to the others.

While this work is being done there are being assembled and manufactured the tools and necessary iron work which will be sent you by Lieutenant Hermenegildo Sal, with whom you will treat directly concerning their receipt, custody and distribution. The same applies to the rations which you will have to distribute to the new pobladores.

Opportunely there will be sent you some tame oxen, some breeding cows and all farm tools.

On the arrival of the Engineer Don Alberto Cordova you will obey his orders in everything he may require. You will make it a particular merit to carry out the orders and instructions which may be sent for the founding of the Villa de Branciforte, which may serve for its betterment.

Our Lord be with you many years.
Diego de Borica
Monterey, May 26, 1797.

The general shelters to which I refer in this communication are such as should be used temporarily for the families which may occupy them. Those on the plaza of the villa may be used thus temporarily but should be more permanent and one house for each poblador.

The enclosed letter to Vallejo I am sending with those which go to San Francisco; the corporal of the escolta there will forward them immediately.

To Senor *Gabriel Moraga.*

SOLDIER AND BROKER

The comisionado of Branciforte had to be a bookkeeper. On March 12, 1797, Hermenegildo Sal, then secretary to Governor Borica, wrote Corporal Moraga:

"Eleven pesos and five and a half reales belong to you as your commission on tobacco sold, and eighteen reales, realized from hides, make thirteen pesos and seven and a half reales to your credit. I charge you with four reales, being the amount you advised me was short from the sale of cigarritos, and two pesos and one and a half reales that you deducted during the past year at San Jose, as commissions, making two pesos and five and a half reales, which, subtracted from the thirteen pesos and seven and a half reales, leaves due you eleven pesos and two reales, which is the amount sent you, and exactly as I have the record. Say no more about the hides, for you are paid for them."

⟳

FIRST FAMILIES OF BRANCIFORTE

THE FIRST FAMILIES of Branciforte came sailing up the coast from San Blas, in the schooner *Concepcion*, arriving at Monterey May 12, 1797, two weeks before Governor Borica wrote to Corporal Moraga.

The eight pobladores for the new pueblo were natives of old Mexico who, running afoul of its rigorous laws, were given choice of a term in the Guadalajara juzgado or going to California.

As inducement they were offered transportation north, 430 pesos spread over five years, houses of adobe and tile as gift of the king, and farm tools to be paid for in installments.

At Governor Borica's request for various crafts they included a carpenter, a tailor, a miner, a merchant, an engraver, two farmers and one unclassified. Three, and perhaps four, brought wives, and two of them children.

On July 24 the party from Guadalajara was escorted around Monterey bay. Thirty-four days later Dolores, scarcely grown daughter of Vicente Moxica, married Jose Isidro Flores of the mission escolta.

Their promised 200-peso houses were not awaiting them and they had to throw up huts of split redwood and tule thatching. The subsidies came, in cash or supplies, however, and at least six of the eight stayed in Branciforte.

Bancroft's history lists nine men in the Guadalajara party but errs. Jose Machuca, by the mission records, is Moxica with his name spelled phonetically.

The eight Guadalajarenos were:

JOSE VICENTE MOXICA. Carpenter. He brought a wife, Victoria de Leon, and five children, Dolores, Josefa, Candelario, Eustagio and Polonio. Venancio was born in 1797, Maria Agapita in 1799 and Dolores Pudencia in 1801. Moxica, first alcalde of Branciforte, elected in 1802, died a few months later. In 1817 his widow married Jose Gordian Higardero of the mission escolta.

JOSE AGUSTIN NARVAEZ. Bachelor; nineteen. Native of Villa Agua Caliente in Guadalajara. In 1806 he enlisted in the San Francisco company and in 1808 he and Maria Josefa Higuera, whom he had married elsewhere, baptised a daughter, Micaela de Jesus, at Santa Cruz. He settled in San Jose where he was alcalde in 1821 and regidor in 1827. In the 1841 San Jose padron he was given as sixty-two years old, with his wife, Josefa Higuera, and five children: Lugarda, born 1826; Maria Guadalupe, born 1828; Teresa, born 1830; Antonio, born 1831; and Maria, born 1833.

JOSE ANTONIO ROBLES. Native of Pueblo de Faltango. He brought a wife, Gertrudis Merlopes of the Pueblo de Aguapulco in the Bishopric of Guadalajara, and an infant daughter, Ines. In the succeeding twenty-five years fourteen more children were born, of whom many descendants are in California today. Ines married Jose Saturnino Castro, son of Mariano, and her descendants constituted a number of that name in Branciforte who were not of the branch of the family founded by Joaquin Castro, whose story is told on page 37.

JOSE IGNACIO ACEDO. Bachelor. Mentioned by Governor Borica in a letter to the comisionado in 1798 as a runaway with Cordero who must be punished. In the mission records he appeared from 1801 to 1811. In 1810 he was a poblador with a wife, Luisa Gonzaga Hernandez, but the baptismal records show no entry of children. In 1808 the Branciforte archives give him as a cattle owner who should pay tithes, but there is no further mention of him.

JOSE MARIA ARCEO. Nineteen. He probably married after his arrival, for the first mention of his wife, Victoria Alegre, came in 1800 when a daughter, Maria Gregoria del Rosario, was born. Other children baptised at Santa Cruz were Felipe de Jesus, 1802, and Nicolas, 1804. His wife died in 1813 when he was recorded as a soldier in the Monterey company. His sons were soldiers at Monterey in the twenties and in 1836 Jose Maria Arceo, undoubtedly the old Guadalajareno, was named juez de campo at Pilarcitos Rancho, near Monterey.

JOSE BARBOSA. Brought a wife, Felipa Estrada, but no children. He was a tailor and recorded as Spanish. His wife died November 6, 1799, when the padres recorded the name of her husband as "Anacleto Barbosa" and stated she was "de razon."

FERMIN CORDERO. Bachelor. In 1798 mentioned as a runaway from Branciforte who should be punished and in 1800 sentenced to a month at hard labor for striking the comisionado. Two years later, however, he was elected regidor. Mission records show him acting as godfather in 1804, 1805 and 1815, but have no further mention of him.

JOSE MIGUEL URIBES. Bachelor. Mentioned only once in the mission records or Branciforte archives, when, in November of 1797, he acted as godfather for an Indian baptised. The priest entered his name as Jose Manuel Uribes.

UNA CAJA DE ESCOPETA

When Peter Lassen, the young Danish blacksmith who had come down from Oregon the previous fall, went over to Branciforte in 1841 to build the iron work for Isaac Graham's

Zayante sawmill he picked up a little loose change by mending "una caja de escopeta," which was the stock of one of the municipal flintlocks. The ayuntamiento gave him twelve pesos for the job.

◄█►

THE INVALIDOS

ITH THE FOUNDING of Branciforte, Governor Borica sent instructions to the presidios to influence young soldiers finishing their ten-year enlistment to settle at the new pueblo.

They were to have the privileges of pobladores and to receive pensions, in return for which they were to be subject to call for military duty, carrying out the scheme of building a population of coast defenders.

In the year after the coming of the Guadalajarenos six young invalidos arrived. With the exception of Sergeant Bravo they were married. Several had served in the Santa Cruz mission escolta and knew the country.

Others followed in the succeeding twenty years, most of whom stayed, but the most notable were Jose Antonio Rodriguez and Joaquin Castro of the 1798 contingent.

The six invalidos of 1798 were:

MARCELINO BRAVO. Sargento retirado. His name, after the record of his coming, appears only twice in the archives. In 1800 he acted as godfather for a son of Pablo Veiar of the escolta and in 1806 his death was recorded. The padres wrote that he was of "el rio de Bravo o Shoquel."

MARCOS BRIONES. Born in Sinaloa and had many relatives in California. His wife, Ysadora Tapia, died in Branciforte in 1812. Four children were born between 1802 and 1806. Marcos was Branciforte comisionado in 1811–12.

MARCOS VILLELA. His wife was Viviana, neophyte of San Carlos mission. Two children, Gertrudis de Jesus and Placida de Jesus, were born before Marcos died in 1805.

JUAN JOSE PERALTA. Member of a well known California family. He appeared in the mission records as a godfather in 1802 but did not stay in Branciforte.

JOAQUIN CASTRO. Came as a boy of seven with his parents and brothers and sisters in the Anza party of 1776 overland from Sonora. While serving his army term he married Antonia, the daughter of his sergeant, Pedro Amador. They brought two children with them to Branciforte, Ignacio and Antonia. Eleven others were born there. After Antonia's death Joaquin in 1833 married young Rosalia Briones, who presented him with three more children. Joaquin and his sons and daughters were grantees of seven ranchos in this region and founded one of the two great families of what is now Santa Cruz county.

JOSE ANTONIO RODRIGUEZ. Founder of the other of the two great families of the north shore of Monterey bay. Literally hundreds of his descendants live there today. The first known record of him in California was as a member of the escolta at Soledad in 1787 but a later record of his son, Sebastian, says the latter was born at Monterey in 1786. Other children were born at San Carlos and San Luis Obispo. Jose Antonio was appointed Branciforte comisionado to succeed Vallejo in 1804 and held the post several years. His wife, who bore him five children before coming to Branciforte and four afterward, was Vicenta de Leon, who died in 1837, aged eighty-six. Three of his sons, all of whom served in the army, were granted ranchos.

A list, perhaps not complete, of the other invalidos who came to Branciforte to stay for a greater or less time is:

Pablo Vejar	Apolonario Bernal
Salvador Higuera	Manuel Romero
Juan Maria Pinto	Antonio Buelna
Julian Rios	Jose Vicente Aguila
Toribio Martinez	Luz Garcia
Jose Francisco Garcia	

⊣⊨⊢

TWO GREAT FAMILIES

TWO GREAT AND WIDE-SPREAD FAMILIES grew out of the households of two veterans of the army of Spain who came to Branciforte in 1798.

Joaquin Castro was twenty-nine years old. Jose Antonio Rodriguez was a few years older. Two score years later their sons and daughters were to own a quarter of a million acres in what is now Santa Cruz county.

Their children were the aristocrats of Branciforte. Their daughters were noted for their dark beauty. The Castro sons were "big handsome men" in the words of William H. Davis, purser of a Honolulu ship which plied the California coast.

Joaquin Castro had trudged with his brothers and sisters in the epochal march of the Anza party in 1776. His father, Joaquin Isidro Castro, had been recruited by Anza because of his family of eight children, which had been increased by the birth of Carlos during the overland trip. His mother, Martina Boutilier, was French or of French descent and, according to legend in the Castro family, of noble blood.

Ignacio, Joaquin's oldest son, was a married man and a soldier when he was drowned in 1817 near San Juan Bautista while carrying the mails. Antonia married Antonio Feliz. Rafaela, born in 1799, became the wife of Francisco Rodriguez, fourth of that family.

Two of the Castro boys, ten-year-old Rafael de Jesus and one-year-old Francisco, died in 1811. Jose Rafael, born in 1803, married Soledad Cota while in the army. Juan Jose, who was born in 1805, married Manuela Juarez and, on her death, Rita Josefa Pinto. Martina had three husbands, Corporal Simon Cota, Michael Lodge and Louis Depeaux. Candida became the wife of Jose Bolcoff, the Russian. Guadalupe, born in 1811, died a bachelor in 1893. Jacinta, noted for her piety in aiding the mission fathers while a girl, became a nun and Mother Superior of the convent at Benicia. Maria de los Angeles married Joseph L. Majors, early American, and presented him with twenty-two children. Ignacio, the last of the sons of Antonio Amador, married Ricarda Rodriguez, granddaughter of Jose Antonio.

In the third generation American, French and English names appeared in the marriages: Francois Poile, Littlejohn, Elden, Lajeunesse, Fourcade, Fallon, Clements, Peck, Averon, Richard, Robinson, Fitzgerald, Winterhalder, Wheeler, Dodero, Bennett. Children and grandchildren went far and wide. Today they are spread over state and nation, but in largest numbers remain in Santa Cruz and nearby counties.

Jose Antonio Rodriguez, when, as an invalido, he settled at Branciforte with his wife, Vicenta Trinidad de Leon, then a woman in her late thirties, had five children. Sebastian, twelve, was the oldest. Alessandro, Margarita, Jose Brigido and Francisco had all made their appearance. In the following ten years were born Antonio Bernave, Francisca Vicenta, Roman and Ana de Jesus.

The boys went into the army before they were twenty and ended their enlistments, married, to receive land grants. The girls took as husbands Jose Maria Perez, Joaquin Escamilla and Juan Gonzales. The brides of the boys were Perfecta Pacheco, Concepcion Martinez, Rafaela Castro, Dolores Galindo, Gertrudis Soto and Ygnacia Alviso.

In the descendants of old Jose Antonio Rodriguez, soldado de cuera in California in 1786 or earlier, are today hundreds of names which show their thorough assimilation in American ways: Trevethan, Dye, Frey, Logan, Post, Howell, Randolph, Chappel, Amaya, Morgan, Newton, Brosius, Merrill, Grant, Dickinson, Triplett, Phillipsen and scores of others.

In the granting of Mexican ranchos the sons and daughters of Joaquin Castro and Jose Antonio Rodriguez received twelve in what is now Santa Cruz county and several elsewhere.

⊲≣⊳

LAND GRANTS

HERDS were too prolific and land too plentiful for the Brancifortians to restrict themselves to their little "house lots" and "farm lots" at the villa.

Life adapted itself to a baronial scale.

Along the coast and El Camino Real homes were established which, in some cases, were occupied for a decade or two before title was acquired.

A three-room adobe near a spring was a mansion. Rawhide thongs tied timbers together. Furniture was scarce and crude.

No Spanish grants were made in what is now Santa Cruz county, but under Mexican rule a quarter of a million acres or more were given.

Three grants were claimed which were not substantiated by the land commission in American days and a number of contests for established grants had to be settled.

A map of the grants in Santa Cruz county which were patented by the United States is shown on page 40.

APTOS. Granted in 1833 to Rafael Castro, son of Joaquin, the 1798 invalido. Along the coast from the Zanjon de Borregas (Lamb gulch) to his father's Rancho San Andres on the southeast. Granted by Governor Figueroa as one square league, it was patented to Rafael by the U.S. as 6,680 acres. In 1851 it was given assessed valuation of $23,000.

SOQUEL. Granted in 1833 to Martina Castro, sister of Rafael. It ran west from the Zanjon de Borregas to the Soquel river. Given by Figueroa as half a square league, the patent by the U.S. was for only 1,668 acres. Martina, who had two daughters by her first husband, Corporal Simon Cota, was the wife of Irish sailor Michael Lodge when she received her land. After Michael was murdered for his gold on his way home from the mines in 1849, she married Louis Depeaux.

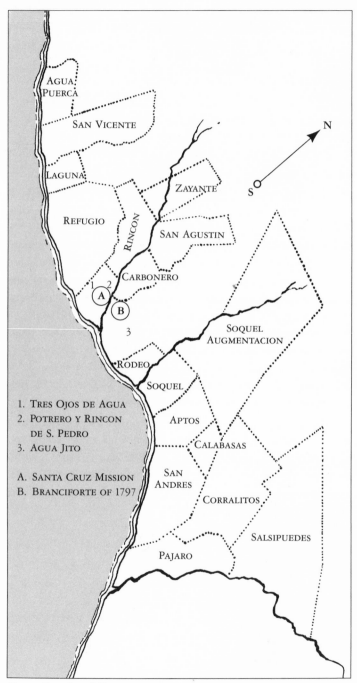

AGUA PUERCA

SAN VICENTE

LAGUNA

ZAYANTE

REFUGIO

RINCON

SAN AGUSTIN

CARBONERO

1 2
(A)
(B)
3

SOQUEL AUGMENTACION

RODEO

SOQUEL

1. TRES OJOS DE AGUA
2. POTRERO Y RINCON DE S. PEDRO
3. AGUA JITO

A. SANTA CRUZ MISSION
B. BRANCIFORTE OF 1797

APTOS

CALABASAS

SAN ANDRES

CORRALITOS

SALSIPUEDES

PAJARO

N

S

Santa Cruz Land Grants   REDRAWN FROM ROWLAND

SOQUEL AUGMENTACION. Granted in 1844 and patented to Martina Castro as 32,702 acres, it extended from her original grant back to Loma Prieta. In 1850 Martina divided her 34,370 acres into nine shares, one for herself and one for each of her children.

SAN ANDRES. Granted in 1833 to Joaquin Castro, the invalido of 1798. It joined the Aptos rancho of his son and was patented as 13,000 acres to Joaquin's bachelor son, Guadalupe. Its name was perverted to San Andreas in late Mexican or early American days.

LAGUNA DE LAS CALA BAZAS. Granted in 1835 to Felipe Hernandez, convict settler of 1798 who had won status of poblador. Patented as 4,000 acres to Charles Morse.

ARROYO DEL RODEO. Granted in 1834 to Francisco Rodriguez, son of one of the 1798 invalidos, and his wife, Rafaela Castro, daughter of another. It adjoined the Soquel Rancho of Rafaela's sister, Martina, on the west, extending from the Soquel river to Arroyo del Rodeo. It was scene of the rodeos at which Castro and Rodriguez cattle were gathered and branded. Patented by the U.S. to John Hames, New Yorker, and John Daubenbiss, Bavarian, who had come to California in 1843, it contained 1,473 acres.

BOLSA DEL PAJARO. Granted by Governor Alvarado in 1837 to Sargento Sebastian Rodriguez, another son of Jose Antonio of the 1798 invalidos, who had finished his army term. It contains the city of Watsonville today. Sebastian, to whom 4,496 acres were patented, sold to Americans before his death in 1855.

AGUAJITO. Smallest of the grants. Its 40 acres were in Arana gulch at the east Santa Cruz city limits. Given in 1837 by Governor Alvarado to Miguel Villagrana, a substantial citizen of Branciforte from 1824 or earlier. His name, occasionally given as Villareal, was shortened to Villa or Via by the Americans. Descendants so known live in Santa Cruz today. The U.S. patent was to Miguel Villagrana, who may have been the grantee or his son.

CARBONERO. Place where charcoal is made. Granted by Governor Alvarado in 1837 to Guillermo Bocle (William Buckle), London-born sailor who came to Santa Cruz in 1824. Patented to him under the name of William Thompson in 1873.

CANADA VERDE SALSIPUEDES. The name Salsipuedes is interpreted as "get out if you can," with various explanations. Occupied as early as 1834 by, and granted in 1840 to, Manuel Jimeno, who came from Mexico in 1830 and was a man of great influence in California government. The Chittenden pass road runs through Salsipuedes, which, with the exception of Martina Castro's holdings, was the largest grant in the county, of 31,201 acres. It was patented by the U.S. to a number of Americans, including William F. White, candidate for governor in 1879.

ARROYO DE LA LAGUNA. Up the coast from Santa Cruz. Granted in 1840 to Gil Sanchez, Branciforte tithe collector, it was patented to James and Squire Williams, two of four American brothers who came in Mexican days and were early-day lumber operators.

REFUGIO. Granted in 1841 to three Castro sisters, Maria de los Angeles, Candida and Jacinta. Jacinta, who became a nun, relinquished her share. Jose Bolcoff, the Russian, married to Candida, informally erased her name and inserted his own. It was patented by the U.S. to two of his sons but later Joseph L. Majors, husband of Maria de los Angeles, was given a third.

SAN AGUSTIN RODEO and ZAYANTE. The two ranchos, up the San Lorenzo six or seven miles, were taken under Mexican law in 1841 by Joseph L. Majors, an American who had been naturalized as a Mexican and married Maria de los Angeles Castro. He was acting for Isaac Graham and perhaps a couple of other Americans. Graham had refused to become a Mexican citizen. Majors immediately sold Zayante to him. The subterfuge was winked at by the authorities. San Agustin and Zayante was assessed at $32,000 in 1851. A grant of Zayante in 1839 to Joaquin Buelna had lapsed.

POTRERO Y RINCON DE SAN PEDRO REGALADO. The potrero of the old mission. Granted in 1842 to Jose Arana and patented by the U.S. to Thomas Russell, who operated a distillery in its hills. Isaac Graham, who had come into possession of the small tract, gave it to Eliza Farnham for aid given by her husband, Thomas Farnham, to Graham at Monterey when Graham was among the exiles of 1840. Mrs. Franham sold it to Russell, who was mysteriously murdered in 1856.

CANADA DEL RINCON. Granted in 1843 to Pierre Sainsevain, French lumberman and millwright, who in American days traded it, for the $150,000 steamer *Santa Cruz*, to Davis and Jordan, who established the lime kilns still operating at Rincon.

AGUA PUERCA Y TRANCAS. Granted in 1843 by Governor Micheltorena to Roman Rodriguez, one of the sons of the old invalido, and to Francisco Alviso.

TRES OJOS DE AGUA. "Three eyes of water." Two hundred acres on what is now High street in Santa Cruz, granted to Nicolas Dodero, Italian sailor who came to California in 1827 in the *Maria Ester*.

LOS CORRALITOS. Occupied as early as 1827 by Jose Amesti, native of Spain who came on the *Panther* in 1822. An early grant was not completed and its 15,400 acres were given him by Governor Alvarado in 1844.

SAN VICENTE. Granted in 1846 to Blas Escamilla, son of Joaquin de los Santos Escamilla and Vicenta Rodriguez, his wife, the daughter of Invalido Jose Antonio Rodriguez.

MESA DE OJO DE AGUA. Small tract on what is now Spring street in Santa Cruz, granted in 1838 to Jose Ramon Buelna and claimed by Thomas Russell, who was given the Portrero y Rincon de San Pedro. The claim was not allowed.

ARASTRADERO. An asserted grant of 1844, east of the San Lorenzo river and up Blackburn gulch, which is now Branciforte drive, to Albert F. Morris. Claim for it by William Blackburn was not allowed. The name denotes a place where ships are careened.

EL JARRO. Up the Santa Cruz coast on what is now known as Scotts creek. Claim for it was presented in U.S. days by Jose de la Cruz Rodriguez but not allowed.

⊐⊏

WAR'S ALARMS

H ARDLY had Branciforte been established than Corporal
Moraga was ordered to maintain a watch of one white
man and two Indians on the cliffs for marauding vessels.
Almost yearly, reports spread of strange ships. In 1800 a
vessel of British appearance was reported anchored off the
Salinas river, and then to have sailed away.

Rebellions in Spain's South American colonies stopped
trade ships from Callao and in 1816 warnings came to Monterey
of a possible visit by insurgent ships from the west coast of
South America.

Governor Sola instructed the padres to be prepared to re-
move their valuables inland. In 1818 an American trader
brought word from Honolulu that two ships flying the flag of
Buenos Aires were coming. When, in November, they appeared
Governor Sola ordered Padre Olbes of Santa Cruz to flee to
Santa Clara and Juez Joaquin Buelna of Branciforte to take
charge of the mission.

Olbes' return brought charges of theft but that was the
extent of the damage for Branciforte. Bouchard, the privateer
commander, sacked Monterey, sailed to the Ortega ranch near
Santa Barbara and on down the coast.

Similar instructions to the priests were repeated in 1820.
Three years later Lord Cochrane, British privateer helping the
revolting South American colonies, touched at Mazatlan and
sent two small ships to California for foodstuffs. His visit,
however, had no effect beyond contribution of half a dozen of
his men to the population of Alta California. Four Branciforte
residents from 1824 were undoubtedly from this source:
William and Samuel Buckle, Julian Wilson and William
Atchison.

◄Ξ►

INSURRECTOS

BRANCIFORTE, like the rest of California, followed in dreamy fashion the revolts in Mexico from 1810 to 1822, little affected by them and always a year late to receive the news.

Not until the California rebellion of 1836 did Brancifortians take any part. Juan B. Alvarado and Jose Castro sent Rafael Pinto, a Branciforte boy who had been their schoolmate, to present a captain's commission to Juan Gonzales, mayordomo of the mission, and to seek recruits around the north shore of Monterey bay.

Pinto and Gonzales enlisted thirty-five men and boys, nearly a third of the army which Alvarado and Castro took south to convince the Los Angelinos and San Diegans that their "free and sovereign state" was to be taken seriously.

Another third of Alvarado's army were "Americanos rifleros," sharpshooting hunters, most of whom had come out over the Santa Fe trail, under the leadership of Isaac Graham, a Virginian, who was running a distillery at Natividad, in the Salinas valley.

The revolution, patterned after that in Texas, subsided when shrewd politicians in Mexico made Alvarado governor. Rafael Pinto, the son of old Serafin Pinto of Branciforte, emerged with a lieutenancy in the Mexican army. In American days he ended his years near Watsonville, where Pinto lake is named after him.

The conviction of the Americans that they had been instrumental in Alvarado's military success made them so overbearing that in 1840 nearly three score "foreigners" were sent by schooner to San Blas. The home government failed to sustain the action of the Californians and most of the "exiles" returned.

Graham and nearly a dozen others came into the redwoods at Zayante, where they formed a colony which was ready, six years later, to join Fremont's Battalion and help in the fighting at Los Angeles to bring those reluctant Spanish Californians under American rule.

⟶

OLD CATTLE BRANDS

C ALIFORNIANS of Spanish and Mexican days measured their wealth in cattle. Registrar of the brands, as well as director of the rodeos and matanzas, was the juez de campo, the judge of the plains.

When the registry book was opened in Branciforte the first to enter his marking was Jose Bolcoff, the Russian-born Brancifortian who became one of the leading citizens of the town and was the last juez de paz of Mexican days, filling his office so well that he was offered the post under American military rule.

Bolcoff, whose rancho was just to the west of the present city of Santa Cruz, obtained his brand in 1821, paying the ayuntamiento of San Jose five pesos for its registration and later recording it at Branciforte.

Next came Juan Gonzales, with a brand inherited from his father, who had registered it in the pueblo of San Francisco.

The Branciforte brands were:

JOSE ANTONIO BOLCOFF

JUAN GONZALES

GUILLERMO BOCLE

JOAQUIN JUAREZ

ANTONIO AMAYA

JOSE ANTONIO ROBLES

TEODORO ROBLES

RAFAEL CASTRO

ROMAN RODRIGUEZ

JUAN JOSE FELIZ

JOSE IGNACIO CASTRO

JOSE DE JESUS LORENZANA

GIL SANCHEZ

FRANCISCO SORIA

FRANCISCO RODRIGUEZ

MIGUEL RAMIREZ

JUAN PEREZ

MIGUEL VILLAGRANA

FRANCISCO DAY
Job Francis Dye

MACEDONIO LORENZANA

ANTONIO RODRIGUEZ

ALEJANDRO RODRIGUEZ

JOSE MECHACAS
Joseph L. Majors

SECUNDINO ROBLES

VENTURO ERNANDEZ

GUADALUPE CASTRO

EUGENIO SOTO

MANUEL RODRIGUEZ

JORGE CHAPEL

JOSE MARIA SALAZAR

NICOLAS ALVISO

CORNELIO PEREZ

PABLO SUIT
Paul Sweet

JUAN JOSE CASTRO

DIEGO WIKIS
James W. Weeks

JOAQUIN CASTRO

SAMUEL BOCLE

LUZ GARCIA

FRANCISCO JUAREZ

JOAQUIN BUELNA

GRAM-NEIL
Isaac Graham–Henry Naile

JUAN PINTO

ROUSSILLON-SAINSEVAIN

MARTIN VELA

◄∃E►

THE ROBLES BOYS

HE ROBLES BOYS were hombres malos, in the estimation of the respectable people of Branciforte.

They tore around the countryside on horseback — not always careful whose horses they rode — and caught the girls' eyes in their velveteen breeches with silver filigree trimming, their satin jackets, their ear rings and silk sashes, which sometimes cost the price of a horse and a mare for a single one.

They made trips over the hills to San Jose, where they frequented the cantinas and the gambling houses, imbibing aguardiente and flinging away pesos as though they were nothing but reales. A ride of forty miles around the bay to Monterey was nothing in their careless young lives.

They were disrespectful to the alcalde and his regidores, who sought to restrain them, and brought sorrow on the head of their father, but they made the hearts of the maidens of old Branciforte flutter.

There were eight of them, but the older ones were more staid. It was Teodoro, Nicolas, Avelino and Fulgencio, the children of the later years of old Jose Antonio Robles, the 1797 poblador from Guadalajara, who ran wild over the countryside and came to a bad end.

Two of them met violent deaths. Fulgencio was shot by Gil Sanchez, the tithe collector, at the bidding of Juz de Paz Juan Gonzales, and Brancifortians mostly agreed he deserved his fate.

Fulgencio rode on horseback right into the adobe of Lawrence Carmichael, while a jovial group of leading Branciforteans was spending the evening gambling. Monterey authorities did not agree with Branciforte opinion and Gonzales and Sanchez were sentenced to a year of exile from Branciforte.

Another result of Sanchez' shot was that dark-eyed Concepcion Salazar, Fulgencio's wife of a few years, had to go to court to recover from his brothers his possessions, which consisted of his gay clothing and his horses.

All that happened, however, three years after the most exciting event in the story of the Robles boys of Branciforte. In 1839 they raised so much disturbance that Prefect Jose Castro, in command of all of northern California, had to send a squad of soldiers over from San Juan Bautista to take them there for trial.

The quartet of hard-riding young Californians resisted and Avelino was so daring in his defiance of military authority that he was shot by Soldado Felipe Espinosa and died in twenty-four hours.

It was an exciting time in Branciforte and Governor Alvarado did not entirely approve. It was, in fact, Avelino's death which probably saved his younger brother, Nicolas, the principal offender, from a severe sentence at hard labor on the fortifications at Monterey. Nicolas already had a bad record for his disregard of ownership of horses he picked to ride.

The older boys of the eight had gone into the army as soon as they were sixteen or seventeen years old. They had married while they were serving their ten-year terms of enlistment and become more settled.

Their story really goes back to Zacatecas, where their father was born. He was married to Gertrudis Merlopes and father of a baby daughter, Ines, when Viceroy Branciforte offered him a chance to go as poblador of a new city in Alta California.

The offer was a handsome one, with traveling expenses, a five-year subsidy, land and a chance to buy tools and cattle on credit.

Only eight young Guadalajarenos who took advantage of the offer reached Branciforte and only the more dependable of them really took hold to make homes, after they got over their disappointment at not finding the promised tile-roofed adobes which were to be theirs by gift of the king.

Antonio and Gertrudis Robles were among those made of sterner stuff and settled down without demur, building their own adobe and thatching it with tule grass.

Gertrudis was kept busy. Baby Ines was only two years old when they came on the *Concepcion* up the coast to Monterey. Jose Antonio de los Nieves was born almost as soon as the family arrived at Branciforte. Eugenia came along in 1800, Rafael two years later, Raimundo in 1804 and Antonio a year later. Teodoro, Avelino, Secundino, Maria Guadalupe, Nicolas, Fulgencio and Estefana came in rapid succession.

Jose Antonio de los Nieves died in 1822, only a few months after he had taken as a bride Petra Vasquez. His son, Policarpio, was born after Jose Antonio's death.

Rafael went into the army and discipline induced in him a sober conduct. Raimundo served his ten-year enlistment in the presidial company of San Francisco, which supplied the guards for the escoltas of the northern missions, came home to marry Perfecta Castro, but died when he was thirty-three.

Teodoro, Avelino, Nicolas and Fulgencio, the wild youngsters, nominally lived with their father and mother in the home adobe on the hill east of Branciforte creek, but herded cattle for many of their neighbors when they were not making surreptitious trips to San Jose or Monterey.

The boys were in continual trouble with the authorities. One of Nicolas' trips to San Jose when he was nineteen was immediately followed by the arrival in Branciforte of Jose Cibrian, sent by Alcalde Pedro Chabolla with a message that a cinnamon-colored horse belonging to Antonio Higuera of that pueblo could undoubtedly be found in the possession of Nicolas, and was to be delivered to Cibrian.

That was in February of 1834. Gray-haired Antonio Bolcoff, the Russian, was juez de paz in Branciforte. He sent Juan Jose Castro, one of his regidores, to interrogate young Nicolas, who met him so belligerently that Bolcoff ordered him under arrest and wrote the Monterey authorities he was sending Nicolas there in handcuffs.

Nicolas' father, the old poblador who had come thirty-seven years earlier, was still influential. He had held his first public office when he was elected regidor in 1805 and by 1817 had been made comisionado. Twice, in 1827 and 1833, he had been picked by his fellow townsmen to be named juez by the governor.

When Nicolas was sent in fetters to Monterey his saddened father called on one of his old friends in the capital and Frederico Antomont went bond for Nicolas until he could be tried.

Manuel Jimeno Caserin, Governor Alvarado's secretary of state, investigated the case and wrote over to Bolcoff that if he would draw up formal charges Nicolas would be tried in the court which had to do with vagrants and petty offenders. Nicolas' punishment was mild, however, and he was quickly back in Branciforte with his brothers.

One of the beauties of Branciforte was dark-eyed Lucia Soria. Her father, Francisco, had already served a year as juez de paz and was later to be juez de campo and, just before the coming of American rule, to be second alcalde.

Young Lucia came of good family. One of her grandfathers had been Jose Soria, alcalde of Monterey, who had died at his country home in Branciforte in 1828. He had been a native of Teguila in the bishopric of Guadalajara. Her maternal grandfather had been an old soldier, Joaquin Juarez.

Fourteen-year-old Lucia caught the eye of the dashing young Nicolas Robles. It is more than likely, too, that Nicolas, despite his known wildness, or perhaps because of it, was observed in his velveteen and satin with filigree buttons and his ear rings, by the youthful Lucia.

Lucia's father did all he could to halt their romance, and quite justifiably, for in 1838 Nicolas was again afoul of the law. Alcalde Dolores Pacheco in San Jose wrote in February that Nicolas Robles was again suspect in a horse stealing case. The animal this time was the property of Jose Romero.

The lawless Nicolas did not this time get off so easily. Feliciano Soberanes, alcalde in Monterey, heard his case. He was fined twenty-five pesos and given a passport to Santa Barbara, with an intimation that he should make his residence there or further south, not to come back to Monterey, Branciforte or San Jose until permitted.

Nicolas, of course, had no worldly goods except his flashing garments, his saddle and his horses. His father, sixty-three years old, retired and full of honors, was called on to pay the fine, which he did by delivery to Alcalde Buelna of two horses, one trained to ride and the other broken to haul a cart.

Terms of "exile" of those days seldom lasted long and early in 1839 Nicolas was back at his father's home, riding again around the shore of Monterey bay with his three brothers, drinking aguardiente and making himself a general nuisance.

Lucia, fifteen years old by this time, was ready to welcome him back but her father was correspondingly sorry. Love found means to circumvent parental opposition. Francisco Soria soon appeared before Alcalde Buelna with a complaint that Nicolas Robles had cut through the laced rawhide of a window in his adobe, helped Lucia out the opening, and that the pair had fled to the hills.

It was decided that the offense was one against the laws of the church and the case was laid before Francisco Soto, administrator of the ex-mission of Santa Cruz, across the river.

Soto agreed with Alcalde Buelna that something had to be done. It was too flagrant a case.

With three men who, trusting to their superior number, did not trouble to arm themselves with any of the municipal muskets, Soto went to the Robles paternal adobe and found Nicolas and Lucia.

"In the name of the nation," Nicolas was arrested.

But Nicolas had no intent of submitting. "Wait until I get my hat," he told the quartet and stepped inside the house, only to emerge with a leveled flintlock.

Soto, however, was not through with his efforts. He spurred away, through Sebastian Rodriguez's rancho on the Pajaro river, to San Juan Bautista.

Prefect Jose Castro detailed Subtenientes Joaquin de la Torre and Victor Linares, with three privates, to go to Branciforte. Arriving at midnight they took advantage of the hour to round up the four Robles, two young members of the Salazar family, and Lucia herself

The next day the male prisoners were fastened together with a rope which bound the neck of each and told they would have to walk to San Juan Bautista.

To the young Californians, accustomed to going even the shortest distance by horse, it was the height of insult. Avelino tore his shirt from his back and threw it at the soldiers, telling them to use it for gun wads.

Soto, the mission administrator, ordered the soldiers to fire. Only one, Felipe Espinosa, obeyed. Avelino called to his brothers that he had been wounded. The soldiers lifted him on a horse and took him back to his house in Branciforte, where he died the next day.

The others were obliged to continue to San Juan Bautista where Castro held court, examining Lucia and her father as witnesses. Avelino's death influenced the court and they were freed except for another short exile to southern California for Nicolas.

The relations of Lucia and Nicolas still troubled Padre Antonio Real at Santa Cruz mission and on April 12, 1839, he wrote Alcalde Buelna:

"In regard to Senorita Lucia Soria I ask that you take most efficacious and active steps to learn where she is; and as soon as you have ascertained the truth have the kindness to notify me, as upon this information will depend my course. If she has gone to be married is the question. I wish to know if she is a wife, or if I should take further steps."

Padre Real's anxiety was ended a year later. Nicolas and Lucia appeared at the mission to be married and on May 1, 1841, was born Felipe Santiago, first of their three children. Nicolas died in 1844 and three years later his widow married Ramon Soto.

⮬

FOREIGNERS ARRIVE

TEN YEARS before San Francisco had its first English-speaking resident, Branciforte and Santa Cruz had four.

They were "foreigners" to the Mexican authorities until they were naturalized and, usually, married to daughters of Hispano-California families.

Thomas Doak, first American settler in California, was briefly in Branciforte in 1823 and was baptised at the mission across the river; the following year four "foreigners" appeared who stayed: Julian Wilson, Virginian, the Buckle brothers and William Trevethan, Britons.

A fifth came soon afterward. Michael Lodge, Dublin sailor, in 1828, with his first wife, a daughter of the old soldier, Luz Garcia, brought a daughter to the mission for baptism.

The Joseph Walker party, offshoot of the Bonneville expedition, which, sent to explore the Great Salt Lake region, found its way across the Sierras to Monterey, left Francois Lajeunesse, and perhaps another, Billy Weare, although the latter may have come by Santa Fe.

Trappers over the Santa Fe trail were Joseph L. Majors, Job F. Dye, Ambrose Tomlinson and probably the Englishman, George Chappel. Henry Hill, a German, and William Chard, New Yorker, were in the records in 1838.

When, in 1840, Monterey determined to deport the "foreigners" Branciforte had a dozen or more English-speaking residents, four of whom were American born.

The return of the "exiles" brought Isaac Graham and his cronies to establish their settlement at Zayante, where they cut timber, operated a grist mill and distillery and, in 1842, set up the first power sawmill in California.

Arrivals in the Branciforte region in 1840, nearly half of whom remained, were Graham, Henry Naile, Henry Jubilee Bee, Charles Henry Cooper, Joseph R. Foster, George W. Frazier, Robert King, Paul Sweet and Alvin Wilson.

Some still came over the Santa Fe trail. Ships brought others and opening of the Oregon trail more.

In 1841 the Branciforte "foreigners" included Josiah Belden, George Bowen, William Brander, Willard and Francis Buzzell, William Garner, Peter Lassen, Albert F. Morris and James Weeks.

By the time of the American occupation in 1846 three score or more were in Branciforte or its vicinity, of whom more than twenty established families and stayed until their deaths. The population of roving adventurers contained many elements of

dissatisfaction and inclination to revolt, with a strong sentiment for making California part of the United States.

UNDER AMERICAN RULE

Santa Cruz, which included Branciforte, was the first community in California to organize under the American rule.

Sixty days after the flag had been raised at Monterey instructions were received for a public assembly to name an alcalde,
but Joseph Majors, the Tennessean, replied that such a meeting
had already elected him.

In the county recorder's office is preserved the tally sheet,
with the votes: Juan Arana 10, Jose Mechas 9, Guadalupe
Castro 6, Juan Emis 3, P. Richar 3, Jose Bolcoff 2. Arana apparently declined and Mechas (Majors) accepted the honor.

William F. Blackburn, generally known as the first American
alcalde of Santa Cruz, was appointed June 21, 1847, by Colonel
Richard B. Mason, acting governor.

Gold discovery in the Sacramento valley started an exodus
to those fields, which brought a rapid succession of alcalde
resignations and appointments. The office went successively to
William Anderson, John Hames, Adna A. Hecox and John F.
Pinkham.

The period 1846–50 saw a local land rush, in which American alcaldes, acting under what they conceived was Mexican
law, parcelled out lots with a free hand, creating a tangle which
had to be straightened out by an act of Congress in 1866.

The Story of
Old Soquel

1940

An early view of Soquel looking southwest

◄ ►

ROSARIO DEL SERAFIN DE ASCULI

ROSARY OF THE SERAPHIN OF ASCULI was the name given
the camp of the Portola party on the night of Monday,
October 16, 1769.

The valley had been first traversed by a white man six days
earlier, when Sargento Jose Francisco Ortega and his squad of
leather jacket pathfinders had pushed ahead marking a course
along the coast of what is now Santa Cruz county.

It had taken three score of soldados de cuera and their Indian
muleteers a week to cover the sixteen miles from the Pajaro
river. Sick with scurvy and exhausted by their three months
march from San Diego, they had rested five days at Corralitos
and then taken two days to push on to Soquel.

The path of the Portola party across the Soquel valley was
probably the same as that later used by the padres as El Camino
Real, crossing the flat and fording the river south of where the
highway now runs.

Miguel Costanso, the engineer, recorded that after a march
of two leagues "within sight of the sea" they came to the bank
of a stream of good water. Portola's diary tells that only two
hours were taken for that day's journey over the level terrain
from Aptos.

Soquel was again site of a night's camp for Portola's men five
weeks and two days later, when they were on their way south
after discovering San Francisco bay.

⇒⇐

FIRST WHITE RESIDENT

S OQUEL'S first white resident was Marcelino Bravo, retired from the Spanish army in California with brevet rank as sergeant.

Bravo came to the north shore of Monterey bay with five other invalido soldiers in 1799. He and Jose Antonio Rodriguez were the only ones of non-commissioned rank and Bravo was possessed of a record which gave him special privileges.

That Bravo established his residence at Soquel in 1800 or soon after is probable from the Santa Cruz mission records. The padres used everyone of Spanish blood who was conveniently nearby as godfathers for the Indians who were baptised, but Bravo's name is absent. Only once, on September 5, 1800, did he appear as padrino, and that was at the christening of Eugenio, newborn son of Pablo Vejar of the mission escolta and his wife, Josefa Miramontes.

The next appearance of Sargento Retirado Bravo's name on the record was on his death on January 16, 1806. The priests wrote that he died at the "rio de Bravo o Shoquel."

The special honor in which Bravo was held is shown in a letter from Lieutenant Hermenegildo Sal, comandante at Monterey, to Comisionado Ignacio Vallejo at Branciforte:

"Always and whenever the corporal of the guard at the Mission of Santa Cruz presents a request to you for any person of white blood to assume the royal service, you must free from other duties two or three of the invalidos, with the exception of Corporal Marcelino Bravo, who is exempt from having to stand guard in case it is required for any situation, and the others are not."

‹∃⊫›

PADRES KNEW SOQUEL

P ORTOLA'S PARTY brought into California the designation "rancheria" for a group or community of Indians. They were not in any sense tribes, as the number in Santa Cruz county shows, nevertheless, so low was the civilization of California's aborigines that it was said those of a rancheria could hardly understand the speech of those in another only a score of miles away.

When the Franciscan missionaries of Santa Cruz began baptising and burying the Indians, they carefully recorded the name of their rancherias, at the same time bestowing the name of a saint upon the community. The Indian name, as recorded, was of course a phonetic spelling in Spanish.

Soquel, Aptos and Zayante were the only rancherias in Santa Cruz county whose Indian names have survived. Soquel rancheria was of sufficient importance of size that the baptism of its chief as "Balthazar" was recorded.

Rancheria names recorded by the padres were:

Achila (Achil)	Chitactac
Achistaca	Chuchumis (Chumistaca)
Alutca	Chruistaca
Asam	Conoch
Aptos (Abtos, Avtos)	Copcha
Ausentaca	Coochi (Coot)
Cajastaca	Cotoni
Cajastac (Cajasta, –aca)	Cucurum
Chaloctaca	Huachi
Chanech	Huocom (Huocon)
Chichutac	Hupnis
Chiputac	Linguamenit

Locobo	Sipieyesi
Luchasme	Somentac
Mallin	Soquel
Mutchas	Suchesum
Notuals	Sumus
Osocalis	Tejey
Partascsi	Tomoi (Tomoy)
Pitac (Pitaca)	Vypu
Sachuen	Yamayan
Sagiianacu	Yasmil
Sayanta	Yeurata

That the rancheria names were used by the Spanish as place names is shown by documents in the old Branciforte archives. In one, dated in 1811, Lieutenant Jose Maria Estudillo, comandante at the Presidio at Monterey, rebukes Comisionado Jose Antonio Rodriguez of Branciforte:

"That which you should have done immediately it was reported to you that the Russian Indians who left here had stolen the cayuco during the night was to have sent two or three invalidos or militiamen who could most easily have followed their trail and compelled their return; now to capture the malefactors will be most difficult.

"It is necessary that with the greatest haste and caution you make inquiry among the Indians of Soquel, who gave the information to the holy padres, and do the same among the Indians who were with the cayuco. Inform me promptly."

The "Rusos Indios" were Aleutians who had come with the Russians from Sitka. Their mention is of interest for only two years before had Alexander Kuskoff made his voyage of exploration south from Alaska to Bodega bay, and only in 1811 did he make his second trip.

For twenty years and more the Californians resisted the efforts of the Aleutians to hunt otter along this coast. In 1817 Estudillo won from Governor Sola recommendation for promotion to a captaincy for having commanded a party of thirteen which prevented seven Russian fishing canoes from landing on Monterey bay, killing one of the occupants and wounding several.

THE LONG WHARF

Huge timbers cut in Soquel in 1849 were taken by schooners from "Soquel Landing" to San Francisco and used to build "the long wharf," which is now Commercial street.

◄▆►

MARTINA CASTRO'S GRANT

S HE WALKED on the land, pulled up grass and three hand-fuls of earth, broke off branches of trees, threw stones to the four winds and performed other ceremonies and acts of possession."

Martina, third daughter of Joaquin Castro and granddaughter of Isidro Castro of the Anza party from Sonora in 1776, thus acquired title to what is now Soquel.

Martina was the handsome, black-haired widow of Corporal Simon Cota when, in 1831, she married Michael Lodge, a Dublin sailor. As was usually the case, Martina and her husband established their home before she asked for land title. Permission to build a house and cultivate the ground was given Lodge on September 8, 1833, by Alcalde Antonio Robles of Branciforte, more than two months before Martina applied to the Monterey government for the area from the Soquel river east to the Sanjon de Borregas.

Governor Jose Figueroa and Agustin V. Zamorano, secretary of the diputacion, referred the application the same day back to the local authorities. The Branciforte ayuntamiento declared the land unoccupied and Martina qualified to receive it. Padre Antonio Real said the mission had no claim to it.

By November 23 the grant was out of the hands of Governor Figueroa, subject only to approval by the diputacion. By the following August the red tape had been unravelled and to the

Russian, Antonio Bolcoff, alcalde by that time, was given the task of naming surveyors. On August 14, 1834, Martina "walked on the land." Today 34,370 acres trace their title back to her act.

Ten years later Martina petitioned for the 32,702 acres back of her original grant, naming it the Rancho de Palo de Yesca (Tinder Tree), but receiving it as Soquel Augmentacion.

Michael Lodge, returning from the gold fields in 1849, disappeared mysteriously, presumably killed by robbers. Martina married Louis Depeaux and in 1850 divided her wide acres among her eight children, with one-ninth reserved for herself, which included her three-room adobe and its garden on the bank of the arroyo east of what is now Bay street. The partition was made in 1860 by Referees C. B. Younger, David Tuttle and Joseph Ruffner.

Carmelita Lodge had married Thomas Fallon, veteran of the Texas war for independence. Her portion, on the river and north of the highway, was bought in 1852 by Joshua Parrish.

Farther east, along the highway, was the share of Helena and her husband, Jose Littlejohn, whose home was where that of Lloyd Bowman is in 1940. Across the highway, where the Izant place is, was the residence of Antonia and her husband, Henry Winegar Peck. The portion of Louisa, the wife of Richard Jean Fourcade, a Frenchman known to the Californians as Ricardo Juan, was south of the highway east of Porter gulch.

Nicanor Cota, who had married Francois Lajeunesse, a French Canadian of the Walker party of 1833, had just moved to Ventura but Pruett St. Clair, another French Canadian who had come over the Santa Fe trail in 1833, believed to have been her assignee, was made owner of land near the present airport.

The flat along the east bank of the river, down toward La Playa de Soquel, went to Josefa, who was Mrs. Lambert Clements, and to the youngest daughter, Maria Guadalupe, who had married Jose Averon, a Frenchman who had been steward on Commodore Sloat's flagship at Monterey in 1846. On Capitola avenue still stands the old Averon home, in which Martina breathed her last in 1890.

Other tracts, sold or mortgaged, were awarded to F. A. Hihn, George K. Porter, Augustus Noble and Frederick Macondray.

In 1864 the Augmentacion was likewise divided by Referees Thomas W. Wright, John W. Turner and Godfrey M. Bockius. Five of Martina's daughters were recipients, the others apparently having sold their rights.

The names of men logging and milling in the upper Soquel valley in 1864 are shown by the assignments. To R. G. Hinckley and his son-in-law, John L. Shelby, went one thirty-sixth of the Augmentacion rancho, in what is still known as Hinckley Basin. George K. Porter received a small piece, as did Richard Savage and Benjamin Farley. Joel Bates' estate got one twenty-seventh, on Bates creek. Other small portions went to Lyman Burrell, Casimero Amaya, John Daubenbiss, Craven Hester, F. A. Hihn and James Taylor.

Martina's distribution of her property did not bring her peace. In her later years her sanity was questioned and six years after her death in 1890 titles based on her deeds were settled by an adjudication which fully vindicated her.

Until a short time before her death in the big Avaron house she lived alone, first in her three-room adobe with its vegetable garden enclosed in upright redwood palings, and then in a little house built for her by Averon. Her old adobe, fallen into disrepair, was torn down in 1925.

HIGH WATER OF 1862

The Soquel valley, like every other part of California, was damaged by the heavy rains of the winter of 1861–62. The home of George Washington Eldridge, wheelwright in Daubenbiss and Hames mill, was washed off its site on the west bank of the river 200 yards north of the highway. He built again across Porter street.

The Old San Jose Road, until the flood, ran straight down the west river bank, but was turned then to its present entrance on Porter street. A redwood log wall built out from the west bank of the river helped throw it slightly to the east, to its present course.

⊐⊏

ARROYO DEL RODEO

THE MEXICAN GRANT of the Rancho Arroyo del Rodeo, west of the Soquel river, was made the same year as that of Soquel to Martina Castro. Its recipient, Francisco Rodriguez, was her brother-in-law, who, with his wife, Rafaela Castro, had lived there a number of years before Alcalde Bolcoff, in September, 1834, made final the grant approved by the territorial diputacion.

Rodriguez was a son of Antonio, an invalido of 1799, and one of a large family, many of whose members were given land.

Rancho Arroyo del Rodeo derived its name from the fact that roundups of the herds of the Rodriguez and Castro families took place in the natural amphitheater half a mile south of the present Rodeo gulch bridge.

Francisco died in 1848 and from his heirs the big tract was bought by Hames and Daubenbiss. Their title was confirmed by the U.S. land commission in 1855 but a survey in 1861 cut it from 2,353 to 1,473 acres.

John Hames was a thirty-two-year-old native of Osage county, New York, who, after interrupting in Peru a round-the-world voyage as ship's carpenter, made his way north to Monterey in 1843. Married by U.S. Consul Thomas Larkin to Drucilla Shadden, an Arkansas girl who had come with her family over the Oregon trail, he had twelve children, most of them born in Soquel.

With his partner, John Daubenbiss, the New Yorker engaged in several sawmill and flour mill ventures, the most notable of which was the four-story flour mill which stood in the sixties and seventies on the lot opposite the present Soquel bank. He was joined here by his brother, Ben, whom he had left in South America.

With John Cummings, Soquel merchant, and perhaps other residents of the town, Hames left in 1880 to prospect for gold

The Daubenbiss house   SOQUEL PIONEERS

in Mexico, hoping to retrieve his fallen fortunes. Word that he
was ill there was received and his son, Ben, brought him back
to Peach Tree, in Monterey county, where he died in 1894.

John Daubenbiss was a Bavarian who, at the age of nineteen,
came to America in 1835 and west over the Oregon trail in
1842. From 1843 he was in California, helping build a sawmill
for Stephen Smith at Bodega and erecting a flour mill for
Mariano Vallejo at Mission San Jose. He served under Sutter
in the Micheltorena campaign and was naturalized as a Mexican
to qualify for a land grant in the Sacramento valley. In 1845
he signed the San Jose call and in 1846 carried dispatches
between Sloat and Fremont. He went south with the California Battalion.

Returning to San Jose in 1847 he married Sarah C. Lard and
moved to Soquel, which he had first visited in 1843 and where
he and Hames had built the sawmill for Martina Castro in 1845.
When Santa Cruz county was organized he was named Soquel
road commissioner in 1850 and in 1858 was elected supervisor.

Of his ten children all but one were born in Soquel. Until his
death in 1896 Daubenbiss was a leading citizen of the county.

Both of the old homes build by Daubenbiss and Hames are
still standing.

The name of Doyle gulch, often applied to Rodeo gulch, came from John Doyle who in the sixties and seventies had a farm two miles north of the highway.

INVITED THE CAPITAL

The people of Soquel in 1868 invited the state of California to move its capital there. They offered the use of the hall over Ned Porter's store and promised use of a "city hall" as soon as it could be erected. The "city hall" was built by the flourishing home town band of the day and became known as the "band hall" where Alf Starkie's service station now stands. Later it was moved north on Main street and became a Methodist church.

━

FIRST SAW MILLS

THE BEGINNING OF SOQUEL as an industrial center was a sawmill erected in 1845 by John Hames and John Daubenbiss, on the east bank of the river opposite the present school grounds.

Hames and Daubenbiss had an agreement with Martina Castro and her Irish husband for logging in the redwoods, but when Commodore Sloat raised the American flag at Monterey both marched away in Fremont's California Battalion, turning their mill over to the owners of the land.

Back in Soquel in 1848 Hames pressed for payment and obtained from Michael Lodge a promise of $5,000. Collection was made difficult, however, by the fact that high water had taken the mill out in December, 1846, while it was being operated by Henry Hill, a German who had come from Mexico with the Hijar and Padres party in 1834, and by Guadalupe Castro, Martina's bachelor brother.

Hames and Lodge were both "at the mines" in 1849 and Lodge was mysteriously killed on his way home. In 1851 Hames went to court but Martina, Lodge's widow, made the defense that under Mexican law she was not responsible for her husband's debts.

After the flood of December, 1846, Lodge hired Adna A. Hecox, a Connecticut carpenter and preacher of Irish descent who was in San Jose, to build a new mill, which Hecox operated until he left for the gold fields in 1848.

The saw mill built by Hecox was on the west bank of the river half a mile farther up, on the site later occupied by a grist mill, a tannery, and finally by O'Neill's paper mill.

ᴴᴱ

JUSTICES OF THE PEACE

SOQUEL was created a judicial township, privileged to have its own justice of the peace, in October of 1852.

The polling place at Soquel's first election, held that year, was at the home of Gervis Hammond. Justices of the peace were elected at large by the county until 1858, but the election of 1852 named two who were Soquel men, J. S. Mattison and Lambert B. Clements.

The need for a justice court in Soquel was ample. With horse and buggy travel distances were great.

At the time of the organization of the county on April 6, 1850, all officers had been appointed. Three justices named then by the legislature had been Dr. George Parsons and Felipe Armas of Santa Cruz and Jose Arano of Aptos.

County-wide election was held in October, 1851, and the names of the two Soquel residents appeared as justices, although Soquel township was not created until a year later. Both Mattison and Clements were elected again in the fall of 1852.

Mattison was an Englishman, born in Yorkshire in 1823, who had crossed the plains in 1849 and in December came to this county where he acquired land on the west bank of Arroyo Rodeo, where his house still stands and Mattison Lane bears his name.

Clements, of Irish descent, had come to California as a member of Colonel Stevenson's regiment of New York Volunteers, who came in 1847 with the understanding they would be discharged from military service in California.

Gervis Hammond had come to Zayante in the middle of 1849 and worked in the timber there. He was the county's first treasurer, auditor and assessor — joint offices in 1850 — and in the fall of 1851 had removed to Soquel where he and Hugh Paul McCall were partners in a timber cutting venture. He died, in his home in Soquel "near the river," in 1854.

Mattison, a strong Christian later to be one of the organizers of the Soquel Congregational church, returned to New York in 1853 and in 1854 was representative of California at a convention of the Sons of Temperance at St. John's, New Brunswick.

In 1859 Mattison, with a bride, Delilah Miles, whom he had married the previous year at Michigan City, Indiana, returned to Soquel, where he was again made justice of the peace.

Clements, who had been a partner of A. C. Sanford in a store in Santa Cruz, had by virtue of his marriage been a Soquel man from 1850. In 1854 he had a brief business career in San Francisco and in 1855 was back in Soquel where he had married, in 1850, Josefa Lodge, second daughter of Martina Castro and her Irish husband, Michael Lodge.

While Mattison was in the east and Clements trying his luck at business in San Francisco, Nathaniel Holcomb was elected justice, but resigned after a month and Andrew J. Rockwell was named to the vacancy. In 1855 Henry W. Peck, another son-in-law of Martina, and Martina's husband, Louis Depeaux, were elected. In 1856 John Miller and Charles Ray took office.

By the early sixties Mattison and Clements were again holding the judicial posts. In the seventies Clements used a room off the bar in Tom Mann's hotel for a court.

CAPTAIN TIDBALL OF COMPANY K

Captain of the infantry company raised in Santa Cruz county for service in the Civil war was T. T. Tidball of Soquel, who lived back of the site of the present apple dryer. Other Soquel men in either the infantry company or the cavalry company which was recruited a year earlier were George Washington Giles, Asa Glover, William Hite, Frank Howard, Jerome Love, Luther White, John Cummings.

◄█►

NED PORTER'S STORE

SOQUEL'S FIRST MERCHANDISER was Edward F. Porter, a native of Vermont. He and his brother, Ben, and six cousins had come in '49 or soon after and most of them established themselves in Soquel in the spring of 1853. Ben Porter and his cousin, George K., established the tannery in what is still known as Porter gulch. Ned founded the first store in the budding village.

A high spot in the annually overflowed flat, where Angell's store is today, was site of the establishment, which catered to every need of the rapidly growing population of woodsmen and farmers, selling groceries, drygoods and hardware, with hard liquor a side line.

After the custom of the time Ned extended liberal credits and frequently took produce or land to settle his bills. His holdings extended up and down Porter street, on which he built a number of rental houses, several of which are still occupied. One of his loans covered part of the land of John Hames, the New Yorker who had bought half of Rancho Rodeo.

When, in the middle fifties, the first post office was opened, Ned Porter's store was its location and he the postmaster.

The Porter store passed, in 1884, into the hands of John Harlan, who had come in 1883 with his family from Missouri, after a short stop in Austin, Nevada. He made his home over it and in 1887 sold to Horatio and Fenner Angell, two enterprising young merchants from Nevada.

Soquel's second store was just across the highway from Ned Porter's. It was established in the late sixties by "Johnny" Cummings, a young Canadian whose sister, Fannie, had married John T. Porter, another cousin of Ned's, who was sheriff just before the Civil War and later superintendent of the state asylum at Agnews. The site, now occupied by Cunnison's garage, was low and a loading platform several feet off the ground ran at its floor level along front and side.

Cummings, whose age was about eighteen at the time, had given it as twenty when in 1861 he had enlisted in Captain Albert Brown's company of cavalry, the first of three raised in Santa Cruz county, which spent the Civil War guarding overland trails from the Indians in Utah.

In 1880 Cummings, with his clerk, Yates C. Lawson, and John Hames, the pioneer of 1845, left on a gold prospecting trip into Mexico, from which he never returned. He married a beautiful senorita there and, after his death, their children were sent back to California to be educated.

Soquel's business district built up rapidly. Tom Mann's hotel was just east of Johnny Cummings' store, with James Dunning's blacksmith shop between. Blacksmiths were many to care for the heavy teaming. One of the first was Samuel Beymer Ewing, who leased from John Daubenbiss a shop across the highway from the latter's home and then moved to Porter and Walnut streets, opposite Getzschmann's Park House. On what is now Kasseroller's corner was a shop run by Henry Hall and later by George Nidever.

J. D. Chace and Co., butchers, had a shop opposite Mann's hotel. Another butcher was Charles Mills, who gave to the school his home site, where the tennis court now is.

John Bowman, a brother of Mayor Gustave Bowman of Santa Cruz, was the tinsmith and hardware dealer, with his home on what are now the school grounds and his shop where Vetterle's building stands next to the bank.

A. Darling, on south Main street, was an early day shoe maker. John Lynam was another. In the early seventies H. Auerbach opened a variety store and when the wooden, three-story, first I. O. O. F. building, which later burned, was erected in 1876, Isaac Fleisig opened a variety store in it.

One of the bars outside the hotels was on north Porter street where "Jack" Frost dispensed liquors. Just south of it, where Fletcher's garage stands, was the four-story flour mill owned by Daubenbiss and Hames.

◄≣►

TURNPIKE TO SAN JOSE

SOQUEL PEOPLE built over the mountain to San Jose the first road passable to stage coaches.

The move for such a highway came in 1855 when Santa Cruz and Santa Clara counties named three men each to "view out" such a route.

Santa Clara residents promptly organized a company to build their end of the turnpike, from Santa Clara to "Santa Cruz Gap."

Soquel made the first move. On January 30, 1858, a meeting in Soquel was presided over by Judge Henry Rice, a North Carolinan who had crossed the plains with an ox team in 1852.

Elihu Anthony, Santa Cruz merchant and postmaster, pioneer of 1847, moved a committee of five to investigate the proposed route and Judge Rice named Anthony; Samuel A. Bartlett, then a resident of Soquel but later to be a furniture dealer and banker in Santa Cruz; Nathaniel Holcomb, farmer and lumberman of Soquel since 1850; F. H. Hihn, the Santa Cruz merchant who later was to develop Capitola; and John Hames, the pioneer mill man and a large land owner.

On March 4, 1858, the "Santa Clara Turnpike Company" published notice of intention to form a joint stock company, signed by Anthony, Bartlett, Holcomb, Hihn, Hames, J. F. J. Bennett, John Daubenbiss, George Parsons, A. W. Rawson and F. M. Kitteridge.

Highways in those days followed the ridges until they reached the "gaps" in the mountains. The Soquel company's route, starting from Nathaniel Holcomb's place, went up the hill west of the Soquel river, where traces of it can be seen today, high above the present "Old San Jose Road."

Santa Cruz' road to rival the one north from Soquel started two months later, as the "Santa Cruz Turnpike," to use the Graham grade and the Mountain Charlie road.

The Soquel road was built at a cost of $12,000; the Santa Cruz turnpike cost only half as much. Both were pushed, to gain the advantage of being put in use first. Soquel won and for many years the San Jose stage coaches stopped at Tom Mann's hotel and then drove west to Santa Cruz.

Holcomb, president of the Soquel organization, went to the county supervisors for permission to charge tolls, which, for travel from Soquel to the summit, were: wagon and span of horses, 50 cents; each additional span, 25 cents; wagon and yoke of oxen, 50 cents; each additional yoke, 25 cents; horse and buggy 37½ cents; horse and rider 25 cents; all loose stock, per head, 5 cents.

SCHOOL HOUSE IN 1853

Soquel had a school house in 1853. The county records show it was used as a polling place that year.

Two little buildings claim the honor. One was built by John Hames on the west side of north Porter street; the other by John Daubenbiss south of the highway near the bottom of the west hill. Each of the pioneers was providing schooling for his children. The first teacher in the Hames school was a man named Cole. In the other one of the first teachers was J. P.

Stearns who, afterward, a lawyer, removed from Watsonville to Santa Barbara.

The first one-room building on the present school site was built about 1860.

SOQUEL'S BIG LEAGUER

Hal Chase, who in the early part of the present century won the reputation of being the "world's greatest first baseman," learned his baseball at his father's sawmill, at the site of the present SRA camp. His father was J. E. Chase. Hal played on Soquel town teams, went to Santa Clara, and played with the New York Yankees.

⊲≣≻

THREE EARLY-DAY HOTELS

GROWTH OF SOQUEL as a lumbering center in the fifties brought hotels to serve and house loggers and mill workers who spent their cash and leisure in the rapidly growing village.

"Black" Bryant and Peter Canares were the original hotel men. It was probably A. F. Bryant who erected a two-story structure on the north side of the highway, between Porter street and the river. The date can not be fixed but it was probably before 1860, as in that year Bryant was tried in justice court on a charge of selling liquors in quantities less than one quart without a license.

The barnlike building had its end to the street; a porch and balcony were across the front; a hall divided both floors. On the ground level to one side was the bar and on the other the parlor, dining room and kitchen. Upstairs over the bar was the dance hall, on the other side were bedrooms.

The hotel passed around 1868 into the hands of genial Tom Wilson Mann, who looked like Mark Twain, and his wife, Elizabeth, who operated it for many years. Later the building was occupied by the blacksmith shop of Mason and Skillinger and their successor, George Ford. It burned in 1911.

Pete Canares, in the early sixties, built a hotel where the Soquel Inn now stands and, with his younger brother, John Baptiste Canares, operated it for a few years, but was in Santa Cruz in 1868. Alex Getzschmann took over the hostelry and its tree-filled grounds; as the Park House it remained in the Getzschmann family more than half a century.

Opposite the I.O.O.F. building stood Soquel's third hotel. James Fitz John Bennett, who had run away from his father's iron discipline at Auburn, New York, in 1850 and come around the Horn, had married the daughter of Judge Henry Rice. He had worked in flour mills of the county until he was elected county clerk-recorder/school superintendent in 1859.

In 1875 he built a square two-story structure, with porch upstairs and down. The hallway on which the big center door opened had the dining room to the right and both a ballroom and bar.

Only a few years after it was built Bennett's hotel burned and he erected a one-story building in which he ran a bar until his death in 1891.

EARLY ROADS FOLLOWED HILLS

Wagon routes of the early days avoided the river lowlands. The highway into Soquel from the west, in the early fifties, turned to the north at what is Forty-first avenue now and circled the hill to ford the river at a point at which was then the sawmill and which later became the paper mill site.

Next came a route which traversed what is now Walnut street, crossed the present school grounds and used a bridge of which the stone abutments are still in place.

The first north and south route was laid out in 1852 by order of the county supervisors, running from Soquel Landing, the present wharf, along what is still marked on the maps as the Soquel Landing road. It followed the west hillside near its top to where the present highway is and then swung around through Hames field, which is the present O'Neill pasture, to reach the river a short distance north of the cemetery.

In 1860 a street was laid out along the west bank of the river in Soquel, but in 1862 a flood forced abandonment of it for the present entry from the north by Porter street.

❧

THE SUGAR MILL

CLAUS SPRECKELS of Aptos shook his head at the fields of sugar beets where the Capitola airport is now. Claus had expanded from his grocery in San Francisco to ownership of refineries in Hawaii but he had doubts of this new German method of making sugar from vegetables.

In a few years, however, Claus was dabbling in sugar beet raising and preparing to put in the fields which still grow near Salinas.

The California Beet Sugar company was Soquel's big industry in the seventies. The machinery, brought from Germany, had been operated for a time at Fond du Lac, Wisconsin, and then brought around the Horn and tried at Alvarado, near Oakland.

In 1873 a Major Flint decided the new beets could be grown around Soquel and spent, it is asserted, $150,000 to bring the plant here. The bridge between Soquel and Capitola was the only one and the machinery, landed at the wharf, was hauled up the Old Soquel Landing road and back to the bank of the river in what is now Riverview terrace.

F. A. Hihn donated ten acres for a site. The refinery was a one-story building, with tanks and boilers in a cellar. Its lumber came from the Comstock mill on the Old San Jose Road above the Iron Bridge. Two 40-horse power engines and four of 8-horse power were wood burning, consuming five thousand cords a year.

Workmen who had come from Germany with the machinery were brought with it. Andreas Otto was superintendent and E. Kleinan, a cripple, his assistant. John Tanke and Adolphe Harboard were foremen and among the crew were Christian Maasberg, Fred Obermuller and W. Weferling.

Homes for employes were built. The residence of Superintendent Otto, a two-story structure, was later moved to the east across Capitola avenue and known prior to its destruction as "Plantation House."

Beets grew on a thousand acres under supervision of the German experts and during the season the plant used 50 to 60 tons a day, turning out 800 tons of sugar in a year.

Operation of the plant ended in 1879, the site reverting to Hihn, and the machinery was held by him until the World War sent junk prices soaring.

A note of interest is that when, in 1882, the mortgage on the home of John Hames was foreclosed while he was prospecting for gold in Mexico, his wife, the Drucilla Shadden whom he had married in Monterey in 1845, found refuge in the old sugar mill, and died there.

EARLY LUMBERING

The Soquel valley succeeded Zayante as the center of lumbering operations in the county in 1851 when Gervis Hammond, Hugh Pablo McCall, G. H. Kirby and a number of others moved to the region, in which Daubenbiss, Hames and Henry Hill had been the only operators.

TWO BRIDGES IN EARLY DAYS

Soquel had two bridges in the seventies, but only a foot plank across the river where the present one is. One, at the paper mill, was probably erected by the mill's owners. The other, whose stone abutments can still be seen on the school grounds, was an extension of Walnut street.

◄❚❚►

CAPITOLA

LA PLAYA DE SOQUEL became Capitola in 1869 when F. A. Hihn laid out "Camp Capitola" as a watering place.

A wharf had been built in the latter fifties at the location of the present one, from which the Old Soquel Landing road ran back along the height west of the river until it dropped down the hill into Soquel.

The first important structure in what is now Capitola was a warehouse. Potatoes were worth "a bit a pound" in California in 1851 and 1852 and the flat lower valley of the Soquel was planted to them. By 1853 everyone in California who could was raising potatoes and the price bubble burst.

Loath to give up their hope of wealth the growers hired Sedgewick J. Lynch, a young Santa Cruz carpenter, to erect a shelter where their crop could await schooners. Ships' captains, however, declined to haul any more potatoes to San Francisco.

Ten years later the warehouse was torn down to provide lumber for other purposes. The dried potatoes were left in a long pile where, well into the seventies, traces of them could be seen on the site where two decades later Hihn built the Capitola hotel.

Overalls and Mother Hubbards were the bathing suits of the seventies. They were rented at Capitola by S. A. Hall, who, a former ship's carpenter, built the Soquel Congregational church. He did the carpenter work for Hihn, and was first lessee of the resort, including a big livery stable.

Bathing was en masse, as a safety measure, on signal of a bell rung each day at 11 o'clock and at 3.

By horse-drawn vehicles the people of San Francisco came to Capitola until the first train on Hihn's Santa Cruz–Watsonville narrow gauge ran on May 18, 1876. The first depot was on the Soquel Landing road, back of the wharf.

Following the advent of the railroad, lots were laid out and privately owned cottages appeared.

Its skating rink of the eighties was transformed into the Hawaiian Gardens, a famed dance hall, which burned, as did Hihn's big Capitola hotel.

On Hihn's death his Capitola interests passed into the hands of his daughter, Mrs. Katherine Henderson, who owned them through the World War and sold them in 1920 to H. Allan Rispin, an oil millionaire, who began elaborate developments, building a twenty-room house and laying out the Monterey Bay golf course. When the 1929 depression hit him his interests were taken over by Benjamin Hayes Smith of Burlingame, subject to mortgages which have been foreclosed.

Not until 1937 were the streets of Capitola deeded to the county.

FIRST COURT HOUSE

Thomas Fallon, who had married Carmelita Lodge, daughter of Martina Castro, sold Santa Cruz county its first court house. It was his home and saddlery shop on the upper Plaza in Santa Cruz. The price was $3500. Later the building was the first county hospital.

THREE PER CENT A MONTH

Three per cent a month was the usual interest on notes in 1861. Records of suits in the court of Justice of the Peace Lambert B. Clements show judgements based on such indebtedness.

ODD FELLOWS LODGE

Soquel's I.O.O.F. lodge was founded in 1867 and on April 26, dedicated its first building on the site of the present one. It burned in 1926.

⊲≣⊳

SOQUEL'S CHURCH

EIGHT GOOD MEMBERS of the Santa Cruz Congregational church withdrew in 1868 and the Soquel Congregational church was formed. Sunday school had been held for several years in the school house and in Joshua Parrish's home, and ministers of several denominations had preached in the town.

Organization of the church followed a visit by the Rev. W. A. Tenney, missionary preacher from San Francisco, who arrived with his family to begin pastoral work the first Sunday in April.

The eight members of the original church were Mr. and Mrs. John S. Mattison, Mrs. Narcissa Parrish, Mrs. Phoebe Feeley, Mrs. Lucy M. Burrell, Mrs. Augustus Noble, Mrs. Rachel Hall and Mrs. Jane McKay.

A lot for a church building was given in 1869 by Joshua Parrish and in March, 1870, its construction was begun by S. A. Hall, a ship's carpenter, who had come the previous year.

Names of Soquel's leading citizens appear through the record of the years. Mattison, strong temperance worker, was deacon and clerk until 1884 and a member until his death in 1890. A. L. Ward, Mrs. Maud Grover and Mrs. Eva Strickland succeeded him as clerk.

Revival services by Dwight L. Moody in Santa Cruz in 1889 added new members to the Soquel congregation and brought a second protestant church, when Methodists bought the old band hall and moved it north on Main street, where it was used for several years until its members united with the East Side

Methodist church in Santa Cruz, contributing its bell to that structure.

Pastors of the Soquel Congregational church have been: W. A. Tenney, 1868–70; J. H. Strong, 1870–75; R. A. Duncan, 1876–79; L. N. Barbour, 1881–85; G. M. Dexter, 1885–87; A. B. Palmer, 1887–91; Howard Mudie, 1891–93; James Parsons, 1893–95; A. B. Snyder, 1895–99; G. H. Wilbur, 1900–02; F. M. Washburn, 1902–04; Franklin F. Pearse, 1904–09; W. J. Spears, 1909–10; J. W. Griffin, 1910–11; C. J. Godsman, 1911–13; Sidney W. Wilcox, 1913–14; W. J. Spears, 1914–17, W. A. Hensel, 1917–18; Frank A. Bissell, 1918–21; W. A. Hensel, 1921–23; Arthur A. Kidder, 1923–24; John J. Kelley, 1924–30; J. C. Bolster, 1930–32; Jessie G. Heath, 1932–.

St. John's Episcopal church in Capitola was organized in 1889 and St. Joseph's Catholic church was dedicated July 24, 1905.

The Seventh Day Adventists organized in 1890 but not until five years later did they erect their first church in Soquel, on the location of the present building, on a site given by Mr. and Mrs. William Kropf. The present stucco structure was built in 1932. Almost across the street from it is the building of the Christian Science Society which, after meeting for several years in the old wooden I.O.O.F. building, erected its own church in 1926, only to see it burn with the nearby Odd Fellows building. The present structure was erected the following year.

WHISKEY CHEAP AS KEROSENE

Whiskey sold for 50¢ a bottle and kerosene for $1.50 a gallon in the store of Ned Porter in 1862. Nails were three pounds for a quarter, coffee three pounds for a dollar, calico 20¢ a yard and tobacco 75¢ a plug.

TWO CHAIR FACTORIES

Soquel, in the height of its industrial status of the seventies and eighties, had two chair factories. One was on the Cahoon place, near the present steel bridge on the Old San Jose Road. The other was on north Main street.

Erected in 1870, Soquel's Congregational Church has been used by motion picture makers as a bit of true New England architecture.

᷈ᴇ᷍

VOTERS OF 1868

O NE PICTURE of Soquel as it existed seventy-two years ago
is its poll list for 1868. Lambert Blair Clements was justice of the peace, Stanley L. Robertson was its physician,
Henry P. Stone was its lawyer and Thomas James Phillips
taught its school.

Unique in its poll list was its woman voter, Charlotte Parkhurst, the stage driver who disguised herself as a man, lived on
a farm east of Aptos and cast her vote in Soquel.

The poll list given below is for Soquel precinct of 1868,
which covered a territory from Arana gulch to a point east of
Aptos. There were only seven precincts. Corralitos and Pajaro
were to the east and San Lorenzo, Scotts Valley, Santa Cruz and
New Years Point to the west.

Of the 329 listed nearly half were still residents in 1875,
when Paulsen's directory of the county was published. Several
score of them have children and grandchildren living in the
mid-county district today.

AIKEN, George,
    Miner, 33, Ireland.
ALBERTS, Albertus Cornelius
    Farmer, 41, Germany.
ALINGER, Frederick,
    Engineer, 52, Switzerland.
ALLBRIGHT, Joseph,
    Farmer, 25, Ohio.
ALLEN, George
    Farmer, 30, Ohio.
ALMENDORES, Vicente,
    Farmer, 29, Mexico.
ARANA, Homobrono,
    Farmer, 29, California.
ARANA, Jose,
    Farmer, 29, Spain.
ARANA, Juan,
    Farmer, 26, California.

ARANA, Marcos,
    Teamster, 37, California.
ARANA, Valose,
    Teamster, 22, California.
ASBURY, Coleman,
    Farmer, 51, Kentucky.

BALL, John Nelson,
    Laborer, 38, New Jersey.
BARKER, Charles Webster,
    Millright, 42, U.S.
BATES, Louis Palmer,
    Millman, 24, U.S.
BATZEL, Charles,
    Farmer, 43, Prussia.
BATZEL, Frederick,
    Farmer, 42, Prussia.

BAUCOM, Joseph,
Farmer, 35, Tennessee.
BEAL, John Monroe,
Farmer, 27, Tennessee.
BECK, William Knight,
Gardner, 62, Kentucky.
BEERS, Scott,
Laborer, 47, New York.
BIGHAM, John,
Farmer, 52, Kentucky.
BIGHAM, John Foster,
Farmer, 35, U.S.
BISCHELL, Henry,
Carpenter, 38, Prussia.
BIXBY, Nelson Alvin,
Wharfinger, 28, U.S.
BOSTWICK, Ebenezer,
Laborer, 63, Vermont.
BOSWELL, Wm. Franklin,
Laborer, 27, Missouri.
BOSWORTH, Almerian Elijah
Carpenter, 22, Maine.
BRADLEY, Elias,
Farmer, Teamster, 39, Ohio.
BREESE, Stephen Decatur,
Merchant, 31, U.S.
BRITTAN, Henry Francis,
Woodsman, 36, New York.
BRODOWSKI, Adolph,
Carpenter, 47, Russia.
BROWN, Augustus,
Saloonkeeper, 22, Missouri.
BROWN, Charles,
Laborer, 32, New York.
BROWN, Henry Skaggs,
Saloonkeeper, 23, Missouri.
BROWN, James,
Laborer, 48, Missouri.
BROWN, John Anderson,
Distiller, 49, Ohio.
BROWN, Joseph Perrin,
Farmer, 26, U.S.
BROWN, Lemuel Augustus,
Laborer, 25, Tennessee.
BROWN, Thos. H. Benton,
Laborer, 28, Missouri.
BROWN, Wm. Hargest,
Farmer, 51, U.S.
BROWNSON, Linus,
Miller, 48, New York.

BRYAN, Thos. Jefferson,
Farmer, 25, Missouri.
BUDDINGTON, John Dabbatt,
Laborer, 40, New York.
BUELTZES, Peter,
Farmer, 49, Holland.
BUNTON, William Arnold,
Farmer, 40, Tennessee.
BUHN, Zacharias,
Farmer, 23, Germany.
BURGES, Ammi Austin,
Laborer, 25, Maine.
BURNS, David Nolan,
Farmer, 40, Kentucky.
BUSELO, Conralto,
Farmer, 50, Germany.
BUSH, James,
Mariner, 35, New York.

CAHOON, Benjamin,
General trader, 65, New York.
CAHOON, Edwin Benjamin,
Farmer, 36, New York.
CALDWELL, Marquis LaFayette,
Laborer, 23, Missouri.
CAMPBELL, Wm. Jackson,
Lumberman, 38, Ohio.
CANARES, John Baptiste,
Farmer, 22, Germany.
CARR, John,
Bricklayer, 25, Massachusetts.
CARTAJAL, Jose Maria,
Teamster, 25, California.
CASTRO, Antonio,
Farmer, 40, California.
CASTRO, Francisco,
Farmer, 43, California.
CASTRO, Jose Maria,
Farmer, 42, California.
CASTRO, Rafael,
Farmer, 65, California.
CASTRO, Vicente,
Farmer, 30, California.
CHALONER, Herbert Alvin,
Woodsman, 21, Maine.
CHASE, William Perry,
Laborer, 30, Maine.
CHRISTIAN, Charles,
Laborer, 44, Sweden.

CLARK, John,
Miner, 37, Ohio.
CLARK, Milton,
Farmer, 27, Missouri.
CLARK, William,
Farmer, 60, Tennessee.
CLINGAN, William Riley,
Farmer, 28, Tennessee.
CLEMENTS, Lambert Blair,
Judicial Officer, 45, U.S.
COLLINS, George,
Carpenter, 50, New York.
CONN, William,
Teamster, 41, Great Britain.
CORCORAN, James,
Farmer, 47, Ireland.
COVENY, John,
Farmer, 46, Ireland.
CRABB, Sylvanus Spencer,
Laborer, 37, U.S.
CRAIG, Samuel,
Carpenter, 40, Virginia.
CULLINAN, Michael,
Farmer, 38, Ireland.
CUMMINGS, David John,
Clerk, 27, Canada.
CUMMINGS, Hiram
Butterfield, Miner, 38,
New York.
CURREN, James,
Teamster, New York.
CURTIS, Edwin Ernest,
Farmer, 21, Maine.

DART, Harrison,
Currier, 48, New York.
DARLING, Abraham,
Miner, 29, New York.
DARLING, Barber,
Lumberman, 34, New York.
DARLING, Jason Jackson,
Laborer, 26, Indiana.
DAUBENBIS, John,
Farmer, 52, Bavaria.
DAUBENBIS, Henry,
Farmer, 39, Bavaria.
DAVENPORT, Curtis,
Farmer, 49, Ohio.
DAVENPORT, David,
Farmer, 24, U.S.

DAVENPORT, Jesse,
Farmer, 49, Ohio.
DAVENPORT, John Pope,
Whaleman, 49, Rhode Isld.
DAVIS, George W.,
Farmer, 39, Virginia.
DEAN, John,
Cooper, 26, New York.
DEXTER, Leonard Warren,
Machinist, 25, Massachusetts.
DOANE, Handley Bushnell,
Farmer, 54, U.S.
DONNELSON, William,
Blacksmith, 35, Maryland.
DOCKERY, John,
Blacksmith, 34, U.S.
DOVER, James Madison,
Farmer, 32, Tennessee.
DOVER, Jesse,
Farmer, 29, Tennessee.
DOWNING, William,
Laborer, 63, Tennessee.
DOYLE, John,
Farmer, 39, Ireland.
DUFFEY, William,
Farmer, 51, Ireland.
DUNCAN, Garner Hiram,
Laborer, 36, Virginia.
DUNN, James Abner,
Woodsman, 46, U.S.
DUNNING, James Monroe,
Blacksmith, 21, Louisiana.
DYER, George,
Clerk, 36, U.S.

ELDRIDGE, Geo. Washington
Wheelwright, 35, U.S.
ELLIS, John,
Farmer, 31, New York.
ELLSMORE, Benj. Gootch,
Lumberman, 24, Maine.
EWING, Samuel Beymer,
Blacksmith, 42, Ohio.

FARGO, Corydon Alonzo,
Blacksmith, 33, New York.
FEELEY, Dennis Carlton,
Farmer, 39, New York.
FENTON, Horatio Reed,
Laborer, 29, New York.

FITZGERALD, Joseph,
Carpenter, 27, U.S.
FOLEY, Patrick,
Farmer, 55, Ireland.
FORSYTH, John Gilbert,
Laborer, 42, Mass.
FOX, Frank,
Teamster, 60, Pennsylvania.
FRESHOUR, Joseph Terre,
Laborer, 24, Indiana.
FREY, Joseph,
Farmer, 43, France.

GALIPHER, Joseph,
Farmer, 56, Maryland.
GARDNER, Daniel Foster,
Lumberman, 48, Maine.
GAULDING, Benj. Franklin,
Blacksmith, 22, Missouri.
GILES, Geo. Washington,
Miller, 33, Ohio.
GLOVER, Asa,
Laborer, 55, New Hamp.
GOOCH, Nicholas Lewis,
Farmer, 31, Indiana.
GOODRICH, Joseph,
Farmer, 40, England.
GOOSEMAN (Guzman),
Andrew, Laborer, 34, Calif.
GOVERS, William,
Laborer, 39, Holland.
GREEN, Wm. H. Harrison,
Blacksmith, 25, Kentucky.
GREINER, Louis Benjamin,
Millman, 30, Pennsylvania.
GROVER, James Lyman,
Farmer, 46, Maine.
GROVER, Stephen Freeland,
Lumberman, 37, Maine.
GROW, G. Timothy,
Mechanic, 37, U.S.
GULLIVER, George William,
Engineer, 22, New Jersey.

HALE, Titus,
Farmer, 32, U.S.
HACKETT, George,
Farmer, 50, New York.
HAIGHT, Lansing,
Millman, 49, New York.

HALL, Samuel Alonzo,
Carpenter, 51, Massachusetts.
HALL, William,
Sawyer, 35, New York.
HAMES, John,
Farmer, 54, New York.
HARMON, Sherlock,
Laborer, 22, Maine.
HARRIS, Benj. Franklin,
Broom Maker, 30, New York.
HARRIS, Willard Carroll,
Laborer, 22, Illinois.
HARSLEY, Abram Mills,
Carpenter, 54, Maine.
HART, Nathan,
Farmer, 35, U.S.
HARTNEY, John,
Tanner, 39, Europe.
HASTINGS, Noah Moulton,
Laborer, 32, New Hampshire.
HATTERY, Ephraim,
Farmer, 30, Ohio.
HEADLEY, James Arnold,
Farmer, 48, Pennsylvania.
HENRY, James,
Laborer, 48, Scotland.
HIMES, Geo. Washington,
Farmer, 45, U.S.
HINCKLEY, Roger Gibson,
Millright, 62, U.S.
HITE, William,
Farmer, 35, Pennsylvania.
HOFFMAN, Adam,
Laborer, 27, Prussia.
HOLCOMB, Isaac Webster,
Farmer, 37, U.S.
HORN, James Monroe,
Joiner, 47, U.S.
HOOPER, Abram,
Laborer, 48, Pennsylvania.
HOWARD, Francis Marion,
Teamster, 25, Missouri.
HOWLAND, Sabin,
Farmer, 44, New York.
HUBBARD, Henry Cutler,
Tanner, 23, Vermont.
HUGHES, Eli Kimber,
Laborer, 41, Kentucky.
HUMPHREY, Verry,
Farmer, 37, New York.

JOHNSON, Calvin,
Miller, 32, U.S.
JOHNSON, Edward,
Laborer, 34, Arkansas.
JOHNSON, Johan Henry,
Farmer, 33, Hanover.
JOHNSON, John,
Farmer, 61, Maryland.

KEATING, John Kavenaugh,
Laborer, 32, Maine.
KINGSLEY, Martin,
Farmer, 34, Ireland.
KIRBY, Charles Henry,
Teamster, 39, Illinois.
KIRBY, Silas Wright,
Laborer, 22, Illinois.
KIRK, William Jonathan,
Laborer, 33, Illinois.
KIRKPATRICK, Charles T.,
Miner, 39, Maine.
KNIGHT, Thomas Dow Wilson,
Engine Turner, 25, R.I.

LANE, Silas Spring,
Woodsman, 30, Maine.
LEE, John Enoch,
Farmer, 32, Tennessee.
LEONARD, James,
Farmer, 63, Ireland.
LEONARD, James,
Farmer, 33, Ireland.
LEONARD, Michael Joseph,
Farmer, 38, Ireland.
LEONARD, Patrick,
Farmer, 36, Ireland.
LISTON, John Franklin,
Teamster, 38, U.S.
LITTLEJOHN, Jose David,
Farmer, 32, California.
LODGE, Jose Ant. Miguel,
Engineer, 27, California.
LOGAN, Gustas,
Miller, 35, Ohio.
LONG, Isaiah Kirk,
Farmer, 32, Indiana.
LOVE, Jerome William,
Soldier, 39, U.S.
LUCERO, Alvino,
Farmer, 32, Mexico.

MACKEY, Hugh,
Currier, 30, Scotland.
MALONEY, James,
Laborer, 70, Ireland.
MALSON, Wm. Thomas,
Laborer, 32, Ohio
MANN, Ervin Francis,
Hotel Keeper, 22, R.I.
MANN, Thomas Wilson,
Hotel Keeper, 23, U.S.
MARTIN, Andrew Jackson,
Engineer, 25, U.S.
MARTIN, Ledyard Hall,
Miller, 27, U.S.
MASON, Swetland,
Teamster, 34, Ohio.
MASON, Sylvester J.,
Farmer, 46, U.S.
MATTISON, John Stead,
Farmer, 44, England.
MATTISON, Robert Wm.,
Farmer, 42, England.
MAXWELL, Wm. Benjamin,
Farmer, 42, U.S.
McAARON, Wm. Henry,
Laborer, 44, Pennsylvania.
McCALL, Hugh Pablo,
Farmer, 74, New Jersey.
McCAWLEY, John,
Laborer, 41, U.S.
McCOY, Daniel,
Teamster, 22, Iowa.
McCOY, James Jackson,
Farmer, 36, Virginia.
McDOUGAL, Thos. Jefferson,
Farmer, 35, U.S.
McELROY, Wilson,
Seaman, 35, Ireland.
McILVENEN, Andrew,
Weaver, 28, Scotland.
McKAMISH, James,
Farmer, 39, Tennessee.
McLAUGHLIN, John L.,
Teamster, 35, New York.
McMULLEN, John,
Farmer, 59, U.S.
MILLER, John Barton,
Farmer, 45, Kentucky.
MILLER, Thomas,
Farmer, 43, England.

MITCHELL, Christopher,
  Woodsman, 34, New York.
MONTIETH, Daniel,
  Farmer, 45, U.S.
MOORE, Amos J.,
  Farmer, 44, U.S.
MOORE, Richard Mount,
  Trader, 62, New Jersey.
MORGAN, John William,
  Farmer, 46, U.S.
MORRISEY, Patrick,
  Papermaker, 25, Ireland.
MURRAY, John,
  Tanner, 32, Ireland.
MUSGRAVE, Alfred,
  Farmer, 41, U.S.

NEFF, John Sherman,
  Teamster, 31, Indiana.
NEWMAN, Benjamin,
  Laborer, 21, Iowa.
NEWMAN, Nathaniel,
  Laborer, 28, Canada.
NICHOLS, Benjamin Cahoon,
  Lumberman, 35, U.S.
NICHOLS, Samuel Merritt,
  Lumberman, 25, U.S.
NICHOLS, Uriah Schemerhorn,
  Lumberman, 27, U.S.
NOBLE, Augustus,
  Farmer, 43, U.S.
NOLAND, William,
  Laborer, 48, Kentucky.
NOONAN, Dennis,
  Laborer, 37, Ireland.
NOYES, Willard Ward,
  Turner, 22, U.S.
NUTTER, Richard,
  Sawyer, 28, England.

O'CONNOR, Bryan,
  Carpenter, 44, Ireland.
OLIVER, William,
  Farmer, 37, Sweden.
ORD, John Stephen,
  Farmer, 33, U.S.
OWEN, John Wesley,
  Saloonkeeper, 32, Kentucky.

PAGE, Charles,
  Teamster, 26, Maine.
PAGLES, Edward,
  Blacksmith, 52, Germany.
PAGLES, Edward,
  Laborer, 21, U.S.
PARKHURST, Charles Darkey,
  Farmer, 55, New Hampshire.
PARRISH, Joshua,
  Farmer, 50, Ohio.
PARSONS, Jacob,
  Blacksmith, 40, U.S.
PARTINGTON, John James,
  Farmer, 33, U.S.
PATTEN, Patrick,
  Teamster, 30, Ireland.
PECK, Henry Winegar,
  Farmer, 48, New York.
PENIX, Jeremiah,
  Laborer, 55, Kentucky.
PHILLIPS, James Brown,
  Teamster, 47, U.S.
PHILLIPS, John Mitchell,
  Laborer, 27, Illinois.
PHILLIPS, John Sayles,
  Farmer, 27, Rhode Island.
PHILLIPS, Thos. James,
  Teacher, 49, U.S.
PIERCE, William,
  Carpenter, 51, Vermont.
PILKINGTON, Thomas,
  Farmer, 53, England.
PORTER, Benj. Franklin,
  Farmer, 35, Vermont
PORTER, Edward,
  Merchant, 40, Vermont.
PORTER, Frank Ford,
  Tanner, 29, U.S.
PORTER, John Thomas,
  Trader, 35, U.S.
POLLARD, Lawrence,
  Farmer, 57, England.

RABEL, Francis,
  Farmer, 42, Prussia.
RAMOS, Jose,
  Teamster, 29, Texas.
REDMON, Henry,
  Laborer, 38, Tennessee.

REED, Robert Samuel,
Dairyman, 33, Missouri.
REED, Wm. James,
Farmer, 29, Massachusetts.
RESSER, Hartman,
Saloonkeeper, 38, Prussia.
RIDDLE, James Martin,
Farmer, 48, North Carolina.
RIGER, John,
Gardner, 45, Germany.
RILEY, Robert,
Farmer, 27, Vermont.
ROBERTSON, James,
Teamster, 31, S.C.
ROBERTSON, Stanley
Littlejohn, Physician, 56, Va.
ROBINSON, George,
Farmer, 56, Delaware.
ROBINSON, John Shelley,
Farmer, 37, Indiana.
ROBINSON, Robert Lee,
Farmer, 21, Iowa.
RODRIGUEZ, Jose Brigido,
Farmer, 74, California.
RODRIGUEZ, Jose de Jesus,
Farmer, 45, California.
RODRIGUEZ, Manrico,
Farmer, 40, California.
RODRIGUEZ, Manuel,
Farmer, 49, California.
ROGERS, Hayden,
Wheelwright, 55, U.S.
ROLLINS, Lyman,
Engineman, 36,
New Hampshire.
ROY, James Morris,
Farmer, 43, Virginia.
RYDER, Charles Henry,
Farmer, 39, U.S.
RYDER, William Rowland,
Farmer, 34, U.S.

SAMUEL, Henry Thomas,
Farmer, 32, Norway.

SAMUEL, Nicholas Andrew,
Farmer, 30, Norway.
SAMUELS, Martin,
Carpenter, 40, Ohio.

SCHWAN, Jacob,
Farmer, 45, Germany.
SERLES, Andonisiana Judson,
Farmer, 37, New York.
SETTLE, Benj. Franklin,
Farmer, 31, Kentucky.
SHELBY, John LaFayette,
Expressman, 38, U.S.
SHEPARD, Bradley Justice,
Blacksmith, 43, New York.
SHUEY, James Edgar,
Farmer, 25, Illinois.
SIMONS, William,
Laborer, 25, Ohio.
SINNOTT, John Edward,
Laborer, 33, Ohio.
SKINNER, Henry,
Clerk, 23, Vermont.
SLOAN, Uriah,
Farmer, 27, Ohio.
SMART, John,
Farmer, 32, Tennessee.
SMITH, Edward,
Laborer, 34, U.S.
SMITH, James,
Laborer, 26, Great Britain.
SMITH, James Mellidge,
Expressman, 39, U.S.
SMITH, William Henry,
Laborer, 37, born at Sea.
SMITH, William Henry,
Laborer, 23, Maine.
SOBERANES, Jose Antonio,
Farmer, 46, California.
STELLE, Frederick,
Farmer, 47, Sweden.
STEVENS, Cyprian,
Laborer, 52, Massachusetts.
STONE, Henry Porter,
Lawyer, 26, U.S.
SWAN, John,
Laborer, 34, Tennessee.
SWEET, Paul,
Farmer, 50, Rhode Island.
SWEET, Timothy,
Miner, 50, New York.

THOMPSON, Uriah William,
Farmer, 36, U.S.

TENNEY, William Alfred,
Clergyman, 40, Maine.
THURBER, Henry,
Farmer, 30, Rhode Island.
THURBER, Ira,
Farmer, 38, Rhode Island.
TOWNE, John Willis,
Farmer, 43, U.S.
TROUT, Emanuel,
Farmer, 46, New York.

VALENCIA, Nicolas,
Farmer, 39, California.

WALSH, John,
Laborer, 36, New York.
WALSH, Patrick,
Hotelman, 52, Ireland.
WARDWELL, Gideon Church,
Farmer, 48, U.S.
WARE, Lewis Talbot,
Farmer, 32, Kentucky.
WEBSTER, Nathaniel B.,
Cook, 41, Connecticut.
WELLER, Henry,
Teamster, 29, England.

WENKLE, Henry,
Farmer, 43, Prussia.
WHITE, Francis Marion,
Teamster, 25, Missouri.
WHITE, Geo. Washington,
Woodsman, 29, Ohio.
WHITE, Harrison,
Laborer, 26, Illinois.
WHITE, John Howell,
Farmer, 22, Illinois.
WHITE, Joseph Charles,
Currier, 34, Pennsylvania.
WHITE, Luther Robin,
Laborer, 22, Illinois.
WHITE, William,
Farmer, 75, U.S.
WHITESIDE, Robert Kiad,
Laborer, 34, Illinois.
WHITTIER, Almon John,
Laborer, 23, Maine.
WILSON, Oscar Paulette,
Miller, 41, U.S.
WRIGHT, David,
Carpenter, 60, New York.
WRIGHT, Thomas,
Teamster, 25, New York.

Annals
of
Santa Cruz

1947

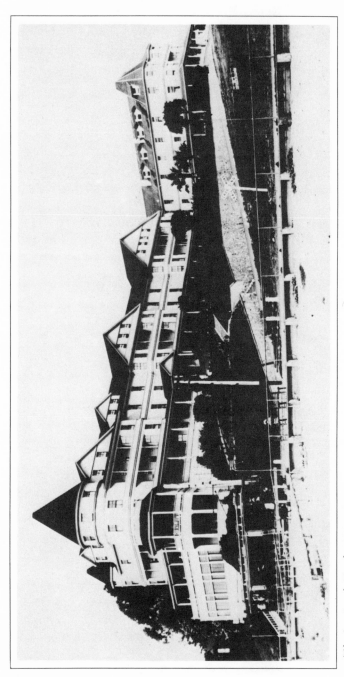

The Sea Beach Hotel, 1888–1912

◄═►

SARGENTO ORTEGA WAS
PORTOLA'S PATHFINDER

A T DUSK of Wednesday, October 14, 1769, Sargento Jose
Francisco Ortega of the Spanish army and eight soldados
de cuera mounted on mules splashed into the waters of
the San Lorenzo river, the first white men to see the site of the
present city of Santa Cruz.

The Portola party, weary and sick after three months' march
from San Diego, had crossed the Pajaro river (the soldiers had
given it the name because they found a bird stuffed by Indians)
on October 11 and camped near it until Ortega returned from
his scouting trip. He reported that he had traveled to the foot
of a high white hill.

The camp was in the region of present day Corralitos. The
hill where Ortega turned back was a week later named by the
chaplain, Fr. Juan Crespi, Alto de Jamon (Ham hill) and the
nearby stream (today's Scotts creek) San Pedro del Jamon. The
hill today is known as Gianone's, sixteen miles up the coast
north of Santa Cruz.

Portola and his main party, the day after being rejoined by
Ortega, moved a league and a half into what is now Valencia
valley; on Monday night they reached the Soquel valley to
which they gave the name of Rosario del Serafin de Asculi,
recording that they found wild roses which reminded them of
those of Spain.

Two leagues on October 17, St. Lawrence day in the Catholic
calendar, brought them to the river which they called San Lorenzo. Concerning the next day Fr. Crespi's diary recorded:
"Five hundred paces after we started we crossed a good arroyo
of running water which descends from some hills where it rises.
We named it Santa Cruz."

The little stream today flows through a residence district and is variously known as Major's mill creek or the Laurel street brook.

Another three days saw the Portola party up the coast at what is now Waddell creek, near the San Mateo county line, which the soldiers called la Canada del Salud, because two days were spent there resting. Crespi named it the arroyo of San Luis Beltran.

The party continued north, still looking for the site of Monterey, which it had failed to recognize as it passed.

Sergeant Ortega was a native of Guanajuato who was five years later commissioned a lieutenant and given command at San Diego. He founded Santa Barbara presidio and, retired with brevet rank as captain, died there in 1798. Bancroft, the historian, remarks of him: "He was an officer whose record was an excellent one." Padre Junipero Serra unsuccessfully proposed him for governor of Alta California.

─◄█►─

MISSION ESTABLISHED BY
ALFEREZ HERMENEGILDO SAL

THE SITE on a little hill a mile back from the mouth of the San Lorenzo river was selected in 1774 for a mission by Fr. Francisco Palou, chaplain of an expedition led by Governor Rivera, which came down the coast from the north.

On December 9, 1774, Palou entered in his diary: "The site is fitted not merely for a town but a city. Nothing is lacking. It has good soil, water, pasture, firewood and timber, all at hand in abundance."

From Monterey, the middle of the next month, Palou forwarded his report to Viceroy Bucarelli in Mexico. On May 24

Bucarelli acknowledged its receipt and wrote to Governor Rivera directing him not to delay in the erection of the proposed new missions.

Rivera was busy and Bucarelli had been succeeded by Antonio Flores and the latter by Don Juan Vicente de Guemes Pachedo de Padilla, Conde de Revilla Gigedo, before the matter was taken up again twelve years later.

Padilla on August 30, 1787, replied to a letter from Fr. Marias de Noriega, temporary head of the Franciscan establishment in Mexico:

"Agreeing to the proposal which your reverence makes in your report of last September, I have resolved that two missions should be established in Alta California, one in the valley called Soledad, close to the Rio de Monterey (Salinas river) between the mission of San Antonio and that of San Carlos; and the other between the mission of San Carlos and that of Santa Clara, about twenty-five leagues from the former, at the place called Santa Cruz."

After Fr. Fermin Lasuen, accompanied by Corporal Luis Peralta and five soldiers, marked the location with a cross on August 28, 1791, Alferez Hermenegildo Sal, commander of San Francisco presidio, sent a mule train of supplies on September 17 and five days later started out himself, guided by Corporal Luis Peralta.

At Santa Clara they picked up Padres Baldomero Lopez and Alonzo Isidro Salazar, more supplies and livestock, and several Indians to be servants and laborers, with which they arrived at the mission site on September 24.

The next morning mass and the Te Deum by the priests and firing of guns by the soldiers constituted the ceremony.

The personnel of the mission establishment in its first month is given by the list of those who acted as godfathers for the Indians, whom the priests immediately began baptising. The first baptism was of an eight-year-old Indian girl on October 9.

Godfathers named in the first month were:

Alferez Sal; Cabo (Corporal) Peralta; Soldados de Cuera Pablo Azebes, Jose Vicente Aguila, Francisco Tapia, Ramon

Linares, Bartholomo Pacheco, Joaquin Bernal and Ignacio Alviso; and Sirvientes Maximo Estrada, Francisco Nisifort, Francisco Gonzales, Anatasio de la Cruz, Salvador Rubio, Manuel Villanueva and Pablo Vejar.

As each Indian was baptised, careful entry was made of his rancheria, which put on the mission books the names of Soquel (or Osocales), Aptos and Zayante, as well as a score of other rancherias whose names are no longer extant.

The first building was a temporary chapel of palisades, slabs of split redwood thrust upright in the ground. On February 27, 1793, cornerstone for a permanent chapel was laid. The structure was completed on May 19, 1794, a stone and adobe building 112 feet long.

The chapel, facing the plaza which later was enclosed by adobes on three sides, was weakened by heavy rains in 1840; a quake in 1857 shook down the front wall. In 1858 a wooden church was built and in 1889 the present brick Catholic church was erected.

The best record of the appearance of the mission chapel is an etching made in 1883 by Henry Chapman Ford, an artist who traveled the California coast, visiting each mission and who, in Santa Cruz, garnered detail from residents who remembered it in Mexican days.

Holy Cross mission of today, built in 1932 with funds given by Mrs. Gladys Sullivan Doyle, was constructed after much research on the same lines and in the same proportions as the chapel of 1794, although about half its size.

The mission priests put their Indian charges to growing corn on the potrero to the north, still called by that name; planted a pear orchard; and had beans and other vegetables growing on the flat which is now Santa Cruz' business district, marking the garden's edge with a ditch and row of willows along what is today Pacific avenue.

By 1800 the mission was producing 4,300 fanegas of wheat, corn and beans annually. Its most prosperous period came in the last dozen years before the religious establishments of California were taken out of the hands of the Franciscans in 1834. The mission then had 3,700 horned cattle, 8,300 sheep and nearly 1,000 horses grazing from Punto Ano Nuevo to Corralitos and was violating governmental orders against Indians on horseback by using its neophytes as vaqueros.

Santa Cruz mission had a martyred priest. On the night of October 12, 1812, Fr. Andres Quintana, temporarily alone while Fr. Marcelino Marquinez was on a trip to Monterey, was called out by the Indians on a pretext and brutally murdered. Investigation by the military four years later brought lashes and imprisonment to the guilty neophytes.

In 1885, when excavation was made for the present church, the body of Fr. Quintana was recognized by its vestments and was reburied in a stone coffin. Quintana was a native of Spain who had landed at Monterey in 1805 and whose sole ministry was at Santa Cruz.

With secularization Governor Jose Figueroa made a short-lived and unsuccessful effort to convert the mission establishment into Villa Figueroa but administration was given over to the authorities of Villa de Branciforte, across the river, and the two communities were merged until American days.

⇥⇤

VILLA DE BRANCIFORTE WAS JUST ACROSS THE RIVER

WHAT IS NOW SANTA CRUZ' east side was for half a century, under Spanish and Mexican rule, a separate village.

Viceroy Branciforte, in Mexico, transmitted orders from Madrid that three pueblos were to be founded in California independent of religious or military, to build a civil population as a guard against encroachment by the Russians already at Sitka and against possible aggression by England or France.

Los Angeles and San Jose, already established, were designated as two of the future cities. For the third a site just across the river from Santa Cruz mission was selected by Lieutenant Alberto de Cordova of the engineering corps of the Spanish army, sent from Madrid to inspect California defenses.

Cordova and Governor Diego Borica from Monterey spent several weeks at the mission in the summer of 1796 laying plans and on May 12, 1797, the schooner *Concepcion* arrived at Monterey from San Blas with eight settlers for Villa de Branci-forte. Three, perhaps four, brought wives; two had children.

They were ex-residents of Guadalajara who, having run afoul of the rigorous law, were given a choice of jail in Mexico or a home in California. They included a tailor, a carpenter, miner, merchant, engraver, two farmers and one unclassified.

As inducements they had been offered free transportation north, 430 pesos spread over five years, houses of adobe and tile as gifts of the king, and farm tools to be paid for in installments.

The eight men were Vicente Moxica, Agustin Narvaez, Antonio Robles, Ignacio Acedes, Jose Maria Arceo, Jose Barbosa, Fermin Cordero and Jose Miguel Uribes.

When the *Concepcion* arrived at Monterey Governor Borica sent orders to Corporal Gabriel Moraga at San Jose to come over to Santa Cruz with a few soldiers, find quarters at the mission and start erecting houses. If the settlers arrived before the building was done they were to turn to and help. Moraga was to remain as comisionado.

The Guadalajarenos arrived, after a march around Monterey bay, on June 24, 1797, to find their adobe homes were not prepared. Those with the most stamina built for themselves, while the others, complaining, found quarters with the soldiers or at the mission.

Another class of settlers was soon found. Borica sent instructions to the presidios to influence young soldiers finishing their ten-year enlistments to settle at the new pueblo. They were to have privileges of pobladores and to receive small pensions; in return they were to be subject to call for military duty, carrying out the scheme for a population for coast defense.

In the year after the coming of the Guadalajarenos six young invalidos settled. With the exception of Corporal Marcelino Bravo, who established himself at Soquel and died there in

1806, they were married. Several had served in the Santa Cruz mission escolta and knew the country.

Two of the invalido soldiers who made homes at Villa de Branciforte in 1797 and 1798 were Jose Antonio Rodriguez, who had served in various mission escoltas for a decade or more, and Joaquin Castro, who had trudged as a boy of six with his father's family in the Anza party overland from Sonora in 1776. Both established large families which have still many members in Santa Cruz county. They and their children were recipients of eight land grants.

Others of the invalidos were Marcos Briones, Marcos Villela, Juan Jose Peralta, Pablo Vejar, Salvador Higuera, Juan Maria Pinto, Julian Rios, Toribio Martinez, Apolonario Bernal, Manuel Romero, Antonio Buelna, Vicente Aguila and Luz Garcia.

Herds were prolific and land plentiful. Life adapted itself to a baronial scale. From the compact little village laid out by Cordova, with its center about where the Branciforte school now stands, the Brancifortians spread over what is today the entire county. Usually they established a ranch home and then applied for a land grant.

The rancho grants in Santa Cruz county, all made under Mexican rule, were:

> **Aptos** (6,680 acres), granted to Rafael Castro in 1883.
> **Soquel and Soquel Augmentacion** (35,000 acres), granted to Rafael's sister, Martina, in 1833 and 1844.
> **San Andres** (13,000 acres), granted their father, Joaquin Castro, 1833.
> **Arroyo del Rodeo** (1,472 acres), Francisco Rodriguez, 1834.
> **Laguna de Calabasas** (2,364 acres), Felipe Hernandez, 1835.
> **Bolsa del Pajaro** (5,496 acres), Sebastian Rodriguez, 1837.
> **Carbonero,** Guillermo Bocle (William Buckle), 1838.
> **Canada Verde de Salsipuedes** (31,201 acres), Manuel Jimeno, 1840.
> **Arroyo de la Laguna,** Gil Sanchez, 1841.
> **Rancho Refugio** (12,137 acres), grant of 1841 to three Castro sisters, Maria de las Angeles, Candida and Jacinta.

San Agustin (4,436 acres), and Zayante (2,658 acres),
Joseph L Majors, 1841.
Potrero Rincon de San Pedro Regalado, Jose Arana,
1842.
Canada del Rincon (5,826 acres), Pierre Sainsevain,
1843.
Agua Puerca y Trancas (4,421 acres), Roman Rodri-
guez, 1843.
Tres Ojos de Agua , Nicolas Dodero, 1844.
Los Corralitos (15,440 acres), Jose Amesti, 1844.
San Vicente (10,802 acres), Blas Escamilla, 1846.

For administrative head Branciforte had a comisionado, at
first a non-commissioned officer in active army service, later
one of the invalidos.

Municipal form of government was attempted. Moxica, one
of the eight Guadalajarenos, was elected alcalde in 1802 but
died the same year, after which there was, so far as records go,
no alcalde until Felipe Hernandez, a convict settler who had
been given full privileges of a poblador by the viceroy, was
elected in 1805.

In 1822 Branciforte was informed by the governor that its
population of 120 gente de razon was insufficient to warrant a
full municipal government, that authorities at San Jose would
take it under their wing and appoint a juez de paz annually. The
change made little difference to the Brancifortians, for they
were usually asked to select the appointee.

Appointment of comisionados stopped in 1834 after which
the juez de paz combined duties of alcalde and comisionado.

Six years later the California government at Monterey began
naming the jueces de paz. The system continued until the
Castro-Alvarado revolution of 1836, when the prefect for northern California, with headquarters at San Juan Bautista, began
making the appointments.

The last juez de paz was Jose Bolcoff, a Russian, born at
Petropaulofski, Kamchatka, who left a Siberian whaling ship in
Monterey bay and settled at Branciforte in 1815. He became a
leading citizen, marrying Candida Castro. Candida was one of
the three Castro sisters to whom Rancho Refugio had been
granted. American courts later held Bolcoff had improperly

erased the names of the sisters from the grant, substituting his own. The courts awarded a third of the ranch (now Wilder's ranch, just west of the city) to Joseph L. Majors, who had married Maria de los Angeles Castro. The third sister, Jacinta, became a nun and relinquished any claim to title. Bolcoff lived in Santa Cruz through the first two decades of American rule after which members of his family moved to Watsonville and to Half Moon Bay in San Mateo county.

Today's visitor who would seek vestige of Villa de Branciforte can do little more than find North Branciforte avenue which, nearly level and a little than a mile long, was laid out in 1796 or 1797 by Cordova, the Spanish lieutenant of engineers, to be a race course for the villagers' horses and the main street of their town. On the lower flat, between Branciforte creek and the San Lorenzo river the Brancifortians held their bull and bear fights.

◄►

JOAQUIN CASTRO'S
SAN ANDRES HOUSE

O N SAN ANDRES RANCHO (which in American days became corrupted to San Andreas) at the end of a hilltop lane that juts off the Larkin valley road, stands the two-story adobe mansion which Joaquin Castro built in his latter years for his seventeen-year-old second wife.

Antonia Amador, his first wife, had lived with him on what is now North Branciforte avenue in Santa Cruz, near her sisters, Donna Serefin Pinto and Donna Francisco Alviso, until her death in 1827 at the age of forty-three. Their children were Martina and Rafael and nine others, most of whom became prominent citizens around the north shore of Monterey bay.

Bereaved, Joaquin married Rosaria Briones, daughter of Manuel Briones and his wife, Antonia Vasquez. For her he built the

San Andres House   UCSC SPECIAL COLLECTIONS

30-by-100-foot home on a commanding position on the rancho granted him north of the mouth of the Pajaro river. It still stands, with its 30-by-50-foot fandango room on the second floor and its two-story porch covered with grape vines.

After Joaquin died in 1838 his young widow married a member of the Espinosa family and lived on in the San Andres home with two of Joaquin's sons, whom she sued over distribution of the property.

EARLY VOTING PRECINCTS

The county got along with three voting precincts, Santa Cruz, Soquel and Pajaro, until 1853 when farming population on the coast of what is now San Mateo county required designation of New Years Point precinct. Butano appeared in 1856 but in 1857 Pescadero was substituted for it.

In 1857 New Years Point and Pescadero went to San Mateo county by legislative act but San Lorenzo, Scotts Valley and Corralitos appeared. By 1879 Mission and Branciforte precincts had been carved out of Santa Cruz and six more rural voting places found necessary, Seaside, Laguna, Ben Lomond (Mountain), Boulder Creek, Summit and Highland.

Six more were in existence by 1886, Aptos, San Andres, Loma Prieta, Castle Rock and Glenwood. Mission and Branciforte had become Santa Cruz Nos. 1 and 2. Pajaro became Watsonville Nos. 1 and 2. Seaside was then Davenport and the old San Lorenzo precinct was Felton.

·≡▰·

BOYS OF BRANCIFORTE WENT FORTH TO WARS

VILLA DE BRANCIFORTE had hardly been established when Corporal Moraga was ordered by the governor to maintain a watch of one white man and two Indians on the cliffs for marauding vessels.

Almost yearly, reports spread through Alta California of strange and perhaps aggressor ships off the coast. In 1800 one of British appearance was said to have anchored off the Salinas river and then sailed out of Monterey bay.

Rebellions in Spain's South American colonies stopped the trade ships from Callao. In 1816 came warnings, which Monterey transmitted to Branciforte, of probable visits by insurgent vessels, although none arrived. Governor Sola instructed priests to be ready to move their mission valuables inland.

In 1818 an American trader brought word from Honolulu that two ships flying the flag of the Republic of Buenos Aires were coming. When, in November, they appeared, Governor Sola ordered Padre Ramon Olbes of Santa Cruz to flee to Santa Clara and Juez Joaquin Buelna of Branciforte to take charge of the mission.

Bouchard, the South American privateer, anchored off Santa Cruz but decided against landing through the winter surf. Crossing the bay he sacked Monterey, after which he sailed south, visiting the Ortega rancho near Santa Barbara and continuing down the coast.

Olbes' return from Santa Clara was followed by charges of theft of mission articles. A military inquiry established that Buelna's laxity had perhaps permitted Indian thievery but that the gente de razon of Branciforte were blameless.

Through the years the boys of Branciforte did their military service, going off for a ten-year enlistment as soon as they were seventeen or eighteen years old, but not until the rebellion of 1836 did the Brancifortians take a general part.

Juan Bautista Alvarado and Jose Castro, the latter a cousin of the Santa Cruz Castros, were leading the effort of Californians to have officials selected from the educated and competent men of California instead of sent from Mexico.

Alvarado and Castro sent young Rafael Pinto, Branciforte boy who had been their schoolmate at Monterey, around the bay with a captain's commission for Juan Gonzales, mayordomo of the mission. Pinto and Gonzales enlisted thirty-five men and boys, nearly a third of the army which Alvarado and Castro led south to convince the reluctant and dubious Angelenos that the newly declared free and sovereign state was to be taken seriously.

Another third of the Alvarado army were "Americanos rifleros," sharpshooting hunters and trappers, most of whom had come over the Santa Fe trail, under leadership of Isaac Graham, a Virginian who was running a little still at Natividad in the Salinas valley.

The rebels succeeded in sending Governor Gutierrez back to Mexico but dropped their effort to found an independent state when the Mexican government shrewdly made Alvarado governor.

Brancifortians again took part in a rebellion when, in 1844–45, Alvarado led a revolt against Governor Micheltorena. The governor had support of Captain John Sutter of Sacramento, who had exacted promise of land grants for himself and his followers. Graham, in Branciforte, offered Micheltorena services of a company of "foreigners" but the Americans and Britons of Santa Cruz repudiated him and his offer.

Alvarado raised a "foreign" contingent in the south and met Micheltorena on February 21, 1845, in the San Fernando valley.

The engagement was without casualties but killed a few days earlier when Alvarado had seized Los Angeles was Juan Tambor, "Johnny the Drummer Boy," who was Juan Higuera of Calabasas rancho of Branciforte.

COUNTY'S LOST AREA

Great was the outcry in May, 1857, when it was learned that a "bill to reorganize San Mateo county" had gone through the legislature transferring to it thirty square miles of coast area which had been in Santa Cruz county. Santa Cruz lost Pescadero and Half Moon Bay.

To top it, another small portion was carved off in 1868 when the line, which had been run straight west from the headwaters of the south branch of San Francisquito creek was changed to follow a ridge of hills to the coast.

AMERICANS WERE
THE FOREIGNERS THEN

IN LATER MEXICAN DAYS Santa Cruz had more English-speaking residents than did Yerba Buena to the north.

Thomas Doak, first American permanent resident of California, was in Branciforte in 1823. A native of Boston, he had come in the *Albatross* in 1816 and been baptised in the Catholic faith at San Carlos five years later.

The following year saw two Americans and two Londoners baptised in Santa Cruz. One, William Ochesson by the mission record, was on his death bed. The others, Julian Wilson, twenty-four-year-old native of Virginia, and William and Samuel Buckle from London, became permanent residents. There is some evidence but no proof that all four had been soldier-sailors in the privateering fleet of Lord Cochrane, the British adventurer who helped South American countries win their independence.

The Buckle brothers for some mysterious reason became the Thompson brothers in the early forties. William, who married Antonia Montero, received Rancho Carbonero as a grant. He had an adobe house on what is today the sixteenth fairway of the Pasatiempo golf course. Samuel remained a bachelor and died in 1872 at the home of Charles Martin at Glenwood. Wilson married Josefa Alviso; their son, Guillermo, married Matilde Buelna; scores of their descendants are in California today.

A year or two later came William Trevethan, a young Briton who had sailed from Plymouth in 1822 on a four-year whaling voyage. When, after touching at Honolulu, his ship, the *Rover,* came to California Trevethan decided to remain. He married Antonia Perez, died in 1875. A street on his land holdings is named after him.

David Spence, young Scotchman who became a prominent Monterey merchant, was baptised at Santa Cruz mission in 1828.

First record of the presence of Michael Lodge, Dublin-born sailor, is the priest's entry when he and his wife, Josefa, daughter of the old soldier Luz Garcia, appeared in 1828 for baptism of a son. Mother and son died the following year and in 1833 Michael married Martina Castro, who was then negotiating for the Soquel grant. Michael went to the mines in 1848 but never returned, indubitably falling prey to robbers.

The Joseph Walker party, offshoot of the Bonneville expedition, which reached Monterey from the Great Salt Lake in the winter of 1833–34, left in Santa Cruz Francois Lajeunesse, young French Canadian, who married one of Martina Castro's daughters by her first husband, Corporal Simon Cota.

With the Hijar and Padre colonists from Mexico came in 1834 Heinrich Hill, a German, who lived out his years working in the timber about Soquel.

Before 1840 the list of "foreigners" in Branciforte included Joseph L. Majors, who became a leading citizen in American days; Job Dye, a Kentuckian who died at Corralitos in 1883; Billy Weare, an Irishman; Ambrose Tomlinson, the American carpenter; George Chappel, an Englishman; John Saunders, the sailor; Jonathan Lucas, an Englishman who engaged in lumbering; William G. Chard, a New Yorker; "Mountain Bill" Anderson, the cockney sailor; George Kinlock, the carpenter; Robert King, a Briton; Nicolas Dodero, an Italian sailor; and Albert F. Morris, English-born sailor.

In the spring of 1840, when Mexican-California authorities decided to rid the territory of "extrangeros" who had not been naturalized, Job Dye and Joseph Majors were running a little grist mill and still up at Zayante. Over at Natividad, in the Salinas valley, Isaac Graham and his protege, boyish Harry Neale, made their headquarters about that little liquor making plant. Many of the extrangeros had been in Graham's rifleros who had helped Alvarado and Castro in 1836.

Ill will had grown because the "foreigners" felt they had not been suitably rewarded. On orders by Castro the "foreigners" were seized. A force of Californians at night invaded Natividad. Morris, the Briton, stopping there, escaped through a window and fled to the Zayante to give warning.

Castro sent orders to Juan Gonzales at Santa Cruz to round up all the extrangeros in his jurisdiction. Gonzales was friendly to the foreigners, apparently gave warning and only put a few under arrest.

Nearly 100 foreigners were gathered in around Monterey bay, of whom 41 were sent by ship to San Blas. The Mexican government repudiated the action of California and the exiles mostly returned. Those sent to San Blas who were arrested at Branciforte or who settled there on their return included Albert Morris, Francois Lajeunesse, William Chard, William Anderson, Charles Henry Cooper (said to have been a Mohican Indian), Henry Neale and Isaac Graham. Dye and Majors, although arrested, were not sent to Mexico as both had been naturalized as Mexicans and had married Spanish girls.

Each of the years from 1840 to 1846 brought into the Santa Cruz area ten or twenty foreigners. Some were roving spirits but nearly half picked the vicinity as permanent home.

Some names are vague because of the uncertainty of the Californians' spelling. A Branciforte document of 1840 mentions an Englishman, Santiago Fadeun. The padron of 1845, last under the Mexican requirement of a yearly census, listed four foreigners who can not be identified: Charles Chaden, William France, Chris Vich and William Wanee.

Arrivals in Branciforte in 1840 included Henry Jubilee Bee, Joseph R. Foster, George W. Frazier, Paul Sweet and Alvin Wilson. A similar list for 1841 includes Josiah Belden, Thomas White, William Brander, Jorge Jose Bonis (probably Bowen), Willard and Francis Buzzell, William Garner and James W. Weeks.

The arrivals in 1842 included Thomas Bowen, Peter Collins, William Dickey, Jean Ricardo Fourcade, James Kennedy, Thomas Lewis, Isaac Stevens, Thomas Turnbull, William Warren and William Wiggins.

In 1843 came William Barton, Thomas Cole, John Daubenbiss, John Hames, Charles Heath, Birnie Dawson, Henry McVicker and the four Williams brothers, James, John, Squire and Isaac. The year 1844 brought Dennis, Jackson, Mansel and Winston Bennett, Carl Labish, Pierre Richard and Charles Rousillon.

In 1845 came Alexander Adrian, William Blackburn, Lawrence Carmichael, Jean Baptiste Mohlier, Louis LaPierre, Jean Baptiste Dabadie, Julian Omnes-Gui, Francois Poile, Pierre Vignes, Thomas Fallon, William H. Hardy, Isaac Hitchcock, Mrs. Elizabeth Patterson, George McDougal, Joseph Frey, Thomas J. Shadden, Jacob R. Snyder, George N. Williams and a Frenchman whose name was recorded as Nertran Cadichi.

The first half of 1846, last period before American occupation brought John Burton and Henry Speale.

Of those listed more than a score established families and stayed in the Santa Cruz region until their deaths. Others in the fifties and sixties removed to other parts of California.

That the large number of foreign settlers about Santa Cruz was regarded with apprehension by the Mexicans is shown by the statement in the Mexican congress of 1844 by Manuel Castanares, member from California, that a thousand armed Americanos were in the "Sierra de Sta Cruz."

The United States flag was raised in Santa Cruz four years before California became American territory. Josiah Belden,

Connecticut Yankee who had crossed the plains in 1841 in the Chiles party, was running in a room of the adobe mission buildings a branch of Thomas Larkin's Monterey store, buying lumber, hides and tallow and selling goods from New England and China.

Commodore Thomas Ap Catesby Jones, sailing hastily north from Callao under belief the British were preparing to seize California, anchored off Monterey on October 19, 1842, and received Alvarado's surrender. The next day two men in a small sailing vessel crossed Monterey bay with the news. Belden produced an American flag which he flew from a pole at the mission. Four days later Commodore Jones, convinced he was in error, turned Monterey back to Alvarado.

Belden closed his branch store in Santa Cruz in November, 1843. Four years later he operated one at San Jose until the gold discovery took him to the mines. He was San Jose's first mayor in 1850. His home was later site of the Vendome hotel. Belden became wealthy by purchase of San Francisco real estate, which he sold to Charles Crocker in 1883. He died April 23, 1892, in New York, director of the Erie railroad and rated several times a millionaire.

THE TROTTING TRACK

From 1870 to 1887 Santa Cruz had its trotting track and yearly race meets when gamblers who made the circuits set up their temporary establishments and a repertory company played nightly at Knight's Opera House. The banked curves of the old oval can still be seen between Swift and Fair avenues a few blocks back from the Cliff Drive.

Mission street had been used for horse racing in the fifties until residents protested to county authorities. In 1865 Ruffner's Lane, which is now Younglove avenue, was scene of contests between locally owned horses.

In 1870 the Santa Cruz Homestead and Real Estate association laid out the track, at first called Ocean View, later Fairview and finally Bay View. It opened with a meet the second week in November, with a race for trotting teams paying a fifty-dollar prize to County Supervisor Portius Festus Dean of Watsonville.

Elias J. Swift, proprietor of the Pacific Ocean House, raced his horses at Fairview and the street to the track was named after him. Attorney James O. Wanzer, made secretary of the racing association on its organization, finally resigned in 1885. Two years later the tract was cut into building lots and the two-story hotel which had housed drivers and owners was removed to Weeks street where it is now a residence.

A track at Opal existed for a short time early in this century.

⬥

AMERICAN ALCALDES
RULED FOR FOUR YEARS

SIXTY DAYS after Commodore Sloat had raised the United States flag at Monterey, Alcalde Walter Colton there received the following letter from Santa Cruz, dated September 6, 1846:

"The commander in chief writes for to hold an election of officers on the 15th inst. As there has been an election of officers already the people are of the opinion that another is not requset at present. If realy nessary you will be so kind as to inform me the first opportunity. I am, sir, very respectfully yours, etc., Joseph L. Majors, by L. Carmichael, sec."

The date of Santa Cruz' local election can not be fixed but the tally sheet is preserved in the county recorder's office. It shows 45 votes cast, with the following results: Jose Arana 10, Jose Mechas 9, Guadalupe Castro 6, Rafael Castro 5, Juan Emis 3, P. Richar 3, Jose Bolcoff 2 and single votes for several others. Apparently Arana declined the honor and it went to Mechas (Majors).

Majors, born near Nashville May 26, 1804, had come over the Santa Fe trail in the same company with Graham, Neale and others. In Los Angeles in November, 1834, he had joined other foreigners in a protest against military duty. In 1835 he settled in the Santa Cruz region, to be naturalized as a Mexican in 1839 and marry that year Maria de los Angeles Castro.

Selected as alcalde, he took up his office in the two-story adobe, largest of the mission buildings, which had served as juzgado for Bolcoff, last of the jueces de paz. His wife's many relatives prompted him to pass a number of cases to Colton in Monterey so that he would not have to adjudicate between his brothers-in-law.

Majors had been nominally grantee of Zayante and San Augustin ranchos but had actually procured them for a syndicate of "foreigners" who declined to become Mexican citizens. He later became possessed of his wife's share of Refugio Rancho, just west of the present city. He built a big home on what is now Allegro Heights which burned in 1879. Just below it, at the upper end of Walnut avenue, was the big Majors mill, begun in 1843 and finished in American days. It blew down in a storm in 1906. Majors died in 1868 and his widow in 1903. They were reputed to have had nineteen children.

On June 21, 1847, Colonel Richard B. Mason, acting governor, appointed as alcalde William Blackburn, cabinet maker and wood worker who had come in 1845 in the Swasey-Todd party, an offshoot of the Oregon immigration. Blackburn, born February 14, 1814, at Harpers Ferry, Virginia, had on his arrival in California joined the American colony at Zayante. After marching in Fremont's battalion to help take Los Angeles he came back to his holdings in Santa Cruz.

Blackburn was building a sawmill four miles out on Branciforte creek when gold was discovered at Colma. Resigning his alcalde-ship he and his employes rushed off to the Sacramento with most of the other men of Santa Cruz but he soon returned, to grow potatoes on his land on the flat near the beach. His three brothers, Jacob, Daniel and James, arrived in the gold rush and Jacob completed the mill, which in 1856 became the property of a New Yorker, Alex McPherson. Its site was that of the Happy Valley resort of today.

Blackburn was married in 1859 to a Massachusetts girl, Harriet Mead, who had come to Santa Cruz with her brother-in-law and sister, Dr. and Mrs. Francis M. Kittredge. He served again briefly as alcalde and when the first legislature, in San Jose, created the county, he was first county judge. Later he served in the legislature. He died March 26, 1867, on a trip to San Francisco. His widow, who inherited considerable property in Santa Cruz and San Francisco, lived until 1920. The home he built just before his death still(1946) stands on Sycamore street.

Santa Cruz had difficulty in keeping alcaldes in office during gold rush days. Apparently each named his successor as he left. Blackburn was succeeded briefly by William Anderson, former English sailor, who turned the post over to John Hames of Soquel. Jonathan F. Pinkham, Kentuckian, forty-niner, served for a time. James G. T. Dunleavy and William Thompson were briefly acting alcaldes, Blackburn was in office a second time, and Adna A. Hecox, Methodist exhorter, was holding the post when state and county governments were instituted.

The American alcaldes named their own court officers to serve papers, designating them sheriffs. Fees made the post attractive. The "sheriffs" included Alexander Simmons, Lorenzo L. Logan, O. K. Stampley and James Gordon.

Under their interpretation of Mexican law the alcaldes made grants of "house lots" and "sowing lots" of the lands about the mission until every man in the village was owner of three or four.

Colonel Jonathan D. Stevenson, New York politician and militia officer who had brought his regiment of volunteers to California in 1847, was a real estate dealer in San Francisco. He dispatched a score of men of his old regiment to petition the Santa Cruz alcaldes for lands which they promptly turned over to him at the uniform price of $100 for a "house lot" and $200 for a "sowing lot."

That Blackburn connived at the wholesale land granting is shown by the fact that on July 11, 1849, Stevenson paid him $1,349 as fees from grantees, all of whom had already deeded their lands to him. Stevenson sold a few tracts for an advanced figure but squatters settled on his holdings. In the sixties he carried a suit to the state supreme court which decided his titles were invalid, holding that the Mexican government had not completed the process of creating a pueblo out of Santa Cruz mission and that the alcalde titles were void because they had not been taken before the federal land commission.

Other alcalde titles were rectified in 1866 when, after Attorney Robert F. Peckham had made a trip east to present a memorial to congress, a special act gave the probate court authority to confirm them to owners of that date.

⊫

Conflict With Mexico
Found Willing Recruits

ZAYANTE, six miles up the San Lorenzo valley, might easily have been the scene of the Bear Flag revolt; had Santa Cruz been of military importance Zayante might have been rendezvous for Americans to raise a crude banner.

The home of Joseph L. Majors, Ambrose Tomlinson, Billy Weare, Isaac Graham, the Bennett brothers and a dozen others of British and American birth, Zayante attracted many of the pioneers who came over the Santa Fe trail in the 1830's and across the plains in the first of the 1840's.

The grist mill there, which made coarse meal from corn and wheat, the little still which made a mountain variety of whisky to compete with the Mexican aguardiente de pais, the "muley" sawmill built in 1841 or 1842, were center of a group of cabins which spread into what is now Mount Hermon and down to the present Big Tree park.

The growing sentiment that California was ripe for becoming a part of the United States was felt. John C. Fremont, lieutenant of topographical engineers in the United States army, whose presence in California precipitated the revolt which antedated by twenty-three days the raising of the American flag at Monterey, was at Zayante on February 24, a week before he made his historic stand on Gavilan peak.

The Fremont party came over from Santa Clara, camping the first night at "wild cat ridge" (Los Gatos), and the next at Mountain Charlie McKiernan's. The night of February 24 it was at Zayante and, as told in Fremont's autobiography, camped in the rain the last three days of February on Thompson's Flat, the present Pasatiempo golf course, which was part of William Thompson's Carbonero grant. Its march on March 1 took it to Soquel.

On March 6 Fremont began erection of his log fort on Gavilan, from which he watched the Californians summoned by Jose Castro assembling on the Salinas plains. Charles N. Weber in San Jose sent John Daubenbiss to Yerba Buena to rouse the Americans there.

Fremont's departure toward Oregon averted a clash which might have made Santa Cruz or the Salinas valley scene of the first revolt by American settlers. The John Daubenbiss whom Weber sent to Yerba Buena had already paid a visit to Santa Cruz in 1843 and was to buy a half interest in Rodeo Rancho here in 1847.

In the part of a day he spent at Zayante, Fremont undoubtedly came in contact with the Americans and Britons there. In the period from 1837 to 1846 more than a score are known to have made its headquarters. Records in the Santa Cruz court house show that Henry L. Ford, who was elected first lieutenant of the Bear Flag revolters, had been at Zayante the previous year, acting as recording clerk for the contract marriage of Isaac Graham and Catherine Bennett.

When, on June 14, 1846, thirty-two or thirty-three Americans who had assembled in the Napa valley marched on Sonoma and took Mariano Vallejo and two or three others prisoners, one of their first actions was to send word that they had raised a flag patterned after that of Texas. The word was intended for

Thomas O. Larkin, American consul at Monterey, but the messenger, Thomas Booker, stopped at Zayante on the way.

Twenty years later Thomas Fallon made a political speech in Santa Cruz in which he recounted the events which followed. "We had an inkling of war," he said, "and Foster came to me and said, 'Let's raise a party and go help them.' Billy Weare and John Daubenbiss went with us."

In the San Jose archives is a document, unsigned, which bears the date of June 25, 1846, reading:

"The twenty-five armed foreigners of Santa Cruz intended to start this morning. It is not known whether they will come this way or as would be more prudent go to the Sacramento."

Events moved fast. Prefect Manuel Castro made a trip around Monterey bay to Branciforte to get horses from the ranch owners. William A. Leidesdorff, the San Francisco merchant, wrote Larkin at Monterey on June 17 that Castro had been in Santa Cruz preparing to go to the Sacramento. Castro arrived at Santa Clara on the day Leidesdorff's letter was sent.

The "armed foreigners" from Santa Cruz rode across the mountains. By July 11 they were camped in the willows on Guadalupe creek. Winston Bennett, who had lived most of the two preceding years at Zayante, was at his mother's home in Santa Clara. Investigating a party of horsemen he found them friends from Santa Cruz.

Bennett rode into San Jose to see how strong the Mexican force was. Henry Pitts had passed through from Monterey with word of the raising of the American flag. With this information Bennett returned to the troop commanded by Fallon and the party rode into the little town and seized the juzgado The next day Fallon sent a courier to Lieutenant John P. Montgomery of the U.S.S. *Portsmouth* at San Francisco:

"I have arrived here with nineteen men with the expectation of joining Captain Fremont but he has not arrived here. I therefore send an express to you for orders what to do. If you can send six guns and pistols, ammunition, etc., I can get men to use them."

Montgomery, providing the guns and ammunition, wrote:

"If you think that your present force at the pueblo of St. Joseph with the accession which I am told by the bearer of your letter you are expecting will be sufficient to that end, I would recommend to you by all means to do as you propose."

The Santa Cruz "armed foreigners" were evidently not too well armed, for on July 16 Fallon sent a courier to Commodore Sloat at Monterey:

"There is a number of lawless characters in the vicinity of this place (principally foreigners), who have taken an active part with General Castro in all underhand measures to annoy the Americans here before we had any protection from our government. Should it meet your views we would wish you to arm the six men of our company who accompanied Lieutenant Gillispie to Monterey and have them placed under the one you think most competent and sent back."

The message to Sloat was signed by "Thomas Fallon, captain; W. Blackburn, lieutenant."

Fallon encountered one difficulty. No United States flag could be found to replace the Mexican flag he had hauled down on the San Jose juzgado. He sent another messenger to Montgomery, who supplied the lack.

Fallon's company grew rapidly as Americans rallied to him. Within a few days it mounted to two score. Fremont was marching from Sacramento in response to Commodore Sloat's request. He and his men came through Pacheco pass and at San Juan Bautista on July 17 met Daingerfield Fauntleroy, purser on the *Savannah*, in command of a company of dragoons. Castro had gone south nearly a week before and occupation of San Juan Bautista gave the Americans every point of importance in northern California. The Santa Cruzans promptly joined Fremont and went south overland or by schooner for the fighting around Los Angeles.

The best source for listing the probable personnel of the nineteen "armed foreigners" whom Fallon led over the little mountain range to seize San Jose is in the names of Santa Cruzans who served in Fremont's California Battalion.

Fallon and Blackburn both went with Fremont. Others known to have served in the battalion included John Daubenbiss,

Alfred Baldwin, P. W. Waggoner, Billy Weare, Otis Ashley,
Winston and Jackson Bennett, William Dickey, R. F. Peckham,
A. A. Hecox and Pruett Sinclair.

Fallon was a veteran of the Texas war for independence who
had reached the Santa Cruz region in the fall of 1845. After
the fighting about Los Angeles he returned to San Jose where
he made a living making saddle trees. Late in 1847 Fallon and
Elihu Anthony crossed the mountains to Santa Cruz by com-
bining an ox team of Anthony's with a wagon Fallon owned.

Fallon continued his occupation of saddletree maker, perhaps
in conjunction with Anthony's blacksmith shop and foundry,
until gold was discovered. Taking some of his own product and
eight dozen picks Anthony made from ships' bolts he went to
Georgetown. The picks he sold for three ounces of gold each.
Back in Santa Cruz a year later he built a story-and-a-half
wooden structure facing the mission plaza on the site now occupied by the reproduction of the original mission chapel. It was
residence, store and hotel. When Santa Cruz county was created in 1850 Fallon sold it to the county for $3,500 to become
the first court house. From 1860 to 1884 it was the county
hospital.

Fallon married Carmelita Lodge, daughter of Michael Lodge
and Martina Castro, in 1848 and was in Santa Cruz for two
years, as shown by records of birth of a daughter and son in
1849 and 1850. He leased the old mission orchard from the
priest in 1848.

Fallon, a native of Ireland who had gone to Canada while a
boy, made a trip to Texas with a view to staying there but was
on his way back to Santa Cruz when three of his children died
in New Orleans in 1854. The next year he settled in San Jose
where he was elected mayor in 1859.

By his first wife, who in later years became well known as
Carmel Fallon, owner of large land holdings in Santa Clara and
Monterey counties, and by a second wife, he had ten children,
of whom five were living at the time of his death in 1885. Both
of his wives had been divorced and when he died he had a
pending appeal from a $10,000 judgment given a Mrs. Elmira
Dunbar by a San Jose jury in a breach of promise action.

Fallon, who left an estate of $300,000, was well advanced in Masonry; his funeral was conducted by the Knights Templar. One of his daughters, Anita Fallon, became well known as an actress.

⟶

CAPTAIN VANCOUVER GAVE
GRIST MILL TO MISSION

CAPTAIN GEORGE VANCOUVER, three and a half years out of Falmouth, had explored the Pacific northwest, made a couple of side trips to the Sandwich islands and was at Monterey for the third time when, in November, 1794, he applied to California authorities for permission to buy vegetables on his voyage home.

Governor Diego Borica, who had begun to doubt the advisability of Vancouver's ships, the *Discovery* and *Chatham*, sailing up and down the coast, told him that Padres Salazar and Lopez at three-year-old Santa Cruz mission had a good garden growing on the flat near their establishment.

Borica hurried a horseback courier around the bay with word that three small boats were coming across from Monterey, that the priests might have their Indians deliver vegetables to the beach, but that the priests were to have nothing to do with the Britons.

The same courier carried instructions to Corporal Jose Antonio Sanchez of the escolta to keep an eye on the transaction. The note, written by the sub-comisario at Monterey, said the boats would be under command of a petty officer named Swain. It is to be wondered if the sub-comisario might not have written, if pressed, that the officer's first name was "Boats."

Corporal Sanchez, reporting to his military superior, Alferez Hermenegildo Sal at San Francisco presidio, gave that officer sufficient apprehension of a landing party that he rushed five more soldiers down to Santa Cruz to help handle the situation.

The three boats left Monterey November 24 and were back on November 28. Corporal Sanchez reported to Borica that none of the sailors had gone to the mission and neither of the priests had gone to the beach, but some contact must have been established. Padre Salazar, on his return to Mexico the following year, wrote an account, "Condiciones Actual de California," in which he recorded that Vancouver had presented to Santa Cruz mission iron work for a grist mill of a value of 1,000 pesos.

Vancouver's fresh vegetables, grown on the flat where Santa Cruz' business district is today, certainly did not last his voyage home. The *Discovery* and the *Chatham* arrived in the Thames October 20, 1795. Vancouver died less than three years later and his account of his explorations was completed by his brother, John, assisted by Captain Puget, both of whom had been with the two-ship fleet.

In 1769 Governor Borica sent artisans who had come up from Mexico over to Santa Cruz to erect the mill. Branciforte records contain a request by the priests to authorities across the river to help in transporting mill stones from San Juan Bautista.

When Santa Cruz mission passed out of the hands of the Franciscans, Jose Antonio Bolcoff, the Russian, obtained possession of the mill. In 1859 the plant, then operated by Bolcoff and Eli Moore, was taken on a mechanic's lien by twenty-four-year-old John Fleck, a Pennsylvania forty-niner. Fleck owned land along what is now Laurel street on which the Kirby tannery was later erected. The mill was at the bottom of the Laurel street hill.

The *Weekly Sentinel* in 1865 referred to it as "the mission mill, along Majors' spring creek, near Kirby's tannery and adjoining the land of Juan Jose Feliz and A. A. Hecox."

Fleck, who lost his mill in 1866 on a $2,586 mortgage to James A. Prewett and Joseph C. Riley, was accused the next year of a murderous attempt on Andrew Thompson, a Norwegian carpenter who had married one of the Feliz girls. Fleck moved to Soquel in 1868 and later to Guadalupe, Santa Barbara county, where he died.

STREET NAMES

The first two streets in Santa Cruz which had names were Main (now Front) and Willow, along the row of willows and ditch which marked the edge of the mission gardens, which became Pacific avenue.

Many of the streets of today were country lanes. Bay street was the "road to the redwoods," Soquel avenue was the road to Monterey and later the Soquel road, Mission street was the "road up the coast."

Civil War influence is seen. Lincoln street was originally Williams Lane and briefly Trust street. Union street was given its name at the same time. Bulkhead street marks a barrier built after the flood of 1862.

➤

HELPING PICK MEMBERS
OF FIRST LEGISLATURE

RESIDENTS of the area which later became Santa Cruz county held their first election under state-wide jurisdiction on November 13, 1849, to help name a governor and legislature.

The adobe juzgado used as court by Adna A. Hecox served as polling place, with voters riding as much as twenty-five miles. Santa Cruz was part of the "District of Monterey," which had two other polling places, at San Juan Bautista and at Monterey.

The Santa Cruz vote for governor totaled 97, of which 52 went for Peter H. Burnett, 42 for W. S. Sherwood, with three scattering.

The district sent to the first state senate Selim E. Woodworth, a Monterey resident. Friends of Dr. John T. McLean of Santa Cruz cast 42 votes for him for the post but the rest of the district gave him only two more, while Woodworth received a total of 252, of which 53 were from Santa Cruz.

Woodworth had, after resigning a commission as lieutenant in the navy, crossed the plains to Oregon in 1846. When the Civil War broke out he returned to the navy, becoming a commodore. He died in San Francisco in 1871, at the age of 55.

For assemblyman Monterey and San Benito favored W. E. P. Hartnell, the Lancashire Englishman who had been in California three decades and had held many positions of trust under the Mexican government. It was the Santa Cruz vote which gave the post to Theron Per Lee, who had come to California in 1847 as a lieutenant in Stevenson's New York Volunteers and who returned to the east in the latter seventies to practice law in New York.

Monterey and San Benito gave Hartnell 107 votes to 94 for Per Lee but Santa Cruz' 51 votes for the latter, with only one ballot cast here for Hartnell, determined the election. Benjamin Allen Case, Connecticut Yankee who had settled in Santa Cruz in 1848, entered the race but while he polled 45 votes in his home town received only 10 in the rest of the district.

The votes of the election, which had been held by proclamation of General Bennett Riley, were canvassed at Monterey on December 10 by a committee consisting of Henry W. Hallack, David Spence, Pacificus Ord, Mariano Malarin and Y. Esquar.

⇥≣⇤

New County Inherited Judicial Problems

THE WIDOW MARY BENNETT rode down from Zayante to ask that Jesse Graham be put under bond to keep the peace. Alcalde Adna A. Hecox was not sure what he could do about it.

The first legislature, over in San Jose, had created the county of Branciforte three months earlier and only two weeks before had yielded to a petition and made it the County of Santa Cruz.

The first set of officers under American form of government had been elected but had not taken office yet.

It was April 21, 1850. Hecox was holding forth in the adobe juzgado. Mary, widow of Vardamon Bennett, the Georgia man who had come to California in 1843, insisted that her sons and Isaac Graham's sons were feuding and that Jesse Graham had made shooting threats.

Calling this the "County of Branciforte," Hecox decreed that Jesse should post $1,000 bond to behave himself. Instead of posting the bond young Jesse rode out the grade to Zayante the next day and not only shot Dennis Bennett at the door of his cabin but took a shot at his mother which wounded her.

Hecox had been born on Grosse Isle on the Detroit river, where his father, a Connecticut man of Irish descent, had just settled. Adna had crossed the plains with his wife, Margaret, and five children, stopped briefly in Santa Clara and arrived in what was to become Santa Cruz county in the spring of 1847 when he lived in a cabin on the Soquel river bank and rebuilt Mike Lodge's washed out sawmill. The next spring he operated the mill on a lease until reports of gold on the Sacramento took him over to investigate.

The forty-two-year-old carpenter and temperance exhorter was one of a party which found the rich diggings at Hangtown. He was at Mokelumne in September but spent the winter back with his family in Santa Cruz and in June, 1849, went to store keeping with Elihu Anthony in the latter's new wooden building on the flat.

Hecox made his home on a farm a mile from the mission on the road up the coast, on land he bought from the Feliz family. The site of his residence today would be the east side of Mission street between Laurel and Rigg streets. In Civil War days he became county treasurer; in 1864 he was made keeper of the new lighthouse, a post his daughter, Laura, was given after his death in 1883.

When Adna, the last of the alcaldes, discovered his peace bond procedure had failed to compel Jesse Graham to conduct himself in an orderly manner he started a legal investigation which, if it accomplished nothing more, absolved Isaac Graham of complicity in his son's act. Jesse rode off into the sand hills, made his way to Texas and fought in the Confederate army in the Civil War. In 1888, a ranch owner near Fresno, he was brought back to Santa Cruz for trial on an indictment returned April 2, 1851. The jury disagreed and 400 Santa Cruzans petitioned to have the charge dropped.

The story of the Graham-Bennett feud, if it has no other part in the history of Santa Cruz, fixes the transition period from government under what the American alcaldes considered Mexican law and that variety set up by the California law makers.

The initial county election was held on April 1, 1850. Votes were cast by 211 male residents, of whom 55 were of Mexican-California descent, 51 were American-, British-, French- or German-born settlers of pre−gold rush days, and 105 were forty-niners.

Legislative act of March 2, 1850, called for election of ten county officials but Santa Cruz emerged from its polling with two or three extra ones, including a juez de campo, a county office created by the legislature a little later, and a pair of public administrators, with no explanation for the fact that there were two.

The first district judge was John H. Watson, a Georgian who had had two years at West Point, studied law, spent three years in Texas and come in the gold rush to California. He had served in the first assembly from San Francisco but had resigned legislative duties on March 1 and was living in the lower end of Santa Cruz county thirty days later to qualify for election. He resigned as district judge after less than a year on conclusion that lawyers made more than judges. In 1859 he went to the state senate from Santa Cruz county. He went to Nevada from Sacramento in the Washoe mining excitement and never returned. At Elko, where he died August 9, 1882, he was credited with being an able attorney in mining law. As district judge he was succeeded by Craven P. Hester.

As county judge and head of the court of sessions was elected William Blackburn, the Harpers Ferry, Virginia, wood worker who had twice been alcalde in the 1846–50 period. Justices of the peace, who elected two of their number as associate members of the court of sessions, were Dr. George Parsons and Felipe Armas of Santa Cruz and Jose Arano of Aptos. Blackburn resigned in September and his place was taken by Attorney Theron Per Lee.

Sheriff was Francisco Alzina, twenty-nine-year-old native of Minorca who had fled political disorders in Spain and arrived at Monterey on the U.S. Frigate *Constitution* in 1846. He had been two years married to Carlota Gonzales, of a family which had lived at the mission for three generations. Francisco, as a native of Spain, was naturalized as an American citizen in September, 1851, a year and a half after he became sheriff. He was succeeded in 1852 by Leander G. Caldwell, a Soquel farmer. Alzina, who had twelve children, died in Santa Cruz in 1887.

The combined offices of clerk, auditor and recorder were given Peter Tracy, an energetic young County Cork Irishman who, but for his death in 1857, would undoubtedly have become one of the county's wealthy men. As it was his estate included land up the coast, around Soquel and a quarter interest in Joel Bates' sawmill.

Coroner was Henry Speale, a forty-six-year-old native of Philadelphia who had crossed the plains in the 1845 Swasy-Todd party with William Blackburn. Speale, an active business man with several town lots, a residence on Willow street and a half interest in Blackburn's mill, came to an untimely end when, in 1858, he was killed in a fall off the cliffs at the beach and was one of the first persons buried in new Evergreen cemetery.

The job of constable, which may not have been elective, was given Robert King, native of London who had been a Santa Cruz resident since 1834. He was arrested in 1840 but was taken sick at Santa Barbara and not taken to Mexico with the exiles. At the time of taking office as the county's first constable he had a wife, who had been Estefana Juarez, and four children. He died before 1860.

The two public administrators were Dr. Charles P. Stevenson and Robert Cathcart. The first was a temporary resident who left no record of himself. The latter was a forty-niner from St.

Louis whose truck garden along the San Lorenzo south of what is now Soquel avenue gave his name to Cathcart street.

Edmund B. Kellogg, elected first county surveyor, was a forty-niner who returned in 1854 to Knoxville, Illinois, and died there in 1856. He served only a few months, being succeeded by Thomas W. Wright, native of Louisiana, who combined his light engineering duties with being a deputy for Tracy. Wright held county office into the eighties, laying out most of the county roads and its first railways. He never married and died November 15, 1897.

Treasurer and assessor was Gervis Hammond, who had found work in the mills around Zayante in the spring of 1849. He followed his election by establishing a home at Soquel and beginning logging there with Hugh Pablo McCall, the old French Canadian who had come over the Santa Fe trail in the middle 1830's. Hammond's residence, "near the river," was Soquel's first polling place, in 1852. He died in 1854.

Road supervisors named by the court of sessions were Antonio Rodriguez for Pajaro (the name of Watsonville was still in the future), Asa P. Sanford for the area east of Aptos, McCall for the Aptos-Soquel zone, Hammond for the roads into Santa Cruz west of Soquel and Thomas Kittleman for those around the county seat.

The county kept the old Mexican post of juez de campo, inspector of brands and arbiter of title to roving livestock. It was given to Jose de la Cruz Rodriguez the first year and in 1851 to Juan Gonzales and Cornelio Perez.

Theron Per Lee was succeeded in the lower house of the legislature by Edmund B. Kellogg. Dr. Francis M. Kittredge was elected in 1852 and in 1853 the southern end of the county put over W. W. Stowe, a farmer on the Amesti rancho, who was elected speaker in 1855. Out of that office, he played briefly with the idea of running for governor but joined the San Francisco legal firm of Wallace, Patterson and Stowe and was known as a railroad lobbyist in the eighties.

Balckburn, elected to the assembly in 1855, was succeeded by Benjamin H. Miles, Watsonville man, who left the following spring for Arizona and was killed in a duel there in 1858.

Santa Cruz and Monterey counties, constituting a senatorial district, sent back to the upper house of the legislature Selim E. Woodworth, the Monterey resident who had served in the first legislature.

‑‑

ELIHU ANTHONY BUILT
TOWN'S FIRST WHARF

UNTIL ELIHU ANTHONY, a God-fearing man and a progressive and hard-working citizen, had been in Santa Cruz half a dozen years the community got along without a wharf. Lumber was dragged through the surf and hoisted aboard schooners. Lighter objects were carried on men's shoulders to small boats which conveyed them to ships.

Anthony came over from Santa Clara in 1847. He laid out Santa Cruz' first two real estate subdivisions; he expanded his blacksmith shop into an iron foundry; he was the first postmaster; he was largely instrumental in founding the first Protestant church.

So, it was characteristic that in 1853, when he was operating a store with Edwin S. Penfield as a partner, they should decide on a wharf as an adjunct to their business. The wharf they built was a plank chute, steep enough to let sacks of potatoes slide into rowboats. Its location was at the edge of the cliff opposite the end of Bay street.

The legislature in 1855 granted a franchise for Santa Cruz' second wharf to David Gharkey, who built it two years later and in 1863 extended it to accommodate larger vessels.

The Anthony-Penfield chute was bought by Davis and Jordan, the firm which began burning lime in Santa Cruz in 1853 and in 1856 paid $150,000 to build on the east coast the steamer *Santa Cruz*. The vessel proved too large for their own business and what freight and passenger traffic Santa Cruz could furnish. In 1859 they traded it to Pierre Sainsevain and his associates for a part of his Rincon rancho, on which were the later lime kilns of the Cowell Lime company, successor to Davis and Jordan. Sainsevain tried the big steamer on a coastal run but sold it to new owners who took it across the Pacific, where it burned on the Yangtse river in 1861.

Until the first railroad linked Santa Cruz with the Southern Pacific at Watsonville in 1876 Davis and Jordan owned a small fleet of schooners which carried their lime up and down the coast, but the ships were so small that the Davis and Jordan wharf remained an incline down which tram cars ran by gravity to be hauled back by horse power. It finally collapsed in high seas on December 31, 1907.

The Davis and Jordan wharf was used by the California Powder works when they began producing explosives in 1863 at the plant three miles up the San Lorenzo river, but they soon began construction of a longer wharf off what is today Santa Cruz' principal bathing beach, opposite Main street, and put up a big wooden warehouse at the top of Beach hill.

When the little seven-mile narrow-gauge Santa Cruz and Felton railroad began operating on October 13, 1875, the Gharkey wharf became the "railroad wharf." It was bought by the South Pacific Coast railroad when that narrow gauge pushed its rails across the hills from Alameda.

In 1877 the powder mill wharf and the railroad wharf were connected but in 1882 the South Pacific Coast gave Joe Roberts a $500 contract to destroy the link. With extension of the wharf it became landing place for vessels of the Pacific Coast Steamship company.

The present city-owned wharf was constructed in 1914.

In Mexican days—perhaps back as far as Spanish times—the only facilities for loading ocean-going freight were cables from the edge of the cliffs to vessels anchored beyond the surf line. Trace of one of these is in a huge iron bolt set in a cliff a mile west of the city limits on the Wilder property which was Jose Antonio Bolcoff's Rancho Refugio.

"Landings" at the mouth of the Pajaro river, on San Andres rancho, at the mouth of the Aptos and on the square league which the Williams brothers had bought in early days from Gil Sanchez, a dozen miles up the coast from Santa Cruz, were all succeeded by wharves of piling and plank.

In 1867 Goodall & Nelson built a 1,000-foot wharf at the mouth of the Pajaro. Rafael Castro built a small wharf at Aptos which was extended to 900 feet by Titus Hale in 1867 and rebuilt into a wharf 1,000 feet long by Claus Spreckels in 1880.

Soquel Landing, the Capitola of today, had a small wharf prior to 1857 when the weekly *Santa Cruz Sentinel* recorded that a new wharf was being built by F. A. Hihn and the Pacific Coast Steamship company. In 1860 it was extended to 1,100 feet but a storm in November, 1865, took away 500 feet of it and left the remainder unsafe. At that time it was said it had cost $6,000 and belonged to Hihn and Captain Robert Sudden of the steamship *Salinas*. It was rebuilt by the steamship company, but in 1879 wheat and lumber shipments began to move by rail and the company posted notices it would no longer be responsible for the wharf or any accidents on it.

In 1868 Captain John P. Davenport, retired from ownership and command of whaling vessels, with John King as partner, built a wharf about fifteen miles up the coast from Santa Cruz at the mouth of Agua Puerca (Muddy Water) creek, for use of which in loading freight charges were made. A considerable town of Davenport Landing grew up, of which the last vestige vanished when the new town of Davenport came into existence about the Santa Cruz Portland Cement company plant established in 1906. The steel cement-loading wharf at Davenport, close to the site of the old Williams Landing, was built in 1933.

Northernmost of the wharves of Santa Cruz county in the days when the big lumber traffic furnished ocean-going freight was built by a Kentuckian, William W. Waddell, who had come from Lexington, Missouri, in 1850, and operated a sawmill in Blackburn gulch until 1860 when he moved his operations to the coastal creek which bears his name, close to the northern county line. His first attempt at a wharf, directly off Waddell beach, ran into a ledge of rock which prevented driving pile to vessel depth, so he ran a tramway down the valley from his mill and a half mile up the coast to a 700-foot wharf.

The second Waddell milll (the first burned in 1864) was large enough that a village grew up about it with a postoffice known as Seaside. The second mill burned in 1883. The little valley is now the Rancho del Oso, owned by Theodore Hoover.

⹀⹀

SHIP BUILDING AND OCEAN TRAFFIC

AMERICAN DAYS in California brought efforts by Santa Cruzans to build ships large enough for coastwise traffic. In 1846 Carlos Rousillon, a French trader who had come from Los Angeles and was briefly associated with Pierre Sainse-vain of Rincon Rancho, constructed a schooner, *Santa Cruz.*

The vessel was built on Beach Hill where its timbers were hauled by ox team, as was material for the ways, 250 yards long and 20 feet from the ground. Spikes, bolts, blocks, sail and rigging were manufactured on the spot. Other articles were obtained from the Sandwich Isles. Pitch for the bottom came from La Brea Rancho in Santa Clara valley.

The *Santa Cruz* had a fifty-five-foot keel, a sixteen-foot beam, ten-foot depth of hold. Its capacity by carpenter's measure was forty-five tons. Flying the French flag it was launched June 25, 1846, and sailed for the Sandwich Isles to be coppered. Two years later it was sold to Manuel Diaz when that native Cali-fornian, former alcalde of Monterey, moved his home and goods to Lower California.

A second *Santa Cruz* built two years later by Isaac Graham and Henry Neale undoubtedly used the same ways. Its picture, reproduced from a photograph of a painting, shows the United

States flag with thirty stars and a house flag with the letters "G" and "N" for its owners. The painting, signed by Joseph Lee as artist, is so far as known, no longer in existence. The photograph of the painting is in the possession of Dr. A. T. Leonard of Villa Fontenay in Santa Cruz county, an active member of the California Historical society.

The third ship constructed in Santa Cruz was the *Creole* by Jean Baptiste Dabadie, French ship's carpenter who had deserted a whaler at Monterey three years before. In the winter of 1848−49 he built a twenty-five-ton schooner on the San Lorenzo river above what is today Riverside avenue. It was used several years in the produce trade between San Francisco and Sacramento.

When in 1850 the Santa Cruz flat was raising potatoes for the mines Elihu Anthony and three associates chartered at San Francisco the schooner *General Morgan,* sailed it down the coast and loaded it with tubers which brought fifteen cents a pound. While loading they heard of the outbreak of cholera and one of the syndicate, of whose name no record exists except that it was Silva, predicted it would sweep the state. He died of the disease twenty-four hours after they reached San Francisco.

Through the fifties shipmasters running for storm shelter found disaster on the north shore of Monterey bay. The *Emily Burns* went ashore there in 1850. In 1851 the *Osceola,* loaded with Chilean flour, broke up at the mouth of the Soquel and the *White Wing*, a flat-bottomed schooner, went to pieces on Santa Cruz beach.

When the *Eagle* was wrecked on the beach in 1852 its cabin was moved to Front street and made part of the Eagle Livery stable. Eight or nine other vessels were driven ashore in the vicinity of Santa Cruz in the next year or two, including the schooner *Oakleaf,* the *James W. Whiting* and the *Luella,* all near the river mouth; the brig *Virginia* and the *Curlew* on the beach; the *Guadalupe* near Woods lagoon; the *Androscoggen* near Aptos; the *Sophia* and the *Traveler.* In 1853 the *Excel* went ashore on the beach where its timbers could be seen at low tide near the powder mill wharf as late as 1875.

In 1854 the schooner *Empire*, loaded with lime in boxes, began burning off Half Moon Bay, put back to Santa Cruz and was scuttled in front of today's boardwalk. In the latter fifties the schooner *Astoria* and the *General Worth* went ashore near Santa Cruz, although the former was got off and resumed its coastwise traffic.

Others in the list of wrecked vessels were Titus Hale's little schooner *Aptos*, driven ashore at Aptos on a storm of 1870, and the steamer *Salinas*, built by James Brennan for the Monterey Bay–San Francisco run in 1860, wrecked up the coast at Pedro Point in 1871.

Until the turn of the century, well past the beginning of rail transportation, Santa Cruz was a recognized port. In 1850 the Alta California advertised that the fast-sailing clipper bark *Hebe* would leave San Francisco for Santa Cruz, Monterey, Santa Barbara, San Pedro and San Diego.

Many of the coastwise steamers of the fifties were side-wheelers but the *Major Tompkins*, plying from Monterey bay points to San Francisco in 1854, was a "propellor."

Before having built on the east coast their $150,000 steamer *Santa Cruz* Davis and Jordan maintained two little sailing vessels, the *Queen of the West* and the *S. D. Bailey*. The former was sold and succeeded by the *Alfred Adams*, and in 1861 the *Adrienne* was bought by the pioneer lime makers.

James Brennan, a forty-niner who had laid out the town of Pescadero and built the hotel which later was the Swanton house, established himself in the Pajaro valley in 1855. He became a property holder in Watsonville, Aptos and Santa Cruz and in 1860 built the steamer *Salinas*, which had the mouth of the Salinas river at Moss Landing as its home port. Brennan developed the landing which later under other ownership became Port Goodall. The *Salinas*, 150 tons burden, plied along the coast until 1871, when it was owned by Goodall & Nelson. Brennan died impoverished in Watsonville in 1885.

A record of one week's shipping at Santa Cruz in March, 1865, in the weekly *Sentinel*, showed the steamer *Salinas* (Captain Robert Sudden) and the schooners *Alfred Adams* (Captain

Levi Hannah), *Adrienne* (Captain William M. C. Hobron), *J. H. Roscoe* (Captain J. J. Smith), *Olivia* (Captain Wells) and *Mary Ellen* (Captain George O. Fake).

About 1865 the *Senator*, a side-wheeler which had come around the Horn in 1848 and plied on the Sacramento river, was put on the short coastwise run. In 1867 it lost its rudder in a storm and was replaced for a year or two by the *Gussie Telfair*, a small steamer which had been a Confederate blockade runner on the east coast and was famed for its strength and speed. Under Captain J. C. Bogart it carried a small cannon which it fired half an hour before leaving. It ran between San Francisco and San Luis Obispo, touching at Santa Cruz, Monterey and San Simeon.

The *Fannie Gilmore*, built at Essex, Massachusetts, in 1865, was brought to Santa Cruz in 1869 by Davis and Jordan and operated in the Santa Cruz–San Francisco lime trade under Captain Dan Farley until 1885 when it was sold to Charles S. Holmes for the Hawaiian inter-island trade.

John D. Chace, New York state man who had come in the gold rush in 1850, fifteen years later owned the brig *Wolcott* which plied to San Francisco with lumber from Williams Landing. The *Wolcott* was commanded by a veteran ship's captain, T. H. Dame, brother-in-law of Chace's wife. Dame, retired for twenty years, died May 19, 1886, at his ranch west of Felton. Chace was twice mayor of Santa Cruz.

In the spring of 1870 two steamers were touching regularly at Santa Cruz, the *Gussie Telfair* which ran as far south as San Luis Obispo and the *Monterey*, successor to the *Salinas* under ownership of Goodall & Nelson. Edward S. West, in charge of the powder mill's interests at the wharf, was agent for the latter. In 1874 the Goodall-Perkins line, known as the Pacific Coast Steamship company, operated the *Kalorama* and *Constantine* along the coast. The Pacific Mail & Steamship company had the *Pacific* for passenger traffic and the tubby little *Gypsy* for freight.

Two more little ships were built in Santa Cruz county in the seventies. In 1875 the *San Vicente*, built at San Vicente creek by

Reis Brothers of San Francisco, who were shipping lime from the San Vicente kiln, went into operation with two trips a week, one of which extended to Santa Cruz. It was sold to the Pacific Coast Steamship company, which used it along the coast until it burned off Pigeon Point in 1887.

In 1878 Brown Brothers, lumber operators, built a sixty-ton schooner near Laurel Grove, which is now known as Swanton. It was named the *Julie Brown*. Its end came in a storm which put it ashore at Lighthouse point in Santa Cruz.

By 1878 the powder mill's trade was attracting larger vessels, not only to carry its product but to bring saltpetre from South America. On their return trips they carried lumber and telegraph poles for Mexico and other southern republics.

In 1877 George H. Sagar, who had commanded coastwise steamers for Goodall-Perkins, settled in Santa Cruz as agent for the Pacific Coast Steamship company. His office at first was on Beach Hill at the powder mill wharf and later back of the railroad wharf when the steamer line began using it. Captain Sagar was a native of Manchester, England, who had served in the British navy. As a youth on the cruiser *Camperdown* he had participated in the bombardment of Sebastopol in the Crimean War. For the eight years before his death in 1897 he was superintendent of the Hihn water system.

In the late seventies and the early eighties Claus Spreckels loaded lumber at Aptos on his schooners for Hawaii. The lumber came from the Grover mill and the shipping so interested the Grover brothers that in 1883 they bought a two-thirds interest in the schooner *Charles G. Wilson* which plied to San Francisco and up the Sacramento river.

By the middle eighties the longer coastwise shipping was in the hands of the Pacific Steamship company, with the shorter hauls on the schooners of Davis & Cowell.

Many of the ships' captains who plied along the coast picked Santa Cruz for their homes. Captain Dan Farley, who commanded the *Alfred Adams*, *Fideliter*, *Los Angeles*, *Eureka* and *Pomona*, was married in Santa Cruz in 1865 to Agnes Liddell, daughter of an early day lumberman whose widow, Elizabeth

Liddell, built one of the first bath houses on Santa Cruz beach. Captain Hannah died in 1896.

Captain T. H. Dame, who had commanded the *Queen of the West*, first of the Davis and Jordan schooners, and had been given command of the steamer *Santa Cruz* in 1856, married Mary Liddell, sister of Mrs. Hannah, and on his retirement made his home near Felton. Captain William M. C. Hobron married in San Francisco in 1860 Minerva Waterman and made a part-time home in Santa Cruz. Captain Robert Sudden lived in Watsonville between voyages.

BASEBALL FLOURISHED

Santa Cruz had a place on the baseball map in the nineties. Two decades earlier town teams had played on grounds back of the Pope House and in 1884 Leibbrandt brothers had mowed the field back of their bathhouse for a diamond.

In 1894 William Ely promoted the "Electrics" to play at Vue de l'Eau at the end of his new trolley line to the west cliffs and secured Bill "Brick" Devereaux, a twenty-two-year-old Oakland boy, from Lincoln in the Western League, to lead them.

The California league had lapsed in 1893 and in 1897 Devereaux gathered a team largely of home town boys to finish third in a round robin tournament sponsored by the *San Francisco Examiner*. In 1898 Santa Cruz finished second in the Pacific Coast League and in 1899 fourth in the California League.

"Alex" Roxburgh, who lived on Mission street near the Plaza, learned his baseball in the eighties on the team led by John Hunolt and in 1887 and 1888 was catcher for the Baltimore Orioles and the Philadelphia Athletics. Frank Arellanes went from Santa Cruz to the Boston Red Sox. Hal Chase, son of a Soquel lumber mill owner, played on the Soquel town teams before he went to Santa Clara and on to be first baseman of the New York Yankees. Harry Hooper of Capitola starred for the Boston Red Sox in the World series games of 1912, 1915 and 1916.

᠊᠊ᗷᐸᖟᗂᖟᐸᗂ᠊᠊

FOUR COURT HOUSES
HAVE SERVED THE COUNTY

S ANTA CRUZ COUNTY has had four court houses — or five if one counts the twenty-one months the new government functioned in William Blackburn's Eagle hotel, the old Mexican juzgado which was then nearly half a century old.

The adobe, two stories and an attic, was largest of the mission buildings. Its site today is fronting on the upper plaza just south of School street.

The county was created by the legislature on February 18, 1850; its first officers took their posts about May 1. On February 6, 1852, the county paid $3,500 for Tom Fallon's story-and-a-half combination store, hotel and residence, built of heavy boards placed vertically, with an outside stair, just across the narrow street north of the Eagle hotel.

When, in 1860, Hugo Hihn erected the still-standing two-story brick building in the point between Main and Willow streets (now Front street and Pacific avenue) the county leased the upper floor. Supervisor Samuel A. Bartlett, who ten years later became president of the county's first bank, failed to find a renter for the old building and it was made a county hospital, to serve that purpose until 1884.

By 1866 the county was ready to erect its own building. A "hill faction" led by R. C. Kirby, the tanner, offered the old Chappel home site on the upper plaza for $400 but the supervisors accepted a tract 110 feet square down on the flat from the Cooper brothers and Thomas W. Moore. A $20,000 bond issue was voted and contract let to Sedgewick J. Lynch and George T. Gragg for a two-story brick building which was completed on October 1, 1867.

The brick building burned in the big fire of April 14, 1894, and the present court house was erected the following year by

R. S. McCabe, to whom the contract was let for $53,475. The present hall of records was built in 1882.

MRS. CASE'S SCHOOL

Mary Amney Case, an energetic thirty-seven-year-old Vermont woman, opened Santa Cruz' first school in the house her husband, Benjamin, had just built in the spring of 1848. They had crossed the plains in 1847. Their home, on the edge of what is now known as Neary's lagoon, just under the west hill, still stands in ruins.

Through the summers of 1848 and 1849 Mary impressed the rudiments of Christianity and education on three children each of Nicholas Dodero, the Widow Patterson and of Pruett Sinclair, and one each of Eli Moore, Nicholas Gann, as well as one of her own.

Benjamin and Mary Case lost their savings in a hotel venture in Los Angeles in 1869 and he died two years later in Mendocino county. She returned to Santa Cruz where she died in 1900 at the home of her son, Rollin.

ᵃᵉ

BLOOMERS HORRIFIED
SANTA CRUZANS OF 1850

SANTA CRUZANS of 1850 were righteously horrified. Two females in their midst were in the habit of wearing baggy bifurcated garments while doing their farm work.

Mrs. Eliza Woodson Burhans Farnham occupied a many-gabled house the two women had helped build on a tract in the mission potrero. The land had been given in 1846 by Isaac Graham to Thomas Farnham in return for the latter's efforts in behalf of Graham and the other exiles of 1840. One story of the house is that Mrs. Farnham and her friend, Georgiana Bruce, attempted to lay the shake roof and began at the top.

Mrs. Farnham, former matron of the women's prison at Mount Pleasant, New York, which later became Sing Sing, had sufficient reputation as a writer and lecturer that the *Alta California* recorded the fact that the ship *Angelique* had arrived in San Francisco without her, and in January, 1850, told of her suit for breach of contract against Phineas Windsor, master of the vessel, alleging he left her at Valparaiso while he sailed with her two young sons to San Francisco.

Mrs. Farnham had already published three books and while here wrote *California Indoors and Out*, in which she told of landing through the surf at Santa Cruz on a man's shoulders.

After an unfortunate marriage to William A. Fitzpatrick, which she ended by divorce, Mrs. Farnham was appointed matron of the Stockton insane asylum. On the outbreak of the Civil War she hurried east to become a nurse on the battlefields. Illness following a cold caught in weeks of tireless effort at Gettysburg caused her death in New York City in December, 1864.

Georgiana Bruce, an English girl, had met Mrs. Farnham at the home of Horace Greeley. She had spent two years at Brook Farm colony of Transcendentalists outside Boston and knew Nathaniel Hawthorne, Ralph Waldo Emerson, George William Curtis, Charles A. Dana, Margaret Filler and Bronson Alcott. After a short time as associate matron at Mount Pleasant under Mrs. Farnham she had taught at Monticello Female Seminary near Alton, Illinois, and tutored in Missouri and near Philadelphia.

In February, 1849, Mrs. Farnham had issued a circular in New York offering to take to California a number of respectable young women each of whom was to contribute $250 for expenses. She became ill and the enterprise lapsed. A few months later Mrs. Farnham's departure for San Francisco to salvage the estate she believed left by her wandering author husband prompted Georgiana to follow. In midsummer of 1850 she reached Santa Cruz, riding horseback from the end of the stage line at San Jose.

Superintendent of farming at Brook Farm had been James Bryant Hill, who in 1851 came from San Francisco to lease land in the southern end of Santa Cruz county to grow potatoes, then bringing a high price at San Francisco and at the mines. To repay Greeley money loaned her for the trip west Georgiana went in the fall of 1851 to spend six months keeping house for Hill. To iron his shirts, in lieu of better utensil, she used a can kept full of boiling water.

On June 22, 1852, in Santa Cruz she married thirty-five-year-old Richard C. Kirby, native of Staffordshire, England, who had deserted in 1845 a whaler off Puget Sound. At Oregon City he met Alfred Baldwin, with whom he joined a party to Sutter's Fort. After operating with Philip Pell a small tannery in San Francisco he had accepted seventy-five dollars a month from William Blackburn to work a tannery on San Agustin Rancho near Santa Cruz, which had been run by Paul Sweet until the latter had joined Fremont's California Battalion.

After discovery of gold Kirby had made a small fortune at the mines but lost it in a trading venture. At the end of two years he was back in Santa Cruz installing a small tannery in Squabble Hollow, which is today Glen Canyon.

Upon his marriage Kirby moved into Santa Cruz, buying a lot and small house on the road up the coast from the mission from George Frick, last teacher of the Methodist academy which preceded the public school. On the lot he built in 1853 a residence which, added to in 1888, is still standing at 129 Mission street.

With Edmund Jones as a partner Kirby bought out a little tannery owned by Charles Brown and installed it on Majors creek (the stream the Portola party had named Santa Cruz). Its site today would be north of Laurel street above and below California street. Its capacity grew to 1,500 hides a month; it operated until 1893 turning out leather which had a coast-wide reputation.

About their home on Mission street the Kirbys planted trees and shrubs from all over the world. In one of the rooms hung the oil portrait of Sir Peter Strudwick, Georgiana's great grandfather.

Bringing five children into the world and maintaining with her husband a reputation for hospitality, Georgiana found time to resume writing. Drawing on her memories of cultural Boston and New York in the middle forties, she sold articles to *Old and New*, a Boston magazine, and "My First Visit to Brook Farm" and "Tale of the Redwoods," the latter fiction, to the *Overland Monthly* of San Francisco. In 1887, just before her death, she published a book, *Years of Experience*.

Mrs. Farnham left her Santa Cruz property to her son Charles, who was in Paris at the time of her death. After her departure it had been occupied by Thomas Russell, whose brother John had operated with convict labor a little file factory at Mount Pleasant. Thomas, a forty-niner, had come to Santa Cruz soon after Mrs. Farnham and took over farming when she failed at it. His murder in a gulch near Evergreen cemetery in 1856 was a never-explained mystery.

Kirby bought the tract from Charles Farnham, deeded 210 acres to the Doderos when they were proved part of Tres Ojos de Agua grant, and gave part of the site for Evergreen cemetery. He gave up plans for a tannery there on his wife's objection because of the site's assiciation with her earlier years there and sold it to Alexander Russell, son of the murdered Thomas.

The house which Eliza and Georgiana had struggled to build in 1851 was replaced in 1868. The land, now frequently used as circus grounds, is known as the Barrett tract.

◄╕╩╕►

BIRTHPLACE OF TEMPERANCE

SANTA CRUZ was birthplace of the temperance movement in California. Adna A. Hecox, who settled his family at Soquel in the spring of 1847, found "Drunkenness exceedingly prevalent" and signed up five "topers." In the spring of 1848 he organized a society with Benjamin A. Case as president and James G. T. Dunleavy as secretary.

The society lapsed when Santa Cruzans left for the gold fields but was reformed in 1849. Eureka Division of the Sons of Temperance was organized in 1852 and the first lodge in California of the Independent Order of Good Templars formed in 1855.

By 1859 seven hundred Santa Cruzans were members of two divisions of the Sons of Temperance, one division of Good Templars and a Temple of honor. Jointly they erected Temperance Hall, a two-story, twenty-five-by-fifty-foot building dedicated March 23, 1861. The structure was center of social activities which did not go to the Exchange hotel. It stood on the north side of Mission street almost opposite Vine. Twice it moved, once directly down fifty feet as the lot was dug away to a new street level and again to Bulkhead and River street where it was razed in 1930.

The W.C.T.U. was organized April 27, 1883, by fifty women in the Congregational church following a meeting two nights before in Knights Opera House which had been addressed by Frances E. Willard.

THE FAIR PAVILION

For thirty-seven years the Fair Pavilion (in its latter years the armory) housed Santa Cruz' civic and social events. It was a barn-like structure, 100 by 150 feet, built in 1883 on Arcan street, which was the present portion of Soquel avenue between Pacific avenue and the river. Its site had been the home of Edward L. Williams.

Built for $10,000 by a company in which F. A. Hihn and R. C. Kirby were leaders, it housed autumn harvest fairs and the ladies' spring rose fairs. In it blazoned on the last night of 1884 the first electric lights in Santa Cruz, from a steam generator brought from San Francisco as a feature of the Pilot Hose company's annual New Year's Eve ball.

It became the armory when the naval reserves used it. Until it burned on the night of January 16, 1920, it was the scene of high school basketball games, community dances and military drill.

⊸≣⊷

THE TWO ADOBES
AND THE ARMAS BROTHERS

N SCHOOL STREET stand two adobes end to end, sole remaining structures of the Franciscan mission. Surmise from the best records is they were built about 1810 for quarters for members of the escolta.

Back of one, known as the Neary adobe since its purchase in 1864 by a young Irishman, Patrick Neary, is a well cared for garden which dates back to Spanish and Mexican days. Neary's purchase was from Felipe Armas, whose story is interesting.

About 1830 King Kamehameha of the Sandwich Isles appealed to California for vaqueros to subdue cattle which, running wild, were becoming a nuisance. Among the vaqueros sent were Felipe Armas and his brother, Joaquin. The former at least was a soldier in the San Francisco presidio company.

In 1845 the Armas brothers returned to California and established homes at Santa Cruz. Felipe had married in the islands and brought two daughers, four and seven years old. Record of their baptism here in 1851 shows their mother as "Maria Richason." Felipe chose a second wife, Antonia, daughter of Sebastian Rodriguez, grantee of Rancho Bolsa del Pajaro, where Watsonville stands.

For residence Felipe bought the adobe from two Indians who had received it in the distribution of mission property. His deed, put on record when the county was formed in 1850, shows the purchase was from "J. Petra y Isidro, indios."

Near the house was the well with its high curb. Back of it was a porch with a flight of steps leading to a little second-floor room in which, while Felipe was still occupant of the building, in 1853, the Santa Cruz Masonic lodge was organized.

When state and county governments were formed in 1850 Felipe was made justice of the peace and member of the court of sessions. He acted on a committee which financed the county's first jail. In 1860 he ran unsuccessfully for supervisor and soon afterward removed his family to Pescadero.

"Maria Richason," who was the wife of Felipe Armas in the Sandwich Isles, has been partially identified by R. S. Kuykendall, associate professor of history in the University of Hawaii. Two Richardson families lived in Hawaii in early days. A son of one, John, probably a brother of Armas' wife, was member of the Privy Council of the kingdom of Hawaii, ten years in the legislature and eight years a circuit judge.

Joaquin Armas died a bachelor in Santa Cruz in December, 1850, leaving a will declaring he had worked for the king of "los Islos de San Dich" and that he and Felipe owned a house there.

The adjoining adobe passed into the hands of Roman Rodriguez, one of the sons of Jose Antonio Rodriguez, the Branciforte invalido settler of 1798, at the time of the distribution of mission property after 1834 and remained in the family until death of his grandson, another Roman, in 1936.

◄►

YOUNG COLLEGE GRADUATE
HEADED FIRST SCHOOL

IN THE COOL SUMMER EVENING the men of Santa Cruz strolled over to the mass meeting or hitched their horses outside the wooden court house on the upper plaza. Most came from homes on the hill but there was a contingent from the flat. The issue was whether Mission Hill or the lower land should be site of the town's first school.

Isaac Pierce wanted $400 for the lot on the hill he had just bought from Hiram Imus, the Connecticut veteran of the War of 1812. Fred A. Hihn offered one almost as large "on the cross street running back from Willow street to the hill" for half the price.

The Branciforte school of 1883   UCSC Special Collections

Tubercular Dr. Asa W. Rawson, who three years before had brought his wife and children from Illinois and was eking out his income by running the Union Livery stable, was elected chairman, an initial victory for the flat as the doctor owned lots on Willow and Main streets.

The hilltop contingent, however, controlled the meeting which voted to buy the Pierce site as nearer most of the homes.

The $400 was raised by subscription, most of it that night. Had Hihn's site been taken Santa Cruz' first public school would have been about where the public library stands.

The building was erected the following year, 1857, at a cost of $2,233, of which $400 came by a county tax, $1,416 raised by subscription and the rest assumed as a debt by the district of which Richard K. Vestal, the wagon maker, William Anthony, the tinsmith, and Richard C. Kirby, the tanner, were trustees. The site, just at the top of Mission street hill, is today that of the administrative buildings of the school system.

Twenty-three-year-old Thomas Milton Gatch had been teacher in Tuolumne county the previous year but one of his pupils had discovered gold nuggets under the building, which was destroyed in the resulting rush. Young Mr. Gatch, who had graduated in 1855 from Ohio Wesleyan university, was not well. He had come to California by the Isthmus and typhoid had ended an attempt to dig gold.

Across the San Joaquin valley he headed and down to Santa Cruz. In the single thirty-by-forty room in August, 1857, school was opened with Mrs. Clara C. Adams teaching the primary grades.

This was the beginning of the notable career as an educator of Thomas M. Gatch. When, in 1913, he died near Seattle he could look back over years in which he had headed three great universities and declined the presidency of a fourth.

In the year and a half that Gatch spent in Santa Cruz in the late fifties he found a wife. Eighteen-year-old Orytha Bennett, who had crossed the plains with her parents and sisters nine years before, lived in a neighboring house on the road up the coast, which means Mission street today, about opposite Union street. The Bennett family had stopped at Sacramento where Sutter had hired Silas F. Bennett to complete the famous sawmill in whose tailrace gold had been discovered. Bennett had met Elihu Anthony at Coloma and with him come to Santa Cruz in 1850.

Silas brought a little gold with him and bought the land where the present Mission Hill school stands. He had, with Adna A. Hecox, given seven acres for the grounds of the first Methodist church.

When, in 1860, Bennett left for Mendocino county, his house was taken by the Rev. John Sheridan Zelie, first Congregational minister of Santa Cruz, who ran a private school in it. In 1867, when a young Vermont-born ex-stage driver named Horace Pope started the Pope House, which became a stopping place for wealthy and social elite of San Francisco, the old Bennett home and the one next door in which Thomas Gatch and his bride had set up housekeeping became part of the establishment. The Bennett cottage was the Pope House office until it was torn down in 1919.

Gatch was grandson of an eminent Methodist divine, the Rev. Philip Gatch, first American-born minister of that church. The grandson was born in 1833 in Milford, now a suburb of Cincinnati. After graduating from Ohio Wesleyan he studied for some months at Lane Theological seminary but was refused a degree when he declined a request of its president, Dr. Lyman Beecher, that he pledge himself to the ministry.

After a seven-and-a-half-month term in Santa Cruz, Principal Gatch became professor of mathematics at the University of the Pacific at Santa Clara. In 1859 he moved north to be head of Puget Sound Wesleyan Institute at Olympia. After a year there he was elected to the chair of ancient languages at Willamette university. Hardly had he and his wife moved to Salem than Willamette's first president, F. S. Hoyt, resigned and twenty-seven-year-old Thomas Gatch was given the position.

At the end of five years as president of the oldest college on the Pacific coast Gatch resigned, returned to Santa Cruz and advertised in the *Sentinel* that he would start a private school in Temperance Hall. The school trustees, however, made him head of the public school, which had grown to such an extent that the old court house and the lower floor of Temperance Hall were being used.

Gatch stayed a year and a half until an offer of $1,600 a year took him back to Willamette where in 1870 he was again its president. He declined the presidency of the University of Oregon when it was organized in 1879 but taught there. In 1886 he became first president of the University of Washington and in 1898 went to Corvallis to be president of Oregon Agricultural College.

Nine years before the start of the first public school Mrs. Mary Amney Case, who with her husband, Benjamin Allen Case, had crossed the plains with Elihu Anthony, had formed a private school in her home, a building still standing in ruins at the upper end of Neary lagoon just under the hill.

In the period between Mrs. Case's school and the first public school the Methodists maintained an academy, at first taught by H. S. Loveland in a little building on the bluff overlooking the river at the end of what is now School street and moved to the new Methodist church on Green street in December, 1850. Succeeding teachers were C. K. Ercanbreck, who became a leading citizen of Watsonville and died there in 1891, the Rev. D. A. Dryden and George W. Frick.

The original public school was soon expanded into two rooms. In 1868 a two-room "Beach school" was erected by a $2,500 tax. It was replaced in 1895 by a two-story wooden building on a nearby location which lasted until the present Laurel school was erected in 1930.

In 1863 residents of "North Santa Cruz" carved out a Santa Cruz District No. 2 and built a one-room structure. In the patriotic fervor of the Civil war it was renamed Grant school. In 1869 it was united with Santa Cruz district.

Branciforte school district, created in 1860, had no building until it was incorporated into the Santa Cruz system, which, by a $2,500 tax, erected in 1869 a two-room structure on the site of the present Santa Cruz hospital. It later was made two stories high and was replaced by the present Branciforte building in 1915.

Well outside the town of those days the residents about Four Corners (the present Bay and Mission streets) organized in 1865 Bay View school district, which included territory several miles up the coast. It opened a "rate school" with Miss Anna Phillips as teacher "well recommended by the trustees," but in 1867 bought a small residence from Moses Meader and installed Nellie Doxie. A new building was constructed in 1885 and the present Bay View school erected in 1908 for $20,000.

In 1876 a three-story wooden building was put up on the original school site by a $20,000 bond issue and a high school course inaugurated. A separate high school building constructed in 1894 burned nineteen years later to be replaced by the present one on the same site. The present Mission Hill school was erected in 1930 out of a $330,000 bond issue which also financed the Laurel and Gault schools.

Several notable private schools flourished in Santa Cruz. In 1867 Mr. and Mrs. Paul Pioda, Swiss, established a "Young Ladies' Seminary" at Pacific avenue and Lincoln street in a building erected for it by Edmund Jones at a cost of $1000. It lasted until Pioda accepted a position at the University of California in 1880. He later had a seminary at Benicia but returned to Santa Cruz where he died in 1892 at his residence on Elm street.

In 1879 Mrs. John L. Gamble of San Francisco, wife of a picturesque graduate of West Point who had served through the Civil War and been secretary to Commodore Parrott of the Asiatic squadron in China, bought Santa Cruz Seminary which had been founded the previous year by Mrs. G. W. Ford, wife of the Baptist minister.

Mrs. Gamble leased the newly built Walnut Avenue House, which still stands at 68 Walnut avenue, until in 1881 F. A. Hihn provided her with new quarters by moving back from Pacific avenue the picturesque Isaac Williams house of 1850, which had for several years been the Methodist parsonage. In the new quarters, which Hihn made three stories high, on a site just a little east of the present telephone company building, the seminary was renamed Quincy Hall and flourished as one of the leading finishing schools of the west, drawing pupils from a wide area. Major Gamble died in 1880 and his widow bought a boarding school on Van Ness avenue in San Francisco. Its lineal descendant is the present Hamlin school on Broadway, in that city.

The three-story building on Walnut avenue became the Auzerais hotel and then the Eastern hotel and burned October 23, 1903.

From the time it was founded in 1884 until 1898 Chestnutwood's Business College drew students from northern and central California, many of whom rose to positions of prominence in the state. John A. Chesnutwood, native of Illinois, had been a teacher at Stockton before he came to establish his Santa Cruz school, which started, like so many other institutions of the city, in a ground-floor room in the Pacific Ocean House.

Chesnutwood's, in the best college tradition, had its baseball teams and gave dances, in addition to teaching bookkeeping and florid handwriting which ran heavily to ornamental scrolls. When Hihn erected the Alta building at Walnut and Pacific avenues Chesnutwood's occupied its entire second floor. Chesnutwood sold out in 1898 and died in 1905 at Stockton. The school under various names continued until 1942.

Holy Cross Academy, founded in 1862 by the Sisters of Mercy in the adobe which was the juzgado of Mexican days, occupied large wooden buildings which were torn down in 1944. The school had, however, moved in 1926 to its present building. From 1891 to 1921 the Christian Brothers maintained a school in Santa Cruz.

Horse-and-buggy days saw more than three score rural schools in Santa Cruz county. Many of them such as the powder mill school, Loma Prieta school and the Dougherty school were abandoned when those little industrial villages went out of existence.

Until 1857 the San Mateo coast line was part of Santa Cruz county and Pescadero, laid out in 1853 by James Brennan, organized in 1857 the second school in the county. In 1859 the growing community in the Pajaro valley formed the Pajaro district out of which was promptly carved Oak Grove, the name of which was in 1871 changed to Corralitos. Soquel district of 1860 contained most of the central part of the county but out of it were carved San Andreas and Union and, a decade later, Aptos, Hazelbrook, Mountain and Summit.

El Jarro district, up the coast, formed in 1865, was changed ten years later to Seaside. Petroleum, formed at the same time, in 1875 became Laguna. The San Lorenzo district of 1863 became Felton in 1875, seven years after Boulder Creek had established its school. The Newell Creek school of 1876 became the Ben Lomond school in 1894.

⊲⊫

LOUDON NELSON BEQUEATHED
ENTIRE ESTATE TO SCHOOL

LOUDON NELSON'S entire fortune was a lot on the San Jose road, which is now Water street, on which he grew vegetables and had his cabin in which he mended shoes for a living.

From his cabin he could see, at the top of Mission hill, the two-room wooden building in which school had been temporarily abandoned for lack of funds. He signed his mark to his will, dedicating his property to giving education to the white folks' children.

In old Evergreen cemetery is the stone with which the white folks honored the ex-slave. Its epitaph is "He was a colored man. He left his entire fortune to Santa Cruz school district No. 1."

His "fortune," put into the hands of Public Administrator Elihu Anthony, included the lot which was sold five years later for $300, a Hugo F. Hihn Co. note for $35, $7 in county scrip, household furniture valued at $15 and a crop of growing onions which brought $15.

Loudon Nelson, born a Carolina slave, had gone with his master to Tennessee and then to California where he was given his freedom. When Anthony in 1875 closed the estate the public school was in sufficient funds to keep open and the $372 was used to augment the school grounds by helping to buy an adjoining lot. The lot and a small cottage were bought from Samuel Richardson Hillman, a sixty-two-year-old bachelor from Delaware, who took the opportunity to retire from his cabinet-making business to a little house on upper Locust street where he died in 1884. The addition to the school grounds was next to the brick Leslie building and today affords entrance to the administrative offices of the city schools.

In tradition the eighth grade class of the present Mission Hill school, successor of District No. 1 when Loudon Nelson died on May 17, 1860, each year cleans and decorates his grave.

INDIAN PLACE NAMES

When the Franciscan priests began baptising, marrying and burying the Indians of the Santa Cruz region they carefully recorded the names of each rancheria, at the same time giving each little group the same of a saint.

Soquel, with its variation of Osocalis, Osoquales and Shoquel; Aptos, which they also wrote Avtos and Abtos; and Zayante are the three which have survived as modern place names.

No statement of the meaning of the words in the Indian tongue of 1791 is possible. The spellings are phonetic, in Spanish, reproduction of the Indian pronunciation.

How small the rancherias were is evidenced by the number recorded. Forty-six show in the mission records, all within an approximate radius of twenty miles. The list ran from Achila and Achistaca to Tomoi and Vypu.

SANTA CRUZANS RALLIED TO UNION'S CAUSE

A STRONG MINORITY FACTION in Santa Cruz county opposed Lincoln in the election of 1860, but when the secession of the southern states came the county rallied patriotically to the flag. A mass meeting on the night of May 8, 1861, in Luther Farnham's Exchange Hotel formed the Union Club, with Postmaster Elihu Anthony as president, Henry W. Peck and boyish Thomas T. Tidball, both Soquel men, as vice presidents and I. C. Willson the attorney as treasurer.

The meeting adopted resolutions beginning, "Whereas insurrectionary war actually exists in our republic . . . ," setting forth that those present declared their unalterable devotion to the American union and were "ready to obey the call of duty in defense of our country wherever it may direct."

Sentiment was not undivided. Before the patriotic resolutions were adopted an alternate set was presented by W. D. Farrand and Judge Henry Rice, southern-born and leading Democrats, which condoned secession and attacked the coercion which the Washington government was assertedly using to keep the slave states in the federation. The alternate resolutions were voted down overwhelmingly.

At Davis & Jordan's lime kilns, at Van Valkenburg's paper mill and at Kirby & Jones' tannery, poles were erected by the employes for flags furnished by the employers. The Union Club staged a Fourth of July celebration with committeemen from every community in the county.

Santa Cruz' first volunteer, impatient to get into the fighting, was thirty-one-year-old George Irving Holt, who took a steamer from San Francisco and joined the California Hundred group from the west coast, whose passage was defrayed by Boston and who fought through the war as members of a Massachusetts regiment. Holt returned to Santa Cruz where he was a painter and died in 1891 to be buried in the I.O.O.F. cemetery.

When, late in August, Governor Downey issued a call for organization of a regiment of infantry and five companies of cavalry for protection of the overland mail routes an enrollment office was opened in the Exchange Hotel. The roll was filled in two weeks.

The government was to furnish horses, so the company went into camp on the flat east of the San Lorenzo river until, on the evening of Sunday, September 22, down a street lined with waving handkerchiefs, it marched to the wharf and embarked on the the steamer *Salinas* with free passage furnished by Davis & Jordan. Landed at San Francisco the men were given breakfast by Davis & Jordan and marched to Camp Alert, the old Pioneer race track, where 25th and Folsom streets now intersect.

On the Friday before departure the company had elected Albert Brown, foreman of the Davis & Jordan quarry, as captain and Alfred H. Hawes, John Quinn and H. B. Stephenson lieutenants. The contingent with its number swelled by recruits from other parts of the state was sworn in at Camp Alert as Company L, Second California Cavalry. Two young Santa Cruzans, Alexander Brown and Asa Anthony, son of George Anthony, died at Camp Alert and were brought home to be buried, the city's first war losses.

With the departure of the cavalry appeared a prototype of the Red Cross. Girls of the town made haversacks each of which contained "stout needles, unbleached linen thread, a yard long coarse crash towel and a handkerchief."

Captain Brown, returning on a down trip of the *Salinas* to secure six extra recruits, voiced formally at the weekly Union Club meeting his appreciation of the efforts of the women, who were led by Miss Maria Field. Miss Field was one of the daughters of Storer W. Field, a Massachusetts man who, after a term in the Wisconsin legislature, had come to Santa Cruz. In 1864 he was partner with F. A. Hihn; in 1868 with James W. Brown he opened a general merchandise store next to Anthony's building. His daughter Maria a few years later married James O. Wanzer but divorced him, studied at Lane Medical school in San Francisco and became California's first woman doctor.

In the early summer of 1863 Company L was in Owens valley; in August it traveled to Salt Lake where it was stationed at Fort Douglas when it was mustered out in September of 1864. Captain Brown re-enlisted at Fort Bridger, Wyoming Territory, and remained a soldier until July 12, 1866. Back in Santa Cruz he served from 1870 to 1874 as county clerk, auditor and recorder. In the eighties in San Francisco he unsuccessfully sought office. Brown died April 12, 1919, at the veterans' home at Yountville.

Even before the cavalry company left, young T. T. Tidball began recruiting an infantry unit. By the middle of November he sent word to Governor Downey that he had thirty-six men enrolled. Benjamin F. Bayley resigned as head of the Soquel school to be first lieutenant.

The people turned out to a military ball at the Exchange Hotel to raise money and townsmen and nearby farmers gave use of teams and wagons to haul the new soldiers to San Francisco, whence they went by boat to Camp Union, near Sacramento. The unit, filled out by volunteers from other parts of the state, was sworn in as Company K, Fifth California Infantry, on November 22, 1861.

There was much talk of a Confederate force from Texas coming to capture southern California and the regiment was rushed south, although Company K, stationed on Alcatraz, was last to go. It was, however, with the California Column when it reached Casa Blanca, Arizona Territory, on March 31, 1863, and marched to Tucson a month later. Peril of a Confederate invasion of Los Angeles lapsed and was followed by plans for a California invasion of Texas which was never carried out, perhaps because it involved a march which would have taken the column across the Mexican border.

The Fifth Infantry stayed on the border with mild service against the Apaches in which Captain Tidball won the following citation:

"Fifteen enlisted men of Company K composed part of the expedition sent under command of Capt. T. T. Tidball against Apache Indians in Canon de Arivaypi, Arizona Territory. The expedition left Tucson May 2 at dusk, made five successive night marches; built no fires; hid during the day. It surprised and attacked an Apache rancheria in the Canon de Arivaypi on the morning of the 7th inst. Killed 47 Indians; took 10 prisoners; captured 66 head of stock with the loss of one man—a citizen of Arizona. Returned to Tucson on the 11th, having marched 180 miles in five days."

In the fall of 1864 the regiment marched from Fort Bowie to Las Cruces to be mustered out. Captain Tidball returned to Santa Cruz where his war record won him immediate election as county clerk and appointment in 1867 to fill a vacancy as assessor. He removed to Jolon and died January 28, 1913, near Monterey.

In 1863 the army recruited Californians of Spanish descent in a separate contingent. Jose M. Rodriguez of Santa Cruz was one of a company of seventy-five under Captain Ramon Pico which went by steamer from San Francisco to Humboldt Bay to hunt hostile Indians.

A third company from Santa Cruz county was sought in 1864 when Captain Claremont C. Smith opened recruiting head-quarters in Watsonville. Company A, Eighth California Infantry, which spent its two years of military duty in garrison service on the Columbia river, was made up largely of men from Wat-sonville, Corralitos, Aptos and Soquel.

With the youngsters off to war, the home guard inevitable in every war was formed with virtually every able-bodied man left in Santa Cruz on its rolls. The Butler Guards drilled with twenty-six-year-old Marcellus P. Fuller, proprietor of the Eagle restaurant, as captain; and James O. Wanzer, deputy county clerk, and six-foot-six George T. Hoff as lieutenants.

In the ranks were such leading citizens as Sheriff Ambrose Calderwood; G. Q. Russell, proprietor of the Washington Stables; Duncan McPherson, editor of the weekly *Sentinel*, and his brother, Alex, the county surveyor; Felix Fiester, the black-smith; I. C. Willson, the lawyer; William W. Broughton, the printer; Lewis T. Ware, the sawyer; elderly Moses Meader, the farmer, who had come with Sam Brannan's shipload of Mor-mons from Brooklyn in 1846; Charles O. Bent, the dairyman; Andrew Trust, the baker; Horace W. Pope, the hotel man; and two score others.

The Butler Guards disbanded but a rival or later organi-zation with Deputy Sheriff Orville Root as captain was kept alive for several years as the Santa Cruz Cavalry, principal duty of which was to turn out for parades.

Veterans of the Civil War began to organize in 1870 when on June 18 General Wright Post was formed at Soquel. Gen-eral W. H. L. Wallace Post was mustered in August 19, 1881, in Santa Cruz, taking its name from an old friend at Earlville, Illinois, of Constable C. T. Sutphen, leader in the organization. In 1889 the Santa Cruz post split over an election in which A. L. Weeks beat Horace Wanzer for commander and Reynolds Post was formed. The two reunited many years later. In 1885 Thomas Amner Post was organized at Boulder Creek.

An 1860's view looking south at the intersection of Front and Pacific

⇥

DOWN TOWN IN 1860

HUGO HIHN had just finished his brick flat-iron building and leased the top floor to the county. Across Main street to the east on approximately the site of today's postoffice were the Franklin House and Santa Cruz House, two of the town's three hotels of that day.

One of the small buildings this side of the Franklin House was the shop of Zebulon Sprague, gun and pistol maker, by the sign. In the distance, past several saloons and Chinese laundries, was the wagon works and blacksmith shop of Edward Pagles.

In the near foreground, on the left, is part of Elihu Anthony's building, first business structure on the flat, which he replaced with a two-story building in 1870. To the right, just out of frame, was the store of Charles D. Eldon. Beyond it, with the flagpole, is the building in which F. A. Hihn had his store with the weekly *Sentinel* upstairs. Past it, not shown was Henry Rice's San Lorenzo Hotel, which burned in 1865 and was replaced by the brick Pacific Ocean House. (Photo page 157.)

Down Pacific was the W. H. Moore home, just south of the present court house site. The dwelling still stands, moved to Short street.

⇥

PIONEER CIRCUSES MADE
THEIR ANNUAL VISITS

CIRCUSES of pioneer California found their way annually to Santa Cruz. Through the fifties the Pioneer Circus, the National, Dan Rice's or Sands, Nathan & Co.'s Elephant Exhibition pitched little tents on Willow street on the present site of the Palomar Hotel.

After the United States Circus and the Combined Basset & Bartholomew shows played in 1861 the Civil War brought a lapse, but in 1864 Wilson & Zoyara's circus with its "vast new hippotheatron" and Lee & Ryland's "equescurriculum and camel show" were both in Santa Cruz.

In 1868 came the Paris Exposition circus and Chiarini's Royal Italian show. By 1870 the grounds shifted to Vine street back of the Pacific Ocean House where Leihy & Lake's Great Overland Circus with 50 Star Performers played.

When, in 1872, the Crystal Palace Circus and the New York Mammoth Circus both came space was found close to Pacific avenue between Walnut and Church, which continued in use during the four or five years that the Montgomery Queen Circus, last of the big one-ring shows, was the yearly attraction.

The Montgomery Queen Circus brought George Hastings, the boy cornetist, who so liked Santa Cruz that he became a permanent resident, leading the town band and playing for the church choir.

Adam Forepaugh's Circus in 1877 found larger space at Walnut and Chestnut avenues on grounds used for several years. In 1880 W. W. Cole's "Electric Lighted, Sun Eclipsing Show" began a series of visits but in 1882 Santa Cruz missed John Robinson's "Ten Big Shows Combined," which was traveling by rail and could not come from Watsonville by narrow-gauge. It made the trip the following year, however. Another show of the early eighties was Barrett's Monster Railroad Show.

Building on Walnut avenue sent the circuses to a lot near Elm street west of Pacific avenue. In the early nineties the John Robinson show used the lot at King street and Walnut avenue, back of the Pope House. By the turn of the century the circus grounds had moved to the Bausch lot at Soquel avenue and Ocean street and later to the Leibbrandt tract near the beach where Ringling's, Barnum and Bailey, Buffalo Bill, Floto, Barnes and others played.

In 1905 a home-town-booster movement raised $1,700 by subscription to buy land near the west cliffs use of which was given the Norris & Rowe Circus which made its winter quarters there until it was sold in 1909 to pay its debts and Norris, whose real name was Andrew C. Cozad, committed suicide.

⇒⊫⇒

MARTINA CASTRO
WAS GRANTEE OF SOQUEL

SOCALES was an alternate phonetic spelling for "Shoquel" in the mission records. Legend is that the Indian word designated a place of willows. Invalido Corporal Marcelino Bravo was its first white settler, dying there January 16, 1806.

Soquel was a place name in 1811. One of the Branciforte documents shows Lieutenant Jose Estudillo, comandante at Monterey, rebuking Comisionado Jose Antonio Robles of Branciforte for not reporting more quickly theft of a boat at Soquel by Rusos Indios — Aleutian Indians brought from Sitka by the Russians to take otter skins.

Two Mexican grants covered the Soquel valley, Soquel and its "augmentacion" to Martina Castro and Arroyo del Rodeo to her brother-in-law, Francisco Rodriguez.

Martina was widow of Corporal Simon Cota when, in 1831, she married Michael Lodge, Dublin sailor. On September 8, 1833, Alcalde Robles gave Lodge and his wife permission to build a home and cultivate the ground at Soquel. Two months later Martina's application for a grant was in the hands of Governor Jose Figueroa in Monterey. On August 14, 1834, formalities had been completed and Martina "walked on the land, pulled up grass and threw handfuls of earth, broke off branches of trees, threw stones to the four winds and performed other ceremonies and acts of possession."

Ten years later Martina petitioned for wide acres back of her original grant, naming it Rancho de Palo de Yesca (Tinder Tree) but receiving it as Soquel Augmentacion. The two grants gave her what was surveyed in American days as 34,370 acres.

Martina, widowed again by the disappearance of Michael, presumably killed for his gold on the way back from the mines in 1849, had married Louis Depeaux when, in 1850, she divided her land, one parcel for herself and one for each of her eight children. Division of Soquel was complete under court supervision in 1860 and that of the Augmentacion in 1864. Litigation after her death in 1890 upheld the titles.

The recipients were Nicanor Cota (wife of Francois Lajeunesse), Luisa Cota (wife of Jean Richard Fourcade), Carmelita Lodge (wife of Thomas Fallon), Josefa Lodge (wife of Lambert B. Clements), Antonia Lodge (wife of Henry W. Peck), Helena Lodge (wife of Jose Littlejohn), Guadalupe Lodge (wife of Jose Averon) and Antonio Miguel Lodge.

Across the Soquel river to the west, Rodeo Rancho, named because in its bottom land nearby ranchers annually gathered their cattle, was given in 1834 to Francisco Rodriguez, son of Jose Antonio Rodriguez, the 1798 invalido. His wife was Rafaela Castro, sister of Martina and of Rafael, who held Aptos Rancho a few miles to the east.

Francisco died in 1848. Title bought from his heirs by John Daubenbiss, the young Bavarian, and John Hames, New York state men, was confirmed by the United States land commission, but a survey of 1861 cut it from 2,353 to 1,473 acres. The two homes built by Hames and Daubenbiss are still (1946) standing. Lumbering, which through Civil War times made Soquel nearly as large and as active as Santa Cruz, got its start when, in 1845, Martina and Michael hired Daubenbiss and Hames to build a little sawmill which stood across the river from the present school site. High water took the mill out in 1848 and in the spring of 1847 Lodge hired Adna A. Hecox, carpenter and preacher, to rebuild it. In 1849 Daubenbiss and Hames erected a mill of their own half a mile up the river. Timbers cut there, taken by schooner from Soquel Landing, built the "long wharf" in San Francisco which is now Commercial street.

Impetus to the lumber industry came in 1852 when Gervis Hammond and Hugh Pablo McCall, who had been working in the timber around Zayante, moved into the Soquel valley. Gershal H. Kirby put a waterpower mill a short distance up stream. Roger Hinckley and John L. Shelby two years later went still further up. In 1857 Joel Bates started the first steam mill in the valley on Bates creek. The Grovers, Benjamin

Cahoon, Lansing Haight and a number of others entered the territory in the sixties.

The timber-working area gradually extended into the hills until past the end of the century when F. A. Hihn's Laurel mill furnished much of the lumber to rebuild a burned and shaken San Francisco in 1906.

Through the roaring sixties and seventies Soquel had three hotels, innumerable blacksmith shops and a corresponding number of saloons. In the seventies a sugar mill flourished on the flat toward Capitola. In 1879 Edward and Frank O'Neill, of a Massachusetts paper-making family, put a paper mill on the site of the Daubenbiss and Hames sawmill. Two chair factories, three tanneries, and a fruit dryer were some of its industries.

Soquel's Congregational church started when on Sunday, May 17, 1868, eight members of the Santa Cruz church gathered in Parson and Blakeley's new blacksmith shop. A lot was given by Joshua Parrish and in March, 1870, S. A. Hall, former ship's carpenter, began erection of the picturesque structure which is still standing.

One of Soquel's claims to fame is that in the polling place in Tom Mann's hotel in 1868 was cast what may have been the first vote by a woman for president of the United States. On her death in her cabin on the road east of Aptos on December 29, 1879, Charles Darkey Parkhurst, veteran stage driver, was found to be Charlotte Parkhurst.

Soquel was made the third township in the county in October, 1852, reaching from Rodeo gulch to Aptos creek. In 1857 it was extended to include Aptos Rancho and Corralitos. In 1879 Corralitos, by petition, was made part of Pajaro township and a little later Aptos township was created. Soquel had its own justice of the peace and constable until the automobile ended horse-and-buggy days.

La Playa de Soquel became Soquel Landing when American days came. The first building of any note was a warehouse erected in 1852 for potatoes which ship's captains refused to haul any longer to a glutted San Francisco market. First record of its wharf was in 1856 when the *Santa Cruz Sentinel* stated an older structure was being repaired and lengthened.

When, in 1869, F. A. Hihn laid out Camp Capitola on the pattern of European watering places he perhaps found inspiration for its name in the fact that Soquel had just gravely invited the state capital, offering a projected town hall and the rooms over Ned Porter's store for state offices.

The Soquel Landing road then, as now, ran back along the height west of the river to the highway. When, on May 18, 1876, the first train ran on the narrow gauge Santa Cruz & Watsonville railroad, the depot was just back of the wharf.

Capitola, except for the lots which were sold, remained in private hands until 1937 when its streets were deeded to the county. Its Episcopal chapel was dedicated in 1898 and its Catholic church in 1905.

⬛▬

APTOS GREW FROM
RANCHO TO VILLAGE

WHEN RAFAEL CASTRO died May 14, 1878, he had lived nineteen years as a subject of the king of Spain, twenty-four years as a Mexican national and thirty-two as a citizen of the United States.

Aptos Rancho, given Rafael in 1833 by Governor Jose Figueroa and increased to 6,680 acres by Governor Alvarado in 1840, was not the earliest grant in what is now Santa Cruz county but those which preceded it had lapsed so Aptos was oldest when titles were confirmed by the United States.

Rafael was born October 15, 1803, in Villa de Branciforte. His father was Joaquin Castro, the boy who had come with the Anza party. His mother was Antonia Amador, daughter of Sergeant Pedro Amador, one of the ablest of Spanish soldiers in California.

Like his father, Rafael married during his ten year military term. He was in the Monterey cavalry company when in 1823

Rafael Castro's house on Aptos Point

he was married to Soledad Cota of a Santa Barbara family. The rank of corporal was the highest Rafael attained. In 1832 he was "cabo licenciado" at Branciforte. Able to read and write Spanish, unusual accomplishment, he was immediately made juez de campo. Through the years he was sindico, alcalde auxiliar and juez de paz until 1844 when he was succeeded in the latter office by Jose Bolcoff.

Aptos as a community first grew on the west bank of the stream. Near the highway Jose Arano, husband of Rafael's youngest daughter, had a store and became Aptos' first postmaster. David Rice, son-in-law of Isaac Graham, had a twelve-room hotel. Toward the bay Rafael built a two-story frame house with porch on all four sides.

Rafael's early concessions of timber, mineral and farming rights were always on a lease basis with prospects of hearty increment. Across the river, where the present village lies, a sawmill built in 1851 by a group of Frenchmen under lease from Rafael was converted by him in 1854 into the Cascade grist mill. Two miles upstream Judge John Watson in 1852 built a shingle mill but, convinced he was not on public land, relinquished it to Rafael who leased it to three young brothers who had been working in Branciforte gulch, Merrit, Ben and Uriah Nichols.

Travel through Aptos had to ford the stream until the county in 1860 spent $2,700 to erect a covered bridge some distance down stream from the present one. It was replaced in 1903. Today's concrete bridge was built in 1930.

On the highway west of the river, Rafael in 1868 gave land for a school house which was built in 1871. The tract was enlarged by donation in 1899 by Claus Spreckels, who financed erection of a new building which still stands. Half a mile to the west Rafael in 1867 gave two acres for a cemetery and church. The church, dedicated October 17, 1875, was torn down in 1935. Its 300-pound bell, bought in 1889 by subscription headed by Ed Arano, is now in the Holy Cross mission in Santa Cruz. The cemetery is still in use.

The village east of the river continued to grow. P. K. Walsh's saloon, established when stages first ran, was enlarged to a livery

stable and hotel. The latter building is still standing, although
Walsh replaced it with a larger one in the middle eighties. In
1871 Arano built a two-story hotel, which twelve years later
he made three stories high.

In 1872 Rafael sold that part of his ranch east of the Aptos
river except what lots were in other hands to Claus Spreckels,
the sugar millionaire who in the succeeding two decades made
Aptos a place of lavish entertaining. He built a hotel with
outdoor dancing pavilion for his guests, erected numerous
cottages, raised thoroughbred horses, put in a race track and
polo field and drive his guests about the countryside in a tallyho
coach. His friend, King Kalakaua of Hawaii, spend a day there
in October, 1881.

The Aptos wharf, built originally by Rafael Castro in the
early fifties, and repaired and enlarged in 1867 when Titus
Hale had a contract to ship firewood on James Brennan's ship,
the *Salinas*, was made big enough to load ocean schooners by
Spreckels, who loaded lumber from it for Honolulu.

In 1882 Spreckels gave right of way to F. A. Hihn for the
Loma Prieta railroad and Aptos became a lumber producing
center, an epoch which lasted until after the end of the century.

Following Spreckels' death his sons, in 1908, put the 2,390
acres on the market for $220,000. In 1925 the Rio del Mar
development began, with its construction of macadam roads,
golf course and club houses.

READY FOR MORMON WAR

Santa Cruzans, having played their part in the Mexican war
which made California part of the Union, retained their martial
spirit. On December 26, 1857, a meeting in Besse & Moore's
saloon organized a company of cavalry to hold itself in readi-
ness to march to Utah to fight the Mormons. The southern end
of the county organized a similar company with Pruett Sinclair
as captain.

The organizations rode in parades and were nucleus of the
first of three companies recruited for the Union army in the
Civil War.

⊲⊟⊳

LOS CORRALITOS
HELD MISSION FLOCKS

LOS CORRALITOS, the little corrals where Santa Cruz mission kept sheep and horses, given as a Mexican grant to Jose Amesti, Monterey merchant, was so attractive that thirty-four American squatters had to be persuaded by court action in 1861 that its acres were not open to homesteading.

Amesti, a Spanish Basque who had come from Mexico on the Panther in 1821, died while the court action was pending. Restoration of the land was to his widow, daughter of Ignacio Vallejo born in Branciforte in 1805. She was a sister of General Mariano Vallejo of Sonoma.

Corralitos' hills were covered with the southernmost of the coast redwood. Lumbering started in 1853 when two farmers, Pruett Sinclair and Jones Hoy, put up a little mill. Ben Hames, brother of John Hames of Soquel, acquired Hoy's interest in 1855.

By 1861 the Santa Cruz weekly *Sentinel* said that Corralitos had a grist mill, two stores, a wagon and blacksmith shop, twenty dwellings, a school house and three sawmills a few miles up the creek. The grist mill belonged to Franklin Aldridge, a pious Kentuckian who preached every Sunday. In 1875 Richmond Bradley, a farmer, donated a lot for a church but not until 1884 was the Congregational church built. Aldridge, after serving a term in the legislature, died in 1900. Thomas Eagar, another Corralitos miller, also served on the county as assemblyman. Robert Orton of Corralitos was an early-day sheriff.

The present Corralitos school site was given by Aldridge in 1872. As Oak Grove the district had been formed in 1859 by seceding from Pajaro. The first teachers, Mr. and Mrs. A. P. Knowles, found themselves instructing pupils from as far as Freedom on one side and the summit of the hills on the other. Organization of Carlton school district in 1863 and of Roache in 1866 relieved the pressure. The building put up in 1872 on the lot given by Aldridge was the third in Corralitos. The present building, erected in 1928, is the third on its site.

In 1877 Peter and James Brown from Santa Clara bought the Aldridge mill and converted it into a plant to make brown paper from wheat straw. It was Corralitos' major industry until it burned in 1898.

✒

ENGLISHMAN WAS FIRST
PAJARO VALLEY SETTLER

EL RANCHO BOLSA DEL PAJARO (the Valley of the bird, the name given by the Portola party) was not formally granted to Sebastian Rodriguez until 1837, but his title was unofficially recognized as early as 1823 and in 1828 he leased it for twenty-five pesos a year to Captain John B. R. Cooper, an Englishman who was half brother of Thomas O. Larkin, American consul at Monterey.

Cooper, who had landed at Monterey in 1827, took a look at Corralitos but found it crowded with cattle. His agreement with Sebastian, who was a sergeant in the Monterey presidial company, was that he would eventually turn over any buildings and improvements he made.

On a bit of high land near what is now the upper end of Watsonville's Main street, Cooper used palisades split from redwood at Corralitos to build corrals, barns, a small grist mill and a house for eight men, which he turned over to Sebastian when the latter quit military service in 1832. The house was replaced with an adobe in 1842.

In 1851 James Bryant Hill, who ten years before had been in charge of farming at Brook Farm, just outside of Boston, came down from San Francisco, leased part of Salsipuedes Rancho and began growing potatoes and other crops for the miners. Hill's home was on what is now known as the Silliman ranch, and there, in 1853, Jesse D. Carr planted the first apple trees in the valley.

John H. Watson, forty-year-old Georgian who had come to California by way of Texas in 1846, resigned as San Francisco member of the first legislature on March 1, 1850, to accept appointment as judge of a district which stretched from Monterey to Contra Costa counties. His selection of the Pajaro valley as his home was followed by the arrival in 1853 of Henry Watson, a Virginia forty-niner, and by Henry's brother, Jacob, in 1854.

With three men of the name in the community the designation Watsonville was natural. Credit for first applying it is given Henry Fell Parsons, a British forty-niner who, as deputy sheriff in 1854 traveled from Santa Cruz to serve legal papers and remarked he was going to "Watsonville."

Judge Watson, who resigned judicial duties after less than a year, operated as lawyer, farmer and lumberman until 1859, when he was elected to the state senate, from which he left for Nevada where he died at Elko on August 9, 1882.

Watsonville was incorporated as a village by legislative act in 1868 and adopted a city form of government in 1903 when W. A. Trafton was elected first mayor.

◄▣►

Felton Was Laid Out
By Edward Stanley

FELTON, laid out as a town in 1868 by Edward Stanley, had been a lumbering center since 1843 when Isaac Graham transferred his pioneer mill from the Zayante to the San Lorenzo river opposite Fall creek.

Stanley was disposing of land which had been taken by his uncle, John A. Stanley, a South Carolinan, on a mortgage from Graham. The name was that of Stanley's lawyer, Charles N. Felton, who twenty-three years later was elected senator from California.

Sawmills had spread up and down the river, all of which

hauled to ford the San Lorenzo and Zayante and go down the Graham Grade. The road down the west side of the San Lorenzo had been pushed south to Gold gulch, where in 1868 Page, Donnell & Lee put up a big mill which was bought in 1870 by George Treat and became famous as the first steam mill in the San Lorenzo valley.

The road north from Santa Cruz had been built past Rincon. Stanley and Eben Bennett took a $6,000 county contract to unite the two. The joined route operated as a toll road until 1872 when its cost had been met.

Mills multiplied around Felton in the fifties and sixties. Otis Ashley, New York state veteran of the Mexican war, worked briefly for Graham and then put in his own mill. Ben Whipple bought the Sainsevain mill at what is now Paradise Park and moved it up.

Stanley named as his agent for sale of Felton lots, Horace Gushee, who had nearly a year earlier begun discussing with other Santa Cruzans feasibility of a railroad up the San Lorenzo. Plans were to run it twenty miles to Kings creek but it was never built past Felton, to which the first train ran October 9, 1875. A year after the Santa Cruz and the Felton, the line's two locomotives, began hauling trains over the narrow-gauge track along the west bank of the river, a syndicate of San Jose men interested in lumbering built the fourteen-mile "V" flume which brought lumber to Felton from near Waterman Gap.

The new Felton boomed. Walter Cooper and J. M. Merrill put up a store, saloon and hotel building. Hubbard W. McKoy, fifty-year-old Vermonter, came from El Dorado county, leased the hotel, and opened a postoffice on agreement to haul mail for nothing on his "express" from Santa Cruz. A couple of years later he installed a blacksmith shop and hired Potter Paschall to run it.

Two young brothers, James F. and Jeremiah Cunningham, natives of New Brunswick who had fought through the Civil War in a Maine regiment, made themselves felt as leaders in the latter sixties. In 1871 J. F. Cunningham and McKoy opened a general store.

San Lorenzo school district, created in 1863 with a school at Ashley's on the San Lorenzo river, in 1875 changed its name to Felton and put up a building there. As the population center of San Lorenzo township Felton had its justice of the peace and constable from the middle seventies. One of the first justices was ex-Sheriff A. L. Rountree, who in 1878 came down from Davenport Landing where he had been running a hotel and took over the Big Tree House.

Stanley provided for a church by donating in 1869 a lot for an Episcopal parish, making Gushee and Joseph Boston of Santa Cruz trustees. The trust was dissolved many years later when Ben Lomond Episcopal parish was declared to include Felton and the lot sold. The Presbyterian church was built in 1893.

With the narrow-gauge outlet to a shipping point at Santa Cruz and the flume funneling most of the lumber of the San Lorenzo valley through it, Felton continued to grow. The county bridged the old ford across the San Lorenzo in September, 1878.

The early eighties were a high point in the town's population and prosperity. Thomas Cramer erected the Central hotel opposite Cunningham's Big Tree House. J. G. Tanner of Santa Cruz put in a branch of his drug store. James F. Cunningham was elected to the legislature. A year later, in 1883, a hose company organized with Wallace B. Drew, the livery man, as chief.

Construction of the South Pacific Coast Railroad branch up the valley to Boulder Creek in 1884 moved the lumber shipping center. The flume between Felton and Boulder Creek was torn down and its right of way used for most of the new rail route. The South Pacific Coast laid out the new town of Boulder Creek; Cunningham & Co. put up a store there; several mills moved up the valley.

An experimental incorporation of Felton as a village with the election April 14, 1884, of D. L. Kent, C. H. Winter and E. J. Rubottom as trustees, Drew as marshal and George Ley as treasurer, lasted only a short time.

A fire on October 29, 1888, took Cunningham's Big Tree House, Drew's livery stable, the town hall and postoffice, a total of five stores and four other buildings. Another blaze on September 17, 1896, destroyed the Kent building and several cottages. A fire in 1907 burned the school house which was replaced with the present building.

⇥

TOWN OF PACIFIC MILLS
BECAME BEN LOMOND

F IRST RESIDENTS of Ben Lomond were two young bachelors, Winston and Jackson Bennett, who put up a cabin and little sawmill at the mouth of Love creek. They went off to the mines late the same year—1848—but were back intermittently until 1855 when Harry Love, who had married their widowed mother the year before, took ownership.

Love, Vermont born, veteran of the Black Hawk Indian war and of the Texas war for independence, brought $5,000 voted him by the legislature for leading the ranger band which killed Joaquin Murietta in the wilds of Tulare county. In the succeeding seven years he laid out a road from Felton which forded Newell creek and logged up the stream which bears his name.

Earliest traffic from the north was down the Love creek grade, with four fords between what is now Boulder Creek and Ben Lomond. In 1873, chiefly by efforts of Isaiah Porter, who was hauling split stuff from the Round Potrero, a road was opened down the west bank of the San Lorenzo over a route still owned by the county.

Napoleon Bonaparte Hicks, a Georgian, settled in 1868 south of Love's mill site and James Priest, who had married a sister of the Bennett brothers, took up land to the north. Hicks' ford and Priest's ford were where the two bridges are today at either end of the town. Hicks and his brother, Achilles Scipio Hicks, ran a sawmill for a time but the latter moved to Scotts valley.

Ben Lomond's first settlers did not stay. Jackson Bennett went to Nicaragua with Walker's filibusterers and died there of yellow fever in 1858. Winston Bennett went mining in New Mexico. Harry Love was killed in a shooting affair at Santa Clara in 1868. Hicks, after selling out to James Pierce, moved to San Bernardino county.

The big timber operation of the vicinity was that of the Pacific Manufacturing company owned by James P. Pierce of Santa

Clara. A Newell creek school of 1876 became the Pacific Mills school in 1881. The town took its name in 1887 when the post-office department objected to Pacific Mills and the name of Ben Lomond Mountain, in use for a quarter of a century, was adopted and Chester B. Fowler, Pierce's bookkeeper, was made postmaster.

The town was laid out in 1888 by Pierce and his mill and log-ging superintendent, Thomas L. Bell. The hills to the south had been logged in the late seventies by Russell, Manson & Cum-mings. Pierce had operated through the eighties on the hills stretching to the north.

Despite efforts at farming the region became one of moun-tain cottages, with the Rowardennan hotel built by Bell on the Pacific Mill site as a leading early-day mountain resort. In 1894 the Newell creek school district became officially the Ben Lomond district; the following year a school house was built.

Electricity came in 1900 when the Big Creek Power Com-pany ran a wire over the hills from the coast. In 1902 a bill to incorporate Ben Lomond failed in the legislature. In 1905 the village briefly had a newspaper, the *News*, printed by C. P. Davis, who also opened a store and announced plans for a bank. The publication lapsed when Davis was recognized as Arthur C. Probert, with a record of promotional activities in the middle west which had caused him to leave hurriedly.

━◀█▶━

GOOD SCOTCH NAME

BEN LOMOND MOUNTAIN was named after the Scotch wine grape district by John Burns, a Scotchman who took up land there in 1850 and with I. C. Willson, a native of Ontario county in the grape-growing region of New York state, put out the county's first vineyard except for a small one near the mission.

Willson, who was Santa Cruz' second county clerk, was mem-ber of the legislature in 1862. His home was where the Rittenhouse building now stands on Pacific avenue between Church street and Walnut avenue.

Burns died in 1880 and the Ben Lomond Winery passed into the hands of F. W. Billing and John Q. Packard, Utah mining men, who put it under the management of Billing's son-in-law, John F. Coope. The company dug the chalk rock caves on Market street to reproduce French methods of aging wine. Their product took prizes in Paris.

The name of Bonnie Doon, applied to part of the mountain top, originated three decades after Burns' arrival, being given by a group of families to whom spiritualism was a religion. In the three decades after the Civil War the region grew to farm, orchards and vineyards.

The Empire Grade, down the ridge of hills to Santa Cruz, was built in 1872 by farmer labor working out the poll tax. Its name derived from the Empire Mining company, one of the many attempts at mining in the county in the fifties.

⟍⟍⟍

BOULDER CREEK OUTGREW
ITS RIVAL VILLAGE

B OULDER CREEK was laid out in 1884 by the South Pacific Coast railroad but it had existed seventeen years earlier. In 1867 the county supervisors ordered a sixty-foot public road laid out from Hicks Ford, now Ben Lomond, to "the forks of the San Lorenzo" and noted that the road would serve Alesworth's mill. A few months later it was extended to "the ranch of King" on the middle fork. "Alesworth" was John W. Ellsworth, who as early as 1863 had put a water power saw-mill on the east side of the river opposite the blue slide.

The hills back of the present town were opened for timber claims in 1865 and the next five years saw a score of homesteaders' cabins. Farthest was that of Tilford George Berry, whose name is perpetuated in the Berry creek falls at the western edge of the Big Basin. Those settlers toward Saratoga Gap found their outlet over the Saratoga grade built in 1868 by Senator Charles Maclay of Santa Clara county.

A mile or two out on Bear Creek settled in 1865 a fifty-four-year-old native of Indiana, Branciford Alcorn. Probably in the same year came William C. Greenleaf. They were followed by Oscar and Austin Harmon, twin brothers from East Machias, Maine; by Ben and Richard Iler, William Parkhurst and John Dobbs. In what is known as the Sequoia district settled in 1867 Daniel Low Crediford and his sons, Winfield Scott and Stephen. The next year William and George Day and W. S. Rodgers established themselves as neighbors. Up the middle fork, on what was referred to as the Saratoga road, settled James Lawrence, followed by Thomas H. Wagstaff and George H. Gibbs on Two Bar creek. The Notley, Brimblecom and Brittingham families came in 1869.

There were enough families in the vicinity in 1868 to need a school and the Boulder Creek district was formed with a little building on what is now West Park avenue.

The site of present Boulder Creek was taken as a timber claim in 1870 by John H. Alcorn, son of the old Branciford, who lived in a cabin on the river bank and erected a little hotel near the school. Angus McKay, a Nova Scotian, opened a blacksmith shop. Jacob S. Perkins put in a store. A postoffice was established with Joseph W. Peery as postmaster.

The community centered just above the present concrete bridge but Peery's mill, established in 1868 a couple of miles to the south, gave employment to several men and in 1875 he established the town of Lorenzo, putting up a thirty-five-by-forty-eight-foot hotel. Charles T. Cottrell from San Jose opened a store. Frank Newell put in a blacksmith shop. Cottrell, made postmaster in 1875, moved the office to Lorenzo but a petition from Boulder Creek returned it in the fall.

Boulder Creek gained a lap in the rivalry when, in 1875, the people organized a society "for purposes local, literary, social" and erected Washingtonian Hall. Any one who donated five dollars in cash, material or labor was a member. The name was supplied by Samuel A. Brimblecom, retired sea captain, who recalled a temperance society of his boyhood of that name. The newly formed division of the Sons of Temperance also used the hall.

Peery's offer of a site in Lorenzo had been rejected and he retaliated by erecting two-story Lorenzo Hall, thirty by sixty feet, for $1,500, which opened with a ball on the Fourth of July of 1877. Lorenzo also scored when Duncan Campbell hired J. W. Farnsworth to drive a daily stage from Santa Cruz.

The fourteen-mile flume, built in 1875 from Waterman Switch to Felton, marked a gain for the upper community by developing the timber lands to the north. Pupils (Lorenzo had no school) increased. Mrs. S. C. Olmstead had been succeeded by Daniel Bracket as teacher in 1879 when the San Lorenzo Flume and Transportation company gave an acre for a new building on a little hill back of the first structure. The people voted a $600 tax for construction and hired David B. Michener when Bracket left for the Felton school.

Arrival of the railroad in 1884 gave Boulder Creek its final impetus. Peery's price for terminal grounds was so high the railroad ran further and bought the Alcorn quarter section, which by that time belonged to Stephen and Demetrius Crediford. That part of the flume south of Boulder Creek was torn down and most of Felton's mills moved to the end of rails. By 1885 it was said twenty-five mills were operating in tributary territory. The hotel started in 1870 by John Alcorn was plastered and given a twenty-four-by-forty-foot dining room.

Henry L. Middleton, born in Healdsburg in 1859, who had in 1882 bought a partnership with the Cunningham brothers, moved with them to Boulder Creek where he gradually took over management of their interests and formed the Big Basin Mercantile company, whose building was razed in 1926.

Middleton, until he became paralyzed in 1921, expanded his holdings over thousands of acres. He was part owner and general manager of the Santa Clara Valley Mill & Lumber company, a Doughterty property; principal owner and manager of the

California Timber company; owner of the Boulder Creek Land & Lumber company; and a large stockholder of the Western Shore Lumber company of San Francisco. Instead of buying stumpage rights he acquired land as he logged it and left a large estate when he died in 1930.

During the first two decades of the present century, Middleton's forty-five-acre home just outside Boulder Creek on the Bear Creek road was one of the show places of the county, with terraces, rock gardens, fountains and lawns.

The railroad definitely decided the rivalry between the two towns. By the spring of 1885 six new residences had been constructed in Boulder Creek. South of the two-story Big Basin Mercantile company building the McAbee brothers, who moved up from Lorenzo, established a livery stable. Across the street J. H. Pickle put in his blacksmith shop. Mason & Pringle opened a butcher shop. To the north, across the creek, the rebuilt Boulder Creek hotel was run by George Dennison, who had succeeded George W. Day in 1883. Opposite it was the store of George H. Chappell, who had bought out Perkins and who had been made postmaster in 1883. Dan Hartman bought the daily stage started by Wallace Drew of Felton and ran a rival service to the railroad.

Chappell retained the postmastership until the end of 1885 when he was succeeded by J. F. Cunningham, who resigned the Felton postmastership and was immediately given the Boulder Creek position.

Lorenzo had the first church, a Methodist edifice erected in 1874 with Peery's backing, when the Rev. Asbury P. Hendon was pastor. It burned and was replaced with a $3,000 building when J. O. Askins was, in 1885, pastor for Lorenzo and Felton. This second building burned in 1906. Halfway between the two towns the Episcopalians, in the spring of 1885, hired John Morrow of Santa Cruz to build a thirty-five-by-fifty-foot church for $2,000. The Presbyterians organized in 1886 and erected a church in Boulder Creek. It and a successor both burned. The present Community church is the third on the site. St. Michael's Catholic church was dedicated October 14, 1900.

Thomas Amner Post of the G.A.R., organized in April, 1885, held its meetings in Washingtonian hall

Eleven years before the arrival of the railroad the pioneers of Bear Creek, led by the Harmon brothers, sought outlet to San Jose and incorporated the Bear Creek Toll Road company, which by 1875 carved a road around the steep mountain sides to connect with a route which the Santa Clara Valley Mill & Lumber Co. had excavated from its mill at the head of Newell creek. In 1888 Brad Morrell's teamsters tore down the toll gate and in 1890 the county bought the route for $500.

The year 1890 saw the Rev. Sam Wallis, just from New Zealand, start the *Boulder Creek Hatchet*. It was successively the *News*, the *Boulder Creek Woodsman* and in the summer of 1896 was the *Boulder Blast*, edited by the Rev. Joseph R. Watson, the Methodist pastor. Late in 1896 C. C. Rodgers started the *Mountain Echo*. He soon took in his brother, W. S. Rodgers who after the older brother's death in 1898 conducted the paper until 1917.

The first of a series of fires struck Boulder Creek on July 16, 1891, burning the hotel, six saloons and six other business places. Only the Big Basin Mercantile company store was left when rebuilding of the business district started. Lorenzo was virtually wiped out on April 14, 1897, when flames took Peery's hall, the Lorenzo hotel and two cottages. Peery rebuilt the hotel.

Electric lights came to Boulder Creek in December of 1896 when Middleton installed a steam plant in the back of his store to operate ninety 16-candlepower lights. He ran a wire to his residence and put ten lights in his planing mill. Not until February 19, 1903, was electricity available to the public. R. G. Elmer of Alameda ran a flume from Peavine gulch to what became known as water works gulch and put in a plant, giving the town ten free lights.

The Boulder Creek Odd Fellows lodge, organized in 1900, erected the same year its two-story building, forty-five by eighty feet. The following year Idlewild lodge of Rebekahs was constituted with seven charter members and Mrs. Emma Dool as noble grand.

Boulder Creek in January, 1902, petitioned for incorporation as a village and voted 107 to 41 on February 15 to incorporate, electing W. H. Dool, I. T. Bloom, J. H. Fuller, Samuel Hubbs and O. L. McAbee trustees, with A. M. Anthony as clerk.

The town had had a justice of the peace for many years and Isiah Hartman was continued in that office. His constable, A. L. Seidlinger, the livery stable keeper, was named by the new municipality to the added offices of marshal, tax collector and poundmaster. The first tax levied by the municipality was a $2 dog license but in September the trustees levied a rate of 75¢ per $100 on $104,695 assessed valuation and ordered a sewer built.

The turn of the century saw Boulder Creek at its height as a lumber production center. Its sawmills made it one of the largest rail shipping points in the state. The town had eleven saloons in 1901, although the number decreased to seven when the county put a license in effect. The village trustees voted a saloon license of twenty dollars a quarter despite which the number of drinking establishments, amply supported by the workers in logging camps and mills, increased to sixteen in 1905, when the license fee was boosted to seventy-five dollars a quarter.

The first school at the present location was a four-room building erected by a $4,000 bond issue and opened in 1891 with W. T. Forsyth as principal. The high school got its start in 1905 when J. H. Aram, J. W. Peery and W. R. McDonald, the Boulder Creek school trustees, called a mass meeting of residents of Alba, Ben Lomond, Boulder Creek, Dougherty and Sequoia districts. A vote of 187 to 9 on March 25, 1905, created the district but a bond issue was rejected. Levying a 75¢ tax the district bought for $550 eight lots south of the grammar school and let a $7,845 contract for a building which was dedicated April 14, 1906. Its first principal was J. W. Dickerson.

In 1905 the experiment in village government ended. To get valuation on which taxes might be levied a wide area had been included; the size of the village drained its treasury for upkeep of its streets. A local option election put saloons out and their license money no longer helped with town expenses. When the electorate favored construction of a bridge across the San Lorenzo, which was opposed by the larger taxpayers, another election was held which voted for disincorporation.

Police judge for the town of Boulder Creek throughout its existence was W. S. Rodgers. When the town ended the township retained its justice of the peace until the county was consolidated into two townships in 1918. The last village clerk was young James M. Maddock, who had been born in a cabin in the present State Redwood Park.

The Boulder Creek hotel, rebuilt and expanded many times from the little building put up by John Alcorn in 1870, burned in 1893.

◄█►

BRICK COURT HOUSE
HAD PICKET FENCE

A PICKET FENCE surrounded the court house of 1885 with ornamental cypress and willow trees on its carefully tended lawn. Hitching racks stood at the edge of the plank sidewalks.

The neat building of brick with stone trim, fifty-five by sixty-five feet, had been turned over to the county in 1867 by its builders, Sedgewick J. Lynch and George T. Gragg. They had made slight profit as the plans had been drawn for construction on the chalk rock of Mission hill and needed more foundation on the soft dirt of the lot on the flat donated by the Cooper brothers and T. W. Moore. The structure had five offices on the ground floor; the court room and clerk's office filled the top floor. The cupola rose to a height of eighty feet.

Occupying part of the present court house lawn was the William F. Ely building with Terry's feed store on the street

An 1880's view of the southeast corner of Pacific and Cooper. The court house is to the left, the Ely building is in the middle and the I.O.O.F. building is to the right. UCSC Special Collections

level and Arthur A. Taylor's print shop and weekly newspaper and Aichberg's photographic gallery upstairs. When the new court house was built after the fire of 1894 the Ely building was moved to face Front street; it was razed when the Palomar hotel was built.

Beyond the Ely building, with a narrow space between, was the nine-year-old Odd Fellows building. Past it was a one-story wooden structure which had been part of the original public school, moved there when the second school had been erected in 1876.

To the north, across Cooper, was the two-story Mike Leonard building with Horace Randall's shoe store in the room on the corner where it was replaced in 1886 by the new City Bank. The building burned, as did the court house, in the big fire of 1894, after which the site was taken by the County Bank. Leonard erected a replica of his old building on the corner a block to the east, a site which had been occupied by the pioneer Cooper Bros. store.

➤

ZAYANTE HAD FIRST
SAW MILL IN CALIFORNIA

ZAYANTE, site of the first power sawmill in California, was a Mexican grant in 1834 to Joaquin Buelna, who had been Branciforte alcalde and earlier teacher in San Jose. Bancroft, the historian, cites the fact that he was a writer of verse.

The scholarly Joaquin let his claim lapse after conferring in 1835 timber rights on Ambrose Tomlinson and Job Dye, thus starting the settlement of "foreigners" which ten years later was a trouble spot in Mexican-Californian politics.

In 1839 a request for Zayante was made by "Don F. Moss," whose real name was Francisco Lajeunesse. He was a French Canadian who had come to the Monterey region in the Walker party in 1833. Despite the fact he had been naturalized and had married Nicanor Cota, "Moss" was not given the grant. Adopting his nickname as surname, he moved to Ventura about 1860.

In the spring of 1841 Isaac Graham and his young partner, Henry Neale, cast eyes on the tract. Neither had become a Mexican citizen so they induced Joseph L. Majors to apply for it. Majors had taken Mexican citizenship and married Maria de Los Angeles Castro. He was granted both Zayante and the adjoining rancho of San Agustin

The grant was made to Majors on April 22, 1841, and on September 11 a syndicate of four signed an agreement to erect a mill, Majors, Graham, a German named Frederick Hoeger, and a young Danish ironworker, Peter Lassen. The mill was a "muley" with a straight saw which worked up and down in a wooden frame. Its site was on the grounds of today's Mount Hermon, where the course of the little flume can be traced on the west bank of Zayante creek opposite the confluence of Bean creek.

Graham and Neale soon took over their partners' interests. In 1843 they built a slightly larger mill on the east bank of the San Lorenzo below the entrance of Fall creek, a mile north of Felton. Graham hauled his lumber up the hill east of the Zayante and along the hilltop across what is today the Pasatiempo golf course to Branciforte creek, which he followed to Santa Cruz and its beach, where he loaded through the surf to coastwise schooners.

Graham was a native of that part of Virginia which became West Virginia in Civil War days. Born in 1800, he had come from Tennessee over the Santa Fe trail. In 1840, when he was seized with the other foreigners and sent to San Blas, he and Neale were operating a little still at Natividad in the Salinas valley.

It is well authenticated that Graham received $36,000 from Mexico as indemnity for his exile. He was one of the wealthy men of Santa Cruz in the fifties when he bought Rancho del Ano Nuevo, on the San Mateo county line up the coast.

Graham's contract marriage in 1845 with twenty-one-year-old Catherine Bennett, which drew the attention of U.S. Consul

Thomas O. Larkin of Monterey, was not successful. In 1850 Catherine, learning that Isaac had left a wife in Tennessee, fled in male garb by schooner from Santa Cruz to San Francisco and Honolulu and then to Oregon. After Isaac located her at Oregon City she returned to Santa Cruz, where she had the marriage annulled in 1852 and the following year married Daniel McCusker, a young Irishman who was starting a dairy ranch in the Elkhorn district south of Watsonville.

The arrival of two of Graham's sons from Tennessee precipitated a feud between them and Catherine's four brothers which brought about the shooting of Dennis Bennett by Jesse Graham. Isaac's first wife had gone to Texas where the law made seven years separation equivalent to divorce and had married again. One of his daughters, married to J. D. Marshall, came from Texas in 1852 and settled on what is known as Marshall creek.

Graham maintained a home at Zayante and in Santa Cruz until his death in 1863 while on a trip to San Francisco. He left his land to his daughter, Matilda Jane, who was Mrs. David M. Rice of Aptos. When, in 1870, George Treat, an Easterner, bought the new Page, Donnell & Lee mill at Gold gulch he acquired also the rich timber holdings of Zayante. Treat mortgaged and lost the tract to Charles McLaughlin. After the latter's death F. A. Hihn bought, divided and sold the tract.

A Santa Clara Valley Mill & Lumber company operation took most of the timber from the upper Zayante valley in the seventies and until the mill burned in 1886 hauled its product by way of Lexington and Los Gatos.

The Zayante school district, created in 1882, had for nearly twenty years as its teacher Josefa Buelna, one of the first graduates of Santa Cruz high school, who was a granddaughter of the Joaquin Buelna who was Zayante's first grantee.

Mount Hermon, modeled after summer religious assemblies to Northfield, Massachusetts, and Winona, Indiana, was instituted in 1906 when a group of church leaders from the San Francisco bay area bought a 400-acre tract from Thomas L. Bell and his associates, who had built Zayante Inn near where the Mount Hermon railroad station later stood.

◄∃⊫►

DAVENPORT LANDING
WAS PROSPEROUS VILLAGE

D AVENPORT LANDING, near the mouth of Agua Puerca creek, eighteen miles up the coast from Santa Cruz, was a booming coast village through the seventies and eighties. The present town of Davenport, two miles to the south, succeeded it when the Santa Cruz Portland Cement plant was built in 1906.

John Pope Davenport, mariner from Tiverton, Rhode Island, had come around the Horn in 1849, gone back by way of the Isthmus and in 1851 returned with his wife and the schooner *Ann McKinn*. Scorning gold mining, he had operated as a whaler at Monterey and Moss Landing and was living in Soquel in 1867 when he and his friend, John King, began building a wharf on El Jarro rancho.

King was declared insane in 1870 but Davenport continued trying out his whales and operating his 450-foot wharf, which ran out to 15 feet of water at low tide. By 1875 the town had L. A. Utt's and Auguste Roque's hotels, William Purdy's store and hall, Benjamin F. Sprague's and W. J. Taliaferro's blacksmith shops, Lorenzen's shipyard and four dwellings. Agua Puerca school was nearby.

Development of better shipping facilities elsewhere ended the wharf's prosperity and John P. Davenport removed to Santa Cruz, where he was a real estate dealer and justice of the peace. Some shipping and fishing remained at Davenport Landing but its population dwindled until in 1886 its postoffice was moved to Laurel Grove, which today is known as Swanton.

Enough of the wharf was left in 1905 for W. J. Dingee's lime kilns of San Vicente Rancho to ship from it, but the following year Dingee's lime company, which had been taken over by John Q. Packard and F. W. Billing, was sold for $400,000 to the newly incorporated Santa Cruz Portland Cement company.

‑ɪ⯑ᴇ‑

BROOKDALE STARTED LIFE
AS REED'S SPUR

J OHN H. LOGAN, superior court judge and bank president in Santa Cruz, laid out Brookdale in 1900. The Grover interests had moved a mill from the Soquel valley in the late seventies and logged over the area now Brookdale and had sold to the Santa Clara Valley Mill & Lumber Co. in 1883. McKoy & Duffey had moved a mill up from Felton in 1880. By 1900 I. T. Bloom had cut the remainder of the accessible timber.

Judge Logan interested Stephen Freeland Grover, still a land owner at what was known as Reed's Spur, in laying out the town, to which the name of Clear Creek was applied until 1902 when it was given a postoffice and the appellation of Brookdale decided on. In 1903 Logan bought Grover's interest.

Judge Logan's name is perpetuated by his discovery in his garden in Santa Cruz of an accidental cross of blackberry and raspberry of peculiar size and lusciousness. He called it the "ruby blackberry" but the public preferred loganberry. Logan, a native of Indiana, erected a little hotel and vigorously sold lots to build the village. Through his influence the state fish hatchery was installed there.

‑ɪ⯑ᴇ‑

THE GREAT FIRE

A T 10:40 O'CLOCK on the evening of Saturday, April 14, 1894, flames shot out of the rear of E. L. Williams' real estate office and Werner Finkeldey's grocery on Cooper street. Fanned by a stiff north wind they spread to Wessendorf

Looking south on Pacific after the fire of 1894

& Staffler's undertaking rooms and to Mike Leonard's two-story wooden building on the corner and leaped the street to the twenty-seven-year-old brick court house.

Of the old tournament hose companies only the Pogonips remained as fire fighters. The Alerts had disbanded. The Pilots had rented their quarters to the city, which hired Charles H. Sanborn to drive the street sweeper and, upon need, to use his horse to pull the fire apparatus.

When, next morning, Santa Cruzans who had battled flames through the night paused to rest, the ground from Pacific avenue to Front street was a stretch of rubble-filled basements and partly standing brick walls. Of the People's bank and the City bank only their brick vaults remained.

The white-fronted John Werner building in the foreground, occupied by A. C. Snyder's dry goods store with Mrs. Sophia Harris' rooming house upstairs, had been gutted, although its walls stood, to be incorporated in the present Hotaling building occupied by the St. George hotel.

⊸⊒⊏⊸

FIRST BANK WAS IN
PACIFIC OCEAN HOUSE

RULING RATE ON LOANED MONEY was fifteen per cent a year when Santa Cruz' first bank opened April 1, 1870, in the corner room of the Pacific Ocean House. It was the Santa Cruz Bank of Savings & Loan. Its president was Samuel Arnold Bartlett, native of Oneida county, New York, who had been fourteen years in Santa Cruz and was with David Hinds selling furniture, building materials and groceries from a store near Locust street. The bank, with its paid up capital of $20,000, rapidly absorbed business which had for two decades been done for Santa Cruzans by the Wells Fargo Express company.

In 1875 the bank moved into the new Delamater building and the Pacific Ocean House location was taken by a "gold" bank with Lucien Heath, the hardware merchant who had come from Oregon in 1868, as its president.

Three years later the two combined with Heath as president. They occupied the Delamater building, and the old location in the Pacific Ocean House was taken by a barber shop.

The Santa Cruz City Bank, which is now the Santa Cruz branch of the Bank of America, was established in 1886 with L. K. Baldwin as president and F. A. Hihn as vice-president. It was doing business in Mike Leonard's two-story wooden building at Cooper and Pacific when the fire of 1894 occurred. Overnight Heath's bank bought the City Bank's site and erected the building it now occupies, Baldwin's bank built at 88 Pacific avenue.

Also victims of the 1894 fire were the two-year-old affiliated People's Bank and People's Savings Bank. They had been organized by A. A. Morey, who came from the Ford store in Watsonville to be cashier while Henry Willey was elected president. The affiliated banks in 1910 put up their own building at Locust street, directly across Pacific avenue from the site on which they began business. In 1914 the People's Bank became the Farmers & Merchants Bank.

VIGILANTE LAW

Vigilantes supplanted civil processes in Santa Cruz in the spring of 1851 when Mariano Hernandez, wanted in the Sacramento valley for murder and theft of gold, was taken from the juzgado where he had been placed for a minor crime and hanged. Records are understandably vague but seem to indicate that the mob took advantage of the occasion to hang two others, one charged with horse stealing and the other later referred to as "a hardened wretch who boasted of the number of Americans he had killed."

In 1852 a posse comitatus hanged "a Scotchman" at the beach for having shot another fisherman back of the Santa Cruz House on Main street.

Pancho Vasquez was shot in 1871 by Sheriff Charles H. Lincoln as Vasquez, wanted elsewhere as a bandit, sought to escape from Matias Lorenzara's barn in Blackburn gulch.

Jose Chamalis and Francisco Arias, both born in or near Santa Cruz, were hanged on the night of May 3, 1877, from cross beams of the Water street bridge by forty men with masked and blackened faces. The pair, just out of San Quentin, had shot a powder mill employe named DeForest at River and Potrero streets to get money to attend a performance of Montgomery Queen's circus, and had been captured the next day at Capitola.

▪️◼️▪️

ORD FAMILY HAD STRAIN
OF ENGLISH ROYAL BLOOD

RAFAEL CASTRO of Aptos in 1852 abandoned an idea of divorcing his wife, Soledad, on advice he would probably have to divide his property. As fee he gave his lawyer, Pacificus Ord, seventy acres on the highway between Aptos and Soquel and brought to the county a family of English royal blood.

A morganatic marriage in 1785 of the Prince of Wales, the future King George IV, with Lady Fitz-Herbert, reigning beauty of London, resulted in the birth of a son who, ineligible to the throne, was sent to the United States in 1800. Taking the name of James Ord, he attended Georgetown university, fought in the War of 1812 and married Rebecca Cresap of Baltimore.

Two of his sons, Lieutenant Edward O. C. Ord, just out of West Point, and Dr. James L. Ord, army surgeon, who arrived in Monterey in 1847, were followed by Pacificus; by John, who settled on the land near Aptos; by Robert; and by William Marcellus. A daughter had married General Trevino of Mexico when he was on a diplomatic mission to Washington. The other, Georgiana, married Samuel Holladay, San Francisco attorney.

The father came to Aptos in 1855 to live with his son, John. His wife died there in 1860 and was buried in the Catholic church yard in Santa Cruz until her body was exhumed in 1931 and taken to Arlington cemetery to rest with that of her husband, with that of her son, who became General Ord of the Civil War, and with that of a grandson who died at San Juan Hill in Cuba in 1898.

James Ord, the father, died in 1873 at Omaha where his son was stationed at an army post. William Marcellus Ord, after serving in the legislature from Butte county, came to Santa Cruz in 1873 and died there in 1882. John, who farmed near Aptos, died in Santa Cruz in 1911.

⊸⊟⊷

PRESENT STREETS LEAD
TO EARLY DAY FORDS

SANTA CRUZANS forded the San Lorenzo with teams or crossed by rowboats in high water until 1864 when the townspeople led by A. R. Meserve, keeper of the general store in Sam Drennan's building, raised money by subscription and piling was driven for a footbridge at the lower ford, at the end of Cooper street.

The slender span was twice washed away and replaced before, in 1868, $3,000 of private subscription and $7,900 of county money financed a wagon span at the upper ford, which is today's Water street.

Despite the fact that contractor Tom Beck built a bridge with a span of 100 feet, supported by struts with iron braces, and laid a roadway of two thicknesses of plank, the high water of 1871 took it out and William Felker and Reuben Button were hired to rebuild it. By 1882 the span was so weak that another was constructed by A. W. Burrell as contractor, which did service until 1913.

The Soquel avenue covered bridge

In 1907 the Union Traction Co. built a narrow concrete bridge at Water street for its trolleys which, six years later, when that line ceased to run, the city took over and widened into the present structure.

The old covered bridge at Soquel avenue, which stood until the present concrete bridge was erected in 1921, was built in 1874 by the San Francisco Bridge Co. on a $14,800 county contract. It had a sidewalk along its north side until in 1903 a separate bridge for trolley cars was built paralleling it on the north, when the pedestrian walk was moved to the south side.

The "Cut Bias" bridge on Riverside avenue, built in 1887, was replaced by the present Riverside avenue bridge in 1930.

◄❚❚►

POPE HOUSE ERA
ONE OF SOCIAL GRANDEUR

IN 1862 Horace W. Pope, a thirty-nine-year-old Vermonter who had driven stage from Santa Clara and, with Luther Farnham, run the San Lorenzo hotel on Willow street, opened a boarding house on Mission street.

He had married in 1859 Anna Farrar of Stockton. With her energetic help he built up the Pope House, a cottage resort which for four decades was patronized by the wealthy and social elite of San Francisco, who brought their ornate barouches and phaetons, their carriage horses and servants, to be a picturesque factor in Santa Cruz summers.

The Pope House which, with its croquet and tennis lawns surrounded by elms, stood in the intersection of Mission and King streets, annually housed the Fairs, Sharons, de Youngs, the Morgan Hills and Murphys and many more of their social set. The hotel was a collection of cottages of which the oldest, built in 1850 by Silas F. Bennett, housed the office and billiard room with card tables for the guests.

Sea Beach Hotel   UCSC SPECIAL COLLECTIONS

Horace Pope died August 31, 1881. His widow, with their two adopted daughters, Evelyn and Mildred, leased the resort for a time in the late eighties to E. J. Swift to operate in conjunction with his Pacific Ocean House, the town's leading commercial hostelry, but retained ownership until 1916. It was razed in 1919.

The era of the Pope House was one of social grandeur for Santa Cruz. During the time it existed many wealthy people established homes and erected large residences.

D. K. Abeel, who had been editor and publisher of the *Kansas City Journal*, came in 1886 to build himself a residence on the Locust street hill while he bought the Douglas House, a hotel on Beach Hill, and added to it until it became the sprawling Sea Beach Hotel, which burned June 12, 1912. Senator James D. Phelan in 1887 bought thirty acres on the west cliff back of the lighthouse and built several cottages in what is still known as Phelan Park.

James P. Smith, merchant of New York and Paris, whose wife, the former Susan Crooks, had spent many summers in Santa Cruz, bought the Kittredge House, a Beach Hill hotel erected in the middle seventies by Dr. Francis M. Kittredge, remodeled it, landscaped the grounds and christened it Sunshine Villa. The building is now the McCray hotel. Smith poured out his ample funds for Santa Cruz. He made possible the Venetian water carnivals of 1895–96, when the river was dammed and its surface used for decorated and illuminated festival craft. Smith built a dancing pavilion at Pacific and Laurel which, as the Palm theater, burned November 24, 1897. It had the distinction of presenting to Santa Cruzans their first movies, on December 28, 1896, when flicker scenes ran of a street in New York city and a ferry boat in motion.

Santa Cruz Tavern, on Beach Hill, was built in 1890 by Major Frank McLaughlin, mining promoter and speculator from Oroville, who bought an old home erected in 1850 by Captain J. J. Smith and replaced it with a twenty-room residence designed for entertaining, which he called Golden Gate Villa. McLaughlin was chairman of the state Republican central committee and many prominent men were his visitors. Faced with vanished fortune, on November 16, 1907, he shot his daughter, Agnes, in her sleep and took poison.

F. W. Billing and John Q. Packard, with Utah mining fortunes, in 1899 bought the William Kerr estate, which is now Pasatiempo, and built big homes, both of which burned. They identified themselves with the community. Both invested heavily in land and utility companies. On the Billing estate golf was first played in Santa Cruz. Billing's son-in-law, J. F. Coope, built a home on Second street, Beach Hill. Packard, on his death in 1908, gave Marysville, scene of his early mining, its public library.

Frederick Hagemann, associate of Claus Spreckels, built the Hagemann hotel (the present Graystone) in 1892; erected the building which is now owned by the Elks; had a home on what is now Hagemann avenue, as well as a country place in Rodeo Gulch and interests in the City Stables, banks and the fair association.

Mrs. J. R. Jarboe, widow of a wealthy San Francisco attorney, built a home on Blackburn Terrace just above the wharf. Her son, Paul, promoted an early golf links back of the west cliffs.

The row of big homes along the hill top above High street started with the erection by Judge John H. Logan in 1880 of his dwelling on "Perry Hill." Next to it Moses Bliss built the home now owned by the Erlanger family of San Francisco. A residence built by an Easterner named Jones was bought by H. A. van C. Torchiana, Netherlands consul general for the Pacific coast, who had practiced law in Santa Cruz around the turn of the century.

An old farm house owned by John Wagner was bought by R. H. Appleby from Minneapolis, who erected the big white house now owned by the Cowells. Next to Spring street Nelson A. Bixby, pioneer wharfinger from New York state, owned a home which was bought and remodeled by Henry Meyrick, an Englishman. It later became the home of C. C. Moore, wealthy San Franciscan, whose father had been an early lumber man in the Soquel valley; it is now (1946) owned by Louis Rittenhouse.

⸺⸺

PROTESTANTS HASTENED
TO BUILD OWN CHURCHES

THE FIRST METHODIST CHURCH in Santa Cruz was a twenty-by-thirty-foot structure at Green and Mission streets, dedicated in December, 1850, with the Rev. William Taylor from San Francisco officiating. Its seats were fitted for a school which H. S. Loveland had been conducting in a shack near the river.

Elihu Anthony, arriving on Christmas eve 1847, had found a nucleus for a church. On the preceding May 1 Adna A. Hecox had, in the adobe juzgado, preached a funeral sermon for a young man killed by a falling tree near Soquel. Services had been held in the home of John D. Green by Hecox and James G. T. Dunleavy. A class of twelve in 1848 elected Anthony minister. In 1848 Hecox and Silas Bennett gave seven acres at Green and Mission streets. Erection of the first church was followed by the coming of the first full time minister, the Rev.

James W. Brier, who with his family had crossed the plains from Michigan by way of Death Valley in 1849.

In 1862, when Peter Y. Cool was minister, the original church was moved back and for $4,500 a new one erected, thirty-six-by-sixty feet, with a steeple, dedicated October 11, 1863. It was enlarged in 1872 when Cool was again pastor.

During the pastorate of E. D. McCreary in 1890 the Methodists vacated the building, which was sold in 1902 to the Catholic church, moved to High street, named Montgomery Hall and used as a gymnasium for the Christian Brothers school. The Methodists retained a parsonage on the hill but bought the Congregational edifice on Church street, enlarging it. They moved their 820-pound bell, which had been bought in 1880 to replace one cracked by Fourth of July celebrants. In 1891 a Methodist chapel was built on Pennsylvania avenue which, moved and enlarged, is the East Side church.

A house adjoining the Church street edifice, which had been built in 1869 for Robert Knowles, was moved to lower Chestnut avenue and in 1901 the present parsonage erected.

The Congregational church originated when the Rev. T. W. Hinds held services in 1851 which resulted in the fourth congregation of that denomination in California. The organization, for which the Apostles creed was doctrinal standard, rented Arcan hall, where the Bank of America now stands, for ten dollars a month, but some of its members moved away and it lapsed.

Hinds reorganized his church in 1857 when, in an adobe on Davis street which had been built in 1836 by Rafael Castro but which later became known as the Boston adobe, William Anthony, a Presbyterian cousin of Elihu, cast the deciding vote to make the church Congregational.

The Rev. John Sheridan Zelie arrived in September and by the following spring a lot on the flat had been bought by $1,800 subscription and church members helped construction with a "raising" in which several were hurt when scaffolding broke.

When, in 1861, the Rev. W. C. Bartlett, later editor of the *San Francisco Bulletin*, succeeded Zelie, he engineered purchase of an 800-pound bell which, larger than the little ones at the

Catholic church or the public school, became the town's fire
bell. In 1890 the Congregationalists erected their present church
at Center and Lincoln streets and sold the one on Church street
to the Methodists, who moved it back, erected an auditorium
and enlarged the grounds by buying a house at the rear which
had been built in 1857 by Bart Stevens and later occupied by
the George Otto family.

The Baptist church got its start in 1857 when the Southern
Baptist convention sent the Rev. Charles N. West with his wife.
On October 24, 1858, West with two other ministers, O. Chittenden and James Webb, conducted a meeting in Rice's hall which
admitted two lay members, adopted the New Hampshire articles
of faith and adjourned to the river to baptise a man named
Stultz.

The little congregation, meeting in the court house and in
Temperance Hall, in 1859 voted against buying a lot on Vine
street. J. B. Knight was minister when, in 1867, Jonathan Guild
donated a site on the Locust street hill and contract was given
John Morrow to build for $2,500 a thirty-two-by-fifty-foot struc-
ture, the same size as the Congregational church. T. M. Merriam
took the pastorate in 1886 on condition the church would be
moved to the flat. The structure was hauled down Mission and
Walnut to Center and twenty-three years later, in 1910, remodeled to the present form. In the eighties the Baptists maintained a chapel on the east side on a lot donated by Calvin
Gault. The structure, moved to Pennsylvania avenue, is now
incorporated in the Seventh Day Adventist church.

The Episcopalians had been holding services two years when,
on July 29, 1864, C. F. Loop, first resident rector, laid the cornerstone for their church on a lot donated by Mrs. Eliza Boston.
They constructed their rectory twenty years later.

Unity Hall, built in 1868 by a congregation organized by the
Rev. Charles G. Ames, was a wooden building with high base-
ment on the north side of Walnut avenue half a block back
from Pacific. When members scattered in 1878 the Methodists
declined to pay $4,000 for it and the edifice went to J. L. Grover
on a mortgage. It was used by the Advent Christian church

before it was bought in 1882 by the Presbyterians and moved to Pacific and Cathcart, where it was razed in 1938.

Ames became pastor of a noted Boston church. The Unitarians, reorganized in 1902 by the Rev. George W. Stone, who later was mayor, built the church on Center street. Beside it is Hackley Hall, designed for a community center, for which $15,000 was given by Mrs. Frances Hackley of Tarreytown, New York.

Organization of the First Christian church in 1884 by the Rev. R. N. Davis, pastor at Watsonville, resulted in a congregation which was meeting in Delamater's hall when the Northern California Conference of Christian Churches erected for $14,000 the octagonal tabernacle in Garfield Park on land donated by Abraham King of San Jose, F. A. Hihn and others. The tabernacle, dedicated August 31, 1890, was scene of the annual church conventions. It burned August 5, 1935. The local congregation, then meeting in the Y.M.C.A. building on lower Pacific avenue, erected its present church at Center and Lincoln streets during the pastorate of the Rev. A. L. McHatton in 1898.

The Advent Christian church, after Unity Hall was sold to the Presbyterians, built on a lot on Elm street presented to them by Duncan McPherson.

Christian Scientists, who began meeting in the old Methodist church on Green street before its purchase by the Catholics, started their present church in 1909.

HOMETOWN RAILROAD
RAN TO FELTON

SANTA CRUZ' first railroad was a seven-mile narrow gauge which ran its first train up the west bank of the San Lorenzo to Felton on October 9, 1875. It was hometown-promoted but built largely by capital from the Santa Clara valley, which was interested in sawmills along the new flume above Felton. Until Mission hill was tunneled a year later it ran trains down Pacific avenue to the wharf.

On May 18, 1876, the Santa Cruz and Watsonville railroad, promoted by F. A. Hihn and Titus Hale, ran its first narrow-gauge train over a twenty-one mile track built by aid of a $100,000 county bond subsidy. The line bridged the river, ran along the beach and up Chestnut avenue and turned east to a depot at Park and Vine streets. Its engine house was on Seabright avenue.

The little Felton line was absorbed by the South Pacific Coast Railroad when that line was built over the mountains from Alameda. Its first train ran May 8, 1880. In 1884 the branch to Boulder Creek was built, with plans never carried out for an extension to the coast at Pescadero.

The Southern Pacific bought the Santa Cruz & Watsonville in 1881 and broad gauged it in 1884. In 1887 it took over the South Pacific Coast which was broad gauged after the earthquake of 1906.

Plans projected through the seventies and eighties for a railroad along the coast found realization in construction in 1906 by the Ocean Shore Railroad of twelve miles of track north from Santa Cruz which never met the rails laid south from San Francisco to Half Moon Bay. The San Francisco earthquake and the financial panic of 1907 ended construction of a line which was projected to extend across the Salinas valley and over the hills to Fresno. The Santa Cruz end of the line operated until 1920 as a logging line for the San Vicente Lumber Co.

The Felton line was first to operate out of Santa Cruz, but the first locomotive here was the snubnosed Betsy Jane, built in San Francisco, which arrived in the middle of October, 1874, to do construction work on the line to Watsonville. Ten years later it helped build the Aptos–Loma Prieta logging road. Its companion locomotive on the Santa Cruz–Watsonville run was the Jupiter, which arrived in 1876.

Motive power for the Felton line was two little locomotives. The Santa Cruz, built by Porter, Bell & Co. in Pittsburgh,

The Betsy Jane: first locomotive in Santa Cruz

crossed the continent by rail but was hauled by team from Watsonville to Aptos, to which point tracks had been laid. In 1880 it was sent by Senator James G. Fair to a logging road he owned which ran east into Nevada from Lake Tahoe. The Felton was taken by Senator Fair to Oakland where it hauled passengers out Telegraph avenue to what is now Sather Gate. Later it returned to pull logging trains on the Dougherty road above Boulder Creek.

THE BETSY JANE

On rails already laid from Woods lagoon toward Capitola the Betsy Jane was placed in October, 1874, to take up its burden of construction of the narrow-gauge Santa Cruz–Watsonville railroad. It had been designed by Francis M. Becker of Santa Cruz but manufactured in San Francisco. It had come over the newly laid rails of the Southern Pacific to Watsonville, where the people turned out in celebration. Its trip to Santa Cruz was ignominiously horse-drawn over the highway.

⇒

HORSE CARS GAVE
CITY RAPID TRANSIT

HORSE CARS began running on Pacific avenue to the wharf in 1876 on rails laid the previous year and used by the Santa Cruz and Felton railroad until contractor M. C. Boyle dug its tunnel under Mission hill.

James Pierce, a Santa Clara lumberman who was a large stockholder in the railroad and the flume above it, and E. J. Cox, an Australian who had come from San Jose and helped organize the County Bank of Savings & Loan, incorporated the Pacific Avenue Street Railroad Co., which extended the rails up Mission street to the Pope House.

Soquel avenue horse car

Hometown men, F. A. Hihn, Elihu Anthony, Amasa Pray and others laid tracks in 1877 on Front street and down the river to Leibbrandt's bath house but quit in 1881, selling their cars to the Pacific avenue line.

A third horse car line operated for a time, running from the lower plaza on Mission, Vine and Cherry to Chestnut avenue, where it switched to the tracks of the narrow-gauge railroad and had to accommodate its schedule to the arrival of the Betsy Jane and Jupiter from Watsonville.

Horse cars extended to the east side in 1890. William Ely, who had quit his job in a woolen mill in Joliet, Illinois, to drive a horse and buggy across the plains in 1850, incorporated for $20,000 the East Santa Cruz Street Railway. Permission was given it to run across the covered bridge and the old rails up Front street gave it a terminus at the lower plaza.

A horse car line for a few years in the nineties ran on Lincoln and Center streets to the Southern Pacific station.

The first electric trolley, the Santa Cruz, Garfield Park and Capitola Railway, promoted by young Fred Swanton, in 1891 started cars from the covered bridge which went west on Walnut avenue and by way of Mission, Younglove and Garfield (now Woodrow) avenue to the cliffs. Ely's retort to electrification was to order from the Baldwin works in Philadelphia a little locomotive. The engine William Ely hauled east side cars until 1895 when residents protested its smoke and noise and the county supervisors ordered it might run from its engine house at Doyle street only twice daily to ply down Cayuga and on to Twin Lakes.

Ely acquired an interest in the Pacific avenue line in 1893 and relaid rails for electrification. J. P. Smith put money into a consolidation. The Garfield Park line ran its rails north from Walnut avenue on Mission to the Pope House, meeting those of the Pacific avenue line. With the same financial backing the tracks were joined and after a few years the Walnut avenue trolley was abandoned. Its rails were taken up in 1909. Tracks on Front street had been removed two years before.

The Santa Cruz, Capitola and Watsonville Railway Co., successor of the Ely east side horse cars, by 1903 had cars running to Opal. All lines were consolidated in 1904 as the Union Traction Company. A line was run to Laveaga Heights; that to Capitola was completed. In July, 1906, the Coast Counties Power Company, dominated by John Martin, bought the Union Traction company.

Physical value of the combined lines was put at $637,000 but the automobile had appeared. In 1927 nearly a million dollars in investment was written off by the Coast Counties Gas and Electric Company, which retained as shops the old car barn at Pacific avenue and Sycamore street, only vestige of the horse cars of 1876 which grew into a gridiron of trolley tracks.

⊪

CONTINUOUS NEWSPAPER
RECORD SINCE 1856

JOHN McELROY, an Ohioan who had served three months in a Louisiana regiment in the Mexican war, had in 1851 with John A. Lewis founded the *Los Angeles Star*, which was also the *Estrella* with some of its columns in Spanish. The following year with Colonel Richard Rust he had published the *Marysville Express*.

In the spring of 1855 McElroy interested Delos R. Ashley, a lawyer who had come from Michigan in 1849, in starting a weekly in Monterey. Type was procured from the *Illustrated Sacramento Union*. Where the press came from McElroy said thirty years later he did not know; Dr. Andrew Randall had procured it. In the library room of the old Mexican cuartal, California and Webster streets, Monterey, the first issue of the *Monterey Sentinel* was printed on June 2, 1855. It was twenty columns in all, with a page twenty-four by thirty inches, subscription price six dollars a year.

Santa Cruz, thriving with its lumber and lime industries, attracted McElroy. When Albion P. Jordan, the thirty-year-old Maine mechanic who was partner in Davis and Jordan, offered free transportation for the plant McElroy accepted. Santa Cruz rallied about the opportunity. A list of eighty-nine paid in advance subscribers was signed and the little printing plant crossed twenty miles of water on the schooner *Queen of the West,* to the indignation of Monterey citizens who had passed the hat to found the paper.

The business district had just moved down from the mission plaza and no building was available until George Inskeep, a young Missourian working in the court house, offered free rent for a year in a tiny cottage on lower Mission street opposite Vine. With the name changed, the *Pacific Sentinel* made its appearance, the first newspaper in Santa Cruz, on June 14, 1856, with twenty columns in all and the price cut to five dollars a year.

In the fall of 1857 McElroy left on a trip east. The publishers became A. M. Parry & Co., the company being McElroy and Ashley. William Vahlberg had put up a building for his bakery on the west side of Main street (today's Front street) and the paper found quarters there. McElroy returned in 1859 and had a succession of partners until his final departure in 1863, to work on various other papers in northern California until he died in the veterans' home at Yountville, May 31, 1892.

For a time two printers, W. W. Broughton and John F. Liston, ran the *Sentinel.* One of its editors was Charles Osgood Cummings, member of a Canadian family who had arrived in the fifties. As Dr. Clearquill he became known as a brilliant writer. He was later part owner of the *Watsonville Pajaronian,* for many years Watsonville postmaster and then editor of the *Stockton Independent.*

Jeremiah Hyde, attorney and politician, acquired a half interest which he sold for $900 to twenty-four-year-old Duncan McPherson, who continued, except for three years when he and a brother published the *San Mateo Gazette* in Redwood City, with the *Sentinel* until his death fifty-seven years later. McPherson had come to California in the spring of 1856 with the family of his father, Alexander, who had been a lumber man and merchant at Riga, near Rochester, New York. The father, after briefly mining at Placerville and hotel keeping at Michigan Bluff, arrived in Santa Cruz in the fall of 1856.

Duncan, after attending the University of Pacific at San Jose and making an adventurous trip to the Frazer river mines, had been hauling lumber by ox team until he bought his interest in the *Sentinel*. The paper had found its third location in upstairs rooms at what is now 54 Pacific avenue in a building belonging to F. A. Hihn, whose family had occupied the rooms until he built a cottage in 1857 on Locust street.

In 1866 a half interest was acquired by Benjamin Park Kooser, a Pennsylvania printer who had enlisted in the artillery in the Mexican war. His regiment had arrived at Monterey in January, 1847, and Corporal Kooser had set type for Walter Colton's *Californian*, the first newspaper in California. His interest in the *Sentinel* continued until his death in 1878 when it was taken by C. W. Waldron, already employed as a reporter.

The paper moved into the second floor of the brick McPherson building, which is now the Alexander hotel, when Duncan's father erected it in 1868. Five years later it occupied the second floor of the frame Whidden building on the site now occupied at Locust street and Pacific avenue by the Farmers & Merchants bank. In 1913 it took a ground floor location on Locust street back of the Alexander hotel and in 1938 erected its present building on Church street.

The *Sentinel* saw rivals come and go. On August 17, 1859, N. W. Slocum issued the *Santa Cruz Weekly News*, which lasted until the following July when he moved the plant to San Jose, bought out F. B. Murdoch of the *Telegraph* and founded the *Mercury*.

The *Santa Cruz Journal*, a Democratic organ, issued its first number on September 3, 1868. Its editor, James Galway, who had come to California in 1847 with Stevenson's regiment, found capital by taking in Charles E. Beane. Immediately after the election Beane sold to Hiram A. Imus and Tom Beck and left for Los Angeles where in 1872 he was editor and half owner of the *News*.

About 1870 W. W. Broughton started the *Weekly Enterprise*, which eight years later was the first attempt at a daily in Santa Cruz. Broughton had, however, sold in 1876 when he loaded a press into a wagon and founded the *Lompoc Record*, which is still in existence. The two-week excursion into the daily field was Henry Coffin's despairing effort to save it. He lost the plant by foreclosure but immediately found another one and founded the *Local Item*.

Green Majors and H. C. Patrick, both of whom had been typos on the *Sentinel*, founded the *Courier*. For two years the three weeklies held the field but Santa Cruz, ranking twelfth in population in the state, attracted another daily effort in the *Echo* which lasted three and a half months in 1881 with Bascom A. Stephens as editor and publisher.

The *Echo*, which had its shop at what is now 42 Pacific avenue, quit at the end of October, 1881, and Stephens went south to a job as reporter on the *Los Angeles Times*.

A. A. Taylor bought the *Courier*'s name and goodwill and both name and plant of the *Item*, to issue the combined *Courier-Item*. Patrick left with his equipment for Washington Territory where he founded the *Tacoma Ledger*. Majors went to Montana to become part owner of the *Butte Inter-Mountain*. Taylor changed the weekly *Courier-Item* into the daily *Surf*, which lasted until June, 1919.

The *Sentinel* became a daily in 1884.

Newspapers of Santa Cruz which have appeared and succumbed include the *Times*, which moved over from Watsonville in 1866; the *Herald* in the late eighties; the *Record*, which tried the daily field in 1892; the *Sunday Tribune*, started in 1907; the *Penny Press* in the nineties; a second *Herald* which started in 1889 on a press moved in from Soquel where a *Soquel Journal* had failed; and the *Evening News*, started in 1907 by E. J. Devlin and H. R. Judah, sold by them in 1938 to Frank Carroll of Indianapolis and absorbed in 1942 into the *Sentinel-News*.

The *Watsonville Register* was born in 1876 as the weekly *Transcript*, with William H. Wheeler running it and George W. Peckham as backer. It absorbed H. B. Watson's *Sun* in 1880 and attempted to issue editions in both Watsonville and Santa Cruz. The Santa Cruz edition, of which E. F. Conway was editor, quit in June, 1882. It became the *Register* in 1904. Fred W. Atkinson, who bought it in 1913, absorbed the *Pajaronian*, which was eight years older than the *Register*, into the *Register-Pajaronian*.

◄═►

MISSION ADOBE WAS CITY'S FIRST HOTEL

J OB FRANIS DYE, forty-three-year-old Kentuckian, leaving for the mines, in July of 1848 sold to Joseph Majors, with whom he had come over the Santa Fe trail in 1832, the big adobe on the mission plaza which had been the juzgado of later Mexican days. Majors named it the Eagle hotel.

The next year, just across what was later called School street, Tom Fallon built the story-and-a-half wooden structure which was residence and store for his saddle trees. In January, 1850, he announced it would be a hotel, too.

The two were short lived. Elihu Anthony was laying out the town's first business district along what was then Main street but is now Front. On the present site of the Veterans' Memorial building was erected a low two-story hotel, the Santa Cruz House. On the west side of Willow street, where the Coast Counties Gas and Electric company's office stands now, Henry Rice, 300-pound Carolinan, in 1852 built the San Lorenzo House.

Up on the hill Fallon in 1852 sold his building to the county for a court house and Majors' adobe was taken over by the Sisters of Charity in 1862 to start Holy Cross school.

In 1856 Rice, elected county judge, sold the San Lorenzo House to W. D. Farrand and James Skene, who unsuccessfully tried to rename it the Steamboat Exchange. It burned in 1865, leaving the site on which Amasa Pray began building the same year the two-story brick Pacific Ocean House, part of which is still standing.

Jacob D. Stagg was running the Santa Cruz House when, in 1859, Henry Harris tired of blacksmithing, bought a building next to Stagg's hotel which had housed a tin shop and began enlarging it into the twenty-three-room Franklin House, which lasted as one of the city's hostelries until it burned in 1886. The Santa Cruz House burned a year later.

The Pacific Ocean House, opened Monday, April 2, 1866, by "Uncle" George Bromley, whom the *Sentinel* described as a "veteran San Francisco club man," assumed metropolitan airs. In 1863 it advertised "an extensive bath house in the rear" and in 1869 it installed gas jets in every room. A third floor was added in 1892 but the hostelry was beginning to be outmoded. It was a lodging house, owned by F. A. Hihn and run by Hedgpeth brothers, when fire badly damaged it on November 7, 1907.

Prosperity of the Pacific Ocean House brought into existence the St. Charles, in the corner of Mission and River streets. A two-story wooden building erected in the late fifties by William Anthony for his hardware store and tin shop, was in 1868 made three stories high and turned into a hotel by Charles Brown, a forty-niner who had come to Santa Cruz with $60,000 made from the sale of San Francisco lots and who died in poverty in 1887. The hotel burned May 7, 1919.

The Riverside hotel, east of the river, was started by Fred Barson, a young Englishman, who in 1870 bought thirty acres from Judge E. H. Heacock.

Far down Pacific avenue Peter V. Wilkins, a young New Yorker who had been lessee of the Santa Cruz House, about 1878 converted a residence which had been built in 1856 by Tom Beck into the Wilkins House. Later it was the Grand Central hotel and was razed in 1940. It stood opposite Cathcart street.

In 1884 A. P. Swanton tore down his Bonner stables on the site of the present postoffice and erected the three-story square Swanton House which burned three years later.

On Beach Hill a cottage resort operated as the Bay View House was bought in 1882 by A. H. Douglas, an artist, from Illinois, who opened it as the Douglas House. In March, 1887, he sold it to D. K. Abeel, former publisher of the *Kansas City Journal*, who expanded it into a sprawling three-story wooden hotel typical of the period. When he sold it in 1901 to J. J. C. Leonard it was said the original cost was $87,000. It burned June 12, 1912.

A three-story building on Walnut avenue which had housed Quincy Hall Seminary was in 1884 opened as the Auzerais House. Later, run by A. N. Hedgpeth as the Eastern Hotel, it was badly burned October 23, 1903, but was repaired and used for a few years.

A building still standing at 68 Walnut avenue, built in 1877 by John Conran as the Walnut Avenue House, was sold by him in 1886 to Mrs. Kate Hubbard of San Francisco. Conran removed to Sacramento.

◄█►

DRAMA AND MINSTRELSY
AT KNIGHT'S OPERA HOUSE

ABOUT WHERE CENTER STREET CROSSES PARK stood Knight's Opera House, for half a century the city's home for grand opera and drama.

Budd Smith was a jaunty thirty-six-year-old Kentuckian who, new in Santa Cruz and established as an auctioneer in Ely's building next to the court house, persuaded F. A. Hihn to sell him a lot for nothing down and James P. Pierce not only to furnish him lumber on the same terms but to haul it on the newly built Santa Cruz & Felton railroad.

On November 23, 1877, the theater opened with "The Bohemian Girl" sung by the Hitchings-Bernard Opera Company,

Knight's Opera House   UCSC SPECIAL COLLECTIONS

just back from Australia, combined with the Ilmar de Murska company. Santa Cruzans filled the rows of kitchen chairs and watched the pictured Atlas rise as the curtain rolled up.

Receipts the first night were $600; for the first four performances were $1,100. Jock Merrill, the Pacific Ocean House bartender, did a rushing business in the little bar he established in the front corner of the theater building.

Budd Smith decided theater patronage justified a stock company and secured James A. Hearne as leading man and Katherine Corcoran to play opposite him. The first week's business was good but the second disastrous. Santa Cruzans who had taken the actors to their hearts and merchants who had extended credit backed a benefit Shakespearean performance in which Hearne played Romeo in white flannel trousers.

Pierce, principal stockholder in the Pacific Avenue horse car line, was compelled to take over the opera house. Budd Smith went to other fields of promotion and in 1887 was in San Francisco as general manager of the California Inventors' Institute. By that time the theater had passed into the hands of Dr. B. Killey Knight, who installed plush seats.

Through the years famous actors trod its boards. A young actress named Minnie Maddern played in "Caprice" in 1887. The Grace Hawthorne company from the Alcazar in San Francisco played "The New Camille" and "Fanchon the Cricket." Paderewski and his piano appeared on its stage. High school classes graduated there. Boxing matches were put on. "The Red Stocking Blondes" for men only appeared. Jack London, Josh Billings and others lectured from the stage.

Race week out at Bay View, with its influx of gamblers, usually brought a "rep show" to present a week's program with changes nightly from "Our American Cousin" to "Led Astray" and "An Unequal Match." Yearly through the eighties Billy Emerson's Minstrels gave a week's stand, with a baseball team of its members playing a Santa Cruz team. Twenty years later George W. Primrose and his Mammoth Minstrel Company came.

Dr. Knight died in 1905 and the old fifty-by-one-hundred-foot building was the property of his widow when in 1921 its timbers were hauled to Capitola and rebuilt into a garage.

Knight's Opera House was not Santa Cruz' first theater. Exchange Hall, in Luther Farnham's hotel provided a stage for traveling entertainers until it burned in 1865. Trust's hall on Front street was used until Elihu Anthony put up his new building with a hall on the second floor in which Fay Templeton, the "wonderful child actress," played with her father's company in "The New Magdalen" on the night of September 28, 1874.

Bob Christy and James Handley had in 1882 moved their variety show from Vienna Gardens near the Bausch brewery on the banks of the Branciforte to 35 Pacific avenue, where they installed seats with beer glass rests. Girls purveyed the drinks. On the night of July 22 a group of men invaded the theater, which had entrances on both Pacific avenue and Front street, smashed furniture, destroyed cases of curios and broke mirrors while the three-man police force turned a deaf ear.

The turn of the century saw the coming of the movies. A livery stable built in 1882 by David Wilson was in 1903 remodeled into the Unique theater and opened with vaudeville on the Grauman circuit. In it Mack Swain's stock company was succeeded by Leo Chrystal Bell's similar organization. On July 1, 1907, the Casino theater at the beach opened with a stage on which many big name thespians appeared. Motion pictures were offered in the Star on Pacific avenue opposite Cathcart, in the Dime on Walnut avenue, the Gem in the St. George block, the Jewel in the Masonic building and the Princess a few doors north of it. The Santa Cruz theater opened in 1920.

⚊

PIONEER SPIRIT
WAS FRATERNAL

SANTA CRUZ LODGE NO. 38 of Masons was organized July 16, 1853, in an upstairs room of an adobe building on School street, with Henry G. Blaisdell, who eleven years later was first governor of Nevada, as presiding officer. The Masons moved to Arcan's hall, then facing Pacific avenue below Soquel avenue, and in 1867 to upstairs rooms in a building which later was bought by the Bank of Santa Cruz county, on the west side of Pacific avenue just above Locust street. Their present building was erected in 1887. Idlewild chapter of Eastern Star was organized February 29, 1876.

Branciforte Lodge No. 68, Independent Order of Odd Fellows, was formed April 26, 1860, in Temperance Hall. San

Lorenzo Lodge No. 96 split from the first unit and was instituted November 6, 1868, in Unity Hall. They met in the McPherson building at Pacific avenue and Locust street until they built the first unit of the present I.O.O.F. building in 1876. The two lodges merged in 1920. Isabella Rebekah Lodge No. 17 was organized April 27, 1874. Soquel Lodge No. 137 of Odd Fellows was formed July 10, 1876, and Martha Washington Lodge of Rebekahs at Soquel on February 28, 1888.

Santa Cruz Elks lodge was established December 27, 1902, and bought its present quarters in 1919.

Minnehaha Tribe, Improved Order of Red Men, organized August 18, 1878, surrendered its charter in 1910. Roxas Tribe was instituted in 1900.

Madrone Circle of Druids was organized November 5, 1871, in Arcan Hall. Manzanita Circle was formed July 7, 1874.

◄≡►

POWDER FOR BLASTING
AND FOR DEWEY'S GUNS

THE CALIFORNIA POWDER WORKS, two miles up the San Lorenzo from Santa Cruz, furnished blasting powder which built the first transcontinental railroads across the Sierras and Rockies. Thirty years later it made the powder for Dewey's guns at Manila.

When the Civil War ran the price of eastern powder to thirteen dollars a keg in California, John H. Baird of San Francisco organized a company which bought in Santa Cruz county the level site where a paper mill had washed away in 1862. Production, started in May, 1864, the first year turned out 150,000 twenty-five-pound kegs. By 1887 the company owned seventeen buildings on 200 acres.

Aristocratic Bernard Peyton, who came as superintendent because of experience in the east, took full place in the community. He was supervisor from San Lorenzo district. He and his son built fine homes on the hill east of the mill, with a switch-back road zigzagging up to them.

Mrs. Peyton, devout Catholic, had a chapel in her home to which men and women from the powder mill village climbed to mass said by a priest from Santa Cruz. In 1888 Mrs. Peyton paid to have three of the bells of old Santa Cruz mission (there were said to have been nine; no record is known of the other six) recast in San Francisco. The three bells, made in Mexico in 1809, weighed 1100 pounds. Tin was added to bring the present bell in Holy Cross church to 1,500 pounds.

When, in the nineties, the "trust" which is the DuPont company began merging powder works of the nation, the one big plant which refused to combine was that at Santa Cruz. Marriage between the Peyton and DuPont families finally effected the consolidation.

In the Spanish–American War the army stationed a guard on powder mill flat after an explosion on May 25, 1898, which killed thirteen men and injured twenty-five. Passing of commerce from ocean routes to railroads made it more economical to manufacture powder elsewhere. The DuPont plant at Hercules, California, is lineal descendant of the Santa Cruz works. Many employes were moved there.

In 1919 powder mill flat was made Paradise Park, site of a cottage colony of members of the Masonic fraternity. Several of the powder mill buildings still stand.

⊰≡⊱

ACKNOWLEDGMENT

Sources: Files of the *Santa Cruz Sentinel*, Branciforte archives in the Santa Cruz county recorder's office, records of Santa Cruz mission preserved by Holy Cross church, the durable and infallible memory of Ernest Otto, Warren Penniman, H. O. Heiner, the Bancroft Library, records of the secretary of state at Sacramento, State Historical Library at Sacramento, State Historical Society. Pictures: Mrs. Robert Rodriguez, Mrs. Rose Rostron, George Otto, Dr. A. T. Leonard, A. G. Finn, Robert S. Tait, Harry Tait, Preston Sawyer, Bob Willey, Peter Jansse.

Los Fundadores

*Herein are listed
the first families of California and also
all other persons with family names that
were in California 1769–1785 except those
who died at San Diego in 1769.*

1951

◄═►

FOREWORD

Los Fundadores presents an attempt to list the names of the men who came from Mexico to northern California in the first fifteen years of its settlement, most of them to remain.

Soldados, pobladores, sirvientes and *presidiarios* compose the list. The mission priests are not included; a complete list of them will be found in the index volume to Englehardt's *Missions and Missionaries.*

The records of the seven central California missions, made available by the Bishop of Monterey-Fresno afford most of the data. Concerning members of the Anza party, Eldredge is largely followed, although not always. For instance, his statement that Santiago de la Cruz Pico was born at San Miguel de Horcasitas in 1733 conflicts with the fact that San Miguel was not established until 1741.

Sources of information and checking include Culleton's *Indians and Pioneers of Old Monterey*, Bancroft's Index in *History of California*, publications of the California Historical Society and the Historical Society of Southern California, Bolton's *Anza* and *Fray Juan Crespi*, and Palou's *Noticias.*

The Spanish phrase *soldado de cuera*, meaning leather jacket soldier, is rendered simply soldier. Other Spanish technical words frequently encountered in the documents are *invalido* (retired soldier), *escolta* (mission guard), *padron* (the annual census), *mestizo* (Spanish and Indian parentage), and *Coyote* (Spanish, Indian and Negro blood).

For the sake of economy the Spanish accents are omitted in the text but will be found in the index. Archaic spellings are corrected in the same section and there, too, will be found several names not alphabetized in the text.

━☰━

HEADS OF FAMILIES IN UPPER CALIFORNIA
1770-1785

ACEVES, Antonio Quitario

He was born in 1740 at Valle de San Bartolome, Durango, and came as recruit soldier in the 1776 Anza party. On the founding of Santa Clara in 1777 he was sent to the guard there. From Durango he brought his wife, Maria Feliciana Cortes, and six children: Maria Petra, 13; Jose Cipriano, 11; Maria Gertrudis, 6; Juan Gregorio, 5; Pablo, 3; Jose Antonio, ——months. Baptised at Santa Clara September, 1777, was Jose Maria. Aceves died in 1820 at San Jose. His wife, Feliciana, had died the previous year. Both were buried at Santa Clara.

Maria Petra married in 1778 at Santa Clara, Jose Antonio Romero, native of Guadalajara. In 1802, a widow, she married at Santa Clara, Francisco Castro, who was later referred to as Francisco Sevilla and was undoubtedly the Indian boy servant who came with the family of Joaquin Isidro Castro in the Anza party. Petra died in 1806 at San Jose.

Jose Cipriano. He was in the Santa Cruz mission guard and in 1791 he married Feliciana, a neophyte, who died at Santa Clara in 1796. Jose was buried at Santa Clara in 1817.

Maria Gertrudis married in 1784 at Santa Clara, Jose Manuel Gonzales, Indian, native of San Bartolome, and as a widow at Santa Clara in 1805 she married Jose Pablo Parras. She died in 1846 at San Jose.

Pablo married in 1794 at Mission Dolores, Petra Regalado Rosales, who died two years later. Pablo died at San Jose in 1803.

Jose Maria, soldier of the Monterey company stationed at San Juan Bautista, married in 1809 at San Carlos, Maria Micaela Mendoza, a native of the Presidio of Monterey. The marriage record stated that she was the daughter of Manuel Buytron and Maria Gregoria Gonzales, both natives of Sinaloa.

AQUEZON, Francisco

Soldier of the California Company. Godfather at San Carlos in February, 1773.

AGUILAR (also spelled Aguiar), Francisco Xavier

Spaniard. In 1769 Portola party. Soldier, remained at Monterey in 1770. Godfather at San Carlos in February, 1773.

ALEGRE, Antonio

Native of Coste-Bachelega of the Republic of Genoa. Aged 40 when, in 1792, at San Carlos, he married Catalina, Indian neophyte, widow of Jose Joaquin Espinosa, who had been massacred on the Colorado river in 1781. In 1795, a widower, at San Carlos, he married Felipa Saens, daughter of Justo Nazario Saens of the Rivera recruits to Los Angeles in 1774 and of Micaela Sotelo, both natives of Sinaloa.

ALSALDO, Francisco Xavier

Lower California Indian. Remained at Monterey in 1770 after coming with the Portola party. Married Angela, a Carmel neophyte.

ALTAMIRANO, Tiburcio de los Reyes

Mexican, ex-sailor, unskilled worker. At Monterey, in 1776 and probably earlier. Married Agueda Maria, a Carmel neophyte.

ALTAMIRANO, Justo Roberto

Veteran soldier in 1776 Anza party. Born in 1745 at Aguage, Sonora. Brought wife, Maria Loreto Delfin, and, a widower, in 1792 at Santa Clara he married Juana Gertrudis Coronado. Justo died in 1825 at San Jose. Two sons came with him in 1776. One, *Jose Antonio*, married in 1787 at Santa Clara, Gertrudis Amezquita, but died two years later, apparently without children. The other, *Matias*, died unmarried at San Jose in 1783.

Justo and Maria Loreto Delfin baptised:

Marcos, 1777, at Mission Dolores. He married in 1803 at Santa Clara, Maria Ygnacia Villavicencio, who bore him nine children before he died in 1821 at San Jose.

Lucas, 1778, at Santa Clara. He married, probably at Mission San Antonio, Geronima Garcia, born at that mission. They baptised eleven children before he died in 1821 at San Jose.

Jose Miguel Capistrano, 1780, at Santa Clara. He married in 1808 at Santa Clara, Maria Agustina Amezquita. They had three children before his burial in 1811 at Santa Clara.

ALVARADO, Bernardo

Arrived at Monterey with pack train from San Diego in 1770. With Portola, says Eldredge.

ALVARADO, Juan Bautista

In 1769 Portola party. Returned to Monterey from San Diego with pack train in 1770. Grandfather of the Juan Bautista Alvarado born at Monterey in 1809.

ALVARADO, Jose Francisco

Son of above, born in Sinaloa. Perhaps with his father in the Portola party. His mother was Maria Dolores Castro. He married in 1808, at San Carlos, when he was sergeant of the Monterey company, Josefa Vallejo, daughter of Ignacio Vicente Vallejo, and was father of Juan Bautista Alvarado. He died in 1809 at San Luis Obispo. Josefa as a widow married in 1809 at San Carlos, Ramon Estrada, cadet of the Monterey company, native of Loreto, Lower California.

ALVAREZ, Ascencio

Soldier at Monterey in 1773.

ALVAREZ, Luis Joaquin

Born in 1740 at Sinaloa. Recruit soldier with Anza in 1776. Brought wife, Maria Nicolasa Ortiz, and two children, Juan Francisco and Maria Francisca. Joaquin was at San Francisco from 1777 to 1782.

ALVIREZ, Claudio

From the Presidio of San Miguel de Horcasitas in Sonora. Born in 1742. He married in 1780 at Santa Clara, Ana Maria Gonzales, Indian, aged 20, daughter, born in Sinaloa, of Manuel Gonzales of San Jose. Claudio, with his name recorded as Manuel Salvador Claudio Alvirez, was buried in 1813 at Santa Clara. His widow died in 1823.

ALVISO, Domingo

Veteran soldier, corporal, in 1776 Anza party. He was buried March 11, 1777, at San Francisco. He brought his wife, Angela Trejo, who married July 20, 1777, at Mission Dolores, Pedro Antonio Bojorgues. Four children who came with Alviso were:

Francisco Xavier, born in Horcasitas, aged 10 in 1776. Married in 1792 at Mission Dolores, Maria Agustina Bojorgues, daughter of Pedro Antonio Bojorgues and his first wife, Francisca de Lara. He died in 1803 at Monterey.

Francisco, born in Horcasitas, aged 9 in 1776. Married in 1792 at San Carlos, Maria de los Reyes Duarte, daughter of Alejo Antonio Duarte and of Gertrudis, neophyte of San Antonio mission.

Maria Loreta, aged 5 in 1776. Married in 1784 at Santa Clara, Luis Maria Peralta, son of Gabriel Peralta of the Anza party.

Ignacio, born in Horcasitas, aged 3 in 1776. Married in 1794 at Mission Dolores, Margarita Bernal, adopted daughter of Juan Francisco Bernal.

AMADOR, Pedro

Service at the Presidio of Loreto, in Lower California, and was sergeant in the 1769 Portola party. After a period back at Cocula he was in 1784 corporal at Santa Barbara presidio. One record has him born in 1739 at Guadalajara; another says in 1742 at Cocula, Jalisco.

AMARILLAS, Juan Angel

Soldier with Portola, says Eldredge. Soldier in the San Gabriel mission guard in 1777, with wife, Maria Loreto de Vega.

AMEZQUITA, Juan Antonio (Mulatto)

Born in 1739 at Matape, Sonora. Enlisted in 1764 at the Presidio of Tubac. Veteran soldier with Anza in 1776. Brought wife, Juana Maria de Guana, and five children:

Manuel Domingo. (In later records Salvador Manuel and Manuel Francisco.) Brought wife, Rosalia Zamora, in Anza party. Widower, Manuel married in 1778 at Santa Clara, Maria Graciana Garcia. The marriage record said Manuel, who was 23 years old in 1776, was born in the Pueblo de San Lorenzo, Sonora.

Maria Josefa, aged 20 in 1776. Married in 1777 at Mission Dolores, Hermenegildo Sal. Three daughters and two sons were born to them at San Francisco before Josefa's death in 1796 at Monterey.

Maria Dolores, aged 10 in 1776. Married in 1791 at Santa Clara, Vicente Antonio Hernandez.

Maria Gertrudis, aged 3 in 1776. Married in 1787 at Santa Clara, Jose Antonio Altamirano.

Juana Maria, few months old in 1776. Married in 1794 at Santa Clara, Jose Antonio Soto. Widow, she married in 1821, at Mission Dolores, Jose Antonio Aguilar.

ANTUNA, Jose Manuel

Soldier with Rivera in October, 1774. Native of Sinaloa. Brought wife, Juana Gertrudis Serna, also a native of Sinaloa, and a daughter, *Maria Valvanera*, born in Sinaloa, who married in 1781, at San Carlos, Manuel Rodriguez, carpenter.

ARBALLO (Orbayo), Maria Feliciana

Widow of Jose Gutierrez, came in 1776 Anza party, bringing two daughters. She married in 1776 at San Gabriel, Juan Francisco Lopez, soldier of that mission guard. The daughters were Tomasa and Estaquia Gutierrez. Feliciana and Lopez baptised Ygnacia Maria de Jesus in 1778 and Ygnacia de Candelaria in 1793, both at San Diego.

Eustaquia Gutierrez married in 1789 Jose Maria Pico and became the mother of Pio Pico.

Maria Ygnacia de la Candelaria married Joaquin Carrillo in San Diego and became the mother of M. G. Vallejo's wife and four other daughters noted for their beauty.

ARBITRE (Alvitre), Juan

With Portola in 1769, says Eldredge. Probably the same as below.

ARBITRE (Alvitre), Sebastian

Soldier in 1769 Portola party. Godfather at San Carlos and San Antonio in 1773. In 1786 sent from San Jose to Los Angeles as incorrigible.

ARCE, Jose Gabriel

With Portola in 1769. As soldier, very old, arrived at Monterey in 1770 with pack train from San Diego.

ARCHULETA, Ygnacio

Spaniard, born at San Miguel de Horcasitas, Sonora, in 1754. Not in 1776 Anza party but at San Francisco in 1777; in 1778 San Jose yearly census. As widower of Gertrudis Martinez, he married July 4, 1777, at Mission Dolores, Ygnacia Gertrudis Pacheco, daughter of Juan Salvio Pacheco of the Anza party.

ARIAS, Miguel

At Monterey in 1773, a sailor-servant from the Principe.

ARRELLANO, Manuel Ramirez

Born in 1742 at Puebla, Mexico. Came as recruit soldier with Anza. Brought wife, Maria Agueda de Haro. One son, Mariano, came with them but died at San Jose in 1786. They baptised at

Santa Clara Jose Teodoro in 1782 and Maria Rosalia in 1784. Arrellano, whose name became Arrellanes, retired from the army in 1786 and went to Los Angeles where he was alcalde in 1790. Ramirez Arrellano was surname of one of the men who came with Cortes and is a family name famous in Spanish–American history.

ARROYO, Manuel

Skilled worker left by the *Santiago* at Monterey in 1774.

ARUZ, Domingo

Catalonian Volunteer. Native of Ciudad de Gerona. At Monterey in 1774 or earlier. Married Serafina, a neophyte of San Carlos; later, widowed, married Gertrudis Quintero.

ARZE, Joaquin

Soldier who came with Rivera in October, 1774.

AVILA, Francisco

Born in 1744 in Villa de Fuerte, Sinaloa. Soldier with Portola in 1769. Married Josefa Quintero, daughter of Luis Quintero, and appeared with her as godparents at Santa Clara in 1790. Francisco, known as a hard case, was at San Jose as late as 1800, according to Bancroft.

AYALA, Pedro Xavier de

Ex-sailor, laborer, left at Monterey by the *San Antonio* in 1771. He married Antonia Rosa, Carmel neophyte.

AZEVEDO, Francisco Antonio

Spaniard, born in 1748 in Sinaloa. Soldier with Portola. Transferred from Monterey to the San Diego company, where he was a corporal in 1790. Settler at Los Angeles 1808–1819.

⚊

BADIOLA, Manuel Antonio

Godparent at Monterey in 1773, a servant.

BASIOLA (also spelled Basilio), Mariano

Unskilled workman left at Monterey by the *San Antonio* in 1771. Sailor, native of Cocotlan.

BELTRAN, Francisco Xavier

Born in 1744 at Chametta, Sinaloa. Came with Rivera recruits from San Blas to San Diego in 1774. At Monterey in 1776 and in the San Jose yearly census in 1778. Brought wife, Gertrudis

Lugo, born 1752 in Sinaloa, a sister of Serafin Lugo of the same party. They brought two adopted children, orphans. Maria Gertrudis Valencia, 8, and Maria Valencia, 1. Beltran was buried in 1808 at San Carlos.

BELTRAN, Joaquin (alias Caravanas)

Born in 1752 in Sinaloa. Came with the Rivera recruits in October, 1774. Soldier at San Antonio in 1786 when daughter was born to his wife, Cecilia Aguilar.

BELTRAN, Nicolas

At Monterey, perhaps as early as 1770. Killed July 18, 1781, in the Yuma massacre on the Colorado river.

BERNAL, Francisco

With Portola in 1769, says Eldredge.

BERNAL, Juan Francisco (Mestizo)

Born in 1737 at Rancho de Tule, Sinaloa. Recruit soldier with Anza. Brought wife, Maria Josefa Soto, a sister of Ygnacio Soto, and seven children:

Joaquin, aged 13 in 1776. Married in 1785 at San Francisco Mission, Josefa Sanchez, aged 16, daughter of Jose Antonio Sanchez. Joaquin died in 1837 at San Jose.

Juan Francisco, aged 12 in 1776. Married in 1782 at Mission Dolores, Petrona Gutierrez. Juan Francisco died before 1804, for in that year his widow, Petrona, married at Mission Dolores, Cornelio Valderrama.

Dionisio, aged 10 in 1776. Married in 1784 at Santa Clara, Maria Manuela Mesa, daughter of Valerio Mesa. Dionisio was in mission guard at Santa Clara, San Luis Obispo and Santa Cruz. His wife died in 1805 at San Jose. Dionisio was retired from the army with rank of corporal when he died at San Jose in 1828.

Apolonario, aged 9 in 1776. Married in 1792 at San Carlos, Maria Apolonaria Soberanes, daughter of Jose Maria Soberanes. Widowed, he married in 1802 at Mission Dolores, Teodora Peralta, daughter of Luis Peralta.

Ana Maria, aged 5 in 1776. Married in 1784, at Mission Dolores, Gabriel Moraga.

Maria Teresa, aged 3 in 1776. Married in 1786 at Mission Dolores, Marcos Chavoya, son of Pascual Chavoya. She died in San Jose in 1830.

Tomas Januario, few months old in 1776.

BERNAL, Manuel Ramon

With Portola in 1769. At San Diego 1782–83. Born 1736 at Real de Alamos.

BERREYESSA, Nicolas Antonio (Coyote)

Born in 1751 in Sinaloa. His parents, who did not come to California, were Cayetano Berreyessa and Micaela Leyva. Nicolas came as civilian colonist with Anza. He married in 1779 at Santa Clara, Maria Gertrudis Peralta, native of the Presidio of Tubac. They baptised *Maria Gabriela* in 1780 at Santa Clara, who in 1795 married Francisco Castro. A son, *Jose de los Reyes*, baptised in 1785 at Santa Clara, married in 1805 Maria Zacarias Bernal.

BERREYESSA, Ysabel (Mestizo)

Born in 1754 in Sinaloa. Sister of Nicolas Antonio. She came in the Anza party and married in 1777 at Mission Dolores, Juan Jose Peralta, brother of Gertrudis who married Nicolas Antonio Berreyessa.

BOJORGUES, Jose Ramon

Born in 1737 in Sinaloa. Soldier in Anza party with his wife, Francisca Romero, and three children. Francisca was buried at Santa Clara in 1818 and Ramon died in 1822. The children who came with them were:

Maria Antonia, aged 15 in 1776, was already married to Tiburcio Vasquez. They baptised seven children in 1778–1789.

Maria Micaela, aged 13 in 1776. She was already the wife of Ygnacio Antonio Anastasio Higuera of the same party.

Maria Gertrudis, aged 12 in 1776. She married in 1777 at Mission Dolores, Jose Francisco Sinova.

BOJORGUES, Pedro Antonio (Mestizo)

Born in 1754 in Sinaloa. Came as soldier in the Anza party, bringing his wife, Maria Francisca Lara, who died January 28, 1777, in San Francisco. Pedro Antonio married July 20, 1777, at Mission Dolores, Maria Angela Trejo, widow of Domingo Alviso. With Bojorgues came his daughter, *Maria Agustina Bojorgues*, who married in 1787 at San Carlos, Francisco Xavier Alviso, native of San Miguel in Sonora, son of Domingo Alviso.

BONBAU, Francisco

Catalonian Volunteer. At Monterey 1771–72, probably came with Fages.

BRAVO, Jose Marcelino

Born in 1749 at San Luis Potosi, son of Antonio Bravo and Ana

Ramona Sambrano. Soldier in San Diego presidio in 1770. Corporal at Monterey in January, 1773, and probably earlier. Married July 24, 1774, at San Carlos, Maria del Carmen Chamorro, born in Guadalajara, daughter of Fernando Chamorro, blacksmith. Retired in 1797 with brevet rank as sergeant. Died at Branciforte in 1806.

BRIONES, Jose Antonio

With Portola in 1769. Wife was Gertrudis Higuera. He was commander of the mission guard at San Juan Capistrano, killed by Indians on August 18, 1777, carrying dispatches from Croix to Neve.

BRIONES, Ignacio Vicente

Born in 1727 in Ciudad de San Luis Potosi. Corporal of the mission guard at San Luis Obispo in February, 1773, and probably earlier. Widower of Antonia Padron, he married at San Luis Obispo, Mariana, neophyte, and baptised there two sons who died in infancy. He was mayordomo of San Carlos mission from 1787 to his death in 1813. Mariana was buried at San Carlos in 1806.

BRIONES, Marcos

He was born in the city of San Luis Potosi in 1760, the son of Ignacio Vicente Briones. He seems to have accompanied his father to California in 1773 or earlier. At San Carlos Mission in 1784 he married Isidora Tapia, aged 13 and the daughter of Felipe Tapia. He was a mission guard at San Antonio, San Carlos, San Luis Obispo and Santa Cruz. Between 1788 and 1806 this couple baptized thirteen children. Isidora died at Santa Cruz Mission in 1812. Marcos was still alive in 1841. His residence is given as San Jose and his age as 87 in the census for that year.

BUELNA, Jose Antonio

Native of Villa Sinaloa, son of Anastasio Buelna He came to California with Rivera in October, 1774. He married in 1776 at San Carlos, Antonia Tapia, daughter of Felipe Tapia. They baptised at least five children from 1777 to 1805 at San Carlos, San Antonio and Soledad.

BULLFERICH, Gervasio

Catalonian Volunteer who came from Guaymas in 1771–72.

BUTRON (also spelled Buitron), Manuel

Catalonian Volunteer. Born in 1727 at Orrela (Origuila) in Valencia, Spain. Remained at Monterey in 1770. Married in 1772 at San Carlos, Margarita, neophyte. They baptised two sons, Manuel and Sebastian, at San Carlos, 1776 and 1778. He died before 1815 when Margarita died, a widow.

⚬

CAMACHO, Jose Anastasio
With Portola in 1769.

CAMACHO, Juan Miguel
With Portola in 1769.

CAMACHO, Jose (probably Jose Anastasio, above)
Soldier at Monterey in 1770, assigned by the presidio commander to the Paquebot *San Carlos* for its voyage south that year, to augment the crew. Seven others were assigned, all Indians.

CAMACHO, Tomas Maria
One San Carlos record said he was a native of Tepic; another of the Pueblo of Magdalena in Guadalajara. He was a sailor and a blacksmith. He was assigned to the Paquebot *San Carlos* to augment its crew for its voyage south in 1770 but was back at Monterey by 1773. He married Tecla, a neophyte, at San Carlos and had two daughters baptised there before he was killed in the Yuma massacre on the Colorado river in 1781.

CANTUA, Ignacio
One record says he was born at Navojoa, Sonora; another that he was a native of Yaqui, Obispado de Sonora. He was a soldier at Monterey in 1784 and probably earlier. He brought a wife, Maria Gertrudis Castillo, a native of Lower California. They brought a daughter, *Dolores*, who was recorded as a native of El Real de Santa Ana en el Sur de California, and her mother native of the same place. Dolores was married in 1787 at San Carlos to Bernardo Ygnacio Pacheco. Cantua and his wife baptised nine children at San Carlos and Santa Clara in 1784–1799. Cantua was buried at Santa Clara in 1822.

(Note: Cantua's wife's name was identical with that of the wife of Anastasio Vasquez who came in the 1776 Anza party).

CANUELAS, Francisco (see Cayuelas)

CARDENAS, Ygnacio
Adopted son of Jose Antonio Sanchez in Anza party. Probably same as *Melchor Cardenas*, a workman at San Francisco presidio in 1777.

CARPIO, Juan Jose and Juan Antonio

Indian vaqueros, natives of Loreto, at Monterey assigned in 1770 to Paquebot *San Carlos* for its voyage south.

CARRILLO, Guillermo

Soldier in 1769 Portola party. Probably remained at Monterey in 1770. Corporal of San Carlos mission guard in 1772; corporal at San Gabriel by July, 1775; sergeant when he died at Monterey in 1782.

CARRILLO, Mariano

Brother of Guillermo. Both born at Presidio of Loreto, sons of Juan Carrillo and Eugenia Millar. Mariano enlisted at Loreto in 1756. He was in the Portola party, going back to San Diego with Portola and then returning in 1770 with a pack train to Monterey. He was alferez and Monterey storekeeper when he died in 1782. Apparently neither brother married.

CARRILLO, Jose Ramon

Nephew of Guillermo and Mariano. Born at Presidio of Loreto, son of Hilario Carrillo and Josefa de Pasos. He was 23 years old in the 1769 Portola party. He was corporal at Monterey when he married in 1781 Tomasa Ygnacia Lugo, daughter of Francisco Lugo. His marriage was at San Carlos but his children were born at San Gabriel, Santa Barbara and San Francisco.

CARRILLO, Pedro Guadalupe

Lower California Indian, who remarried at Monterey in 1770. Married Victoria Maria, Carmel neophyte, and later Francisca Maria, Carmel neophyte. No record of children.

CASILLAS, Juan Manuel

With Portola in 1769. No other record.

CASTELO, Agustin

Born in 1737 in Sinaloa. With Portola in 1769. Appeared in records at San Antonio in 1773 and at San Carlos in 1774.

CASTRO, Joaquin Isidro

Born in 1732 in Sinaloa. Came as a soldier in 1776 Anza party. He brought his wife, Martina Botiller, also a native of Sinaloa. When Santa Clara mission was established in 1777 he was sent to the guard there They lived in or near San Jose until Joaquin Isidro died at Monterey in 1802. Martina died in Santa Cruz in 1813. They brought eight children and an 8-year-old Indian boy servant, *Francisco Antonio.*

The children were:

Ygnacio Clemente, aged 20 in 1776. Married in 1780 at Mission Dolores, Maria Barbara Pacheco, daughter of Salvio Pacheco, who died in 1810 at San Jose. Ygnacio Clemente then married Clementina Montero, daughter of Manuel Montero. He was drowned carrying the military mail in 1817 and was buried at San Juan Bautista.

Ana Josefa, aged 18 in 1776. Married in 1776 at San Carlos, Jose Maria Soberanes. As widow she married in 1816 at San Carlos, Jose Miguel Uribe.

Maria Encarnacion, aged 12 in 1776. Married in 1782 at Santa Clara, Surgeon Jose Davila and returned to Mexico with him, being in Mexico City in 1800.

Jose Mariano, aged 9 in 1776. Married in 1790 at Santa Barbara, Josefa Romero, native of Lower California, daughter of Juan Maria Romero.

Joaquin, aged 6 in 1776. Married in 1791 at Mission Dolores, Antonia Amador, native of Loreto, daughter of Pedro Amador. They baptised 11 children at San Carlos and Santa Cruz. Antonia died at Santa Cruz in 1827 and Joaquin in 1830 married Rosalia Briones, aged 14, daughter of Manuel Briones of San Jose. They had four children. Joaquin died in 1838 at Santa Cruz.

Francisco Maria, aged 2 in 1776. Married in 1793 at Santa Clara, Gabriela Berreyessa, daughter of Nicolas Berreyessa. Francisco died in 1831.

Maria del Carmen, aged 10 in 1776. Married in 1814 at Santa Clara, Ventura Amezquita.

Carlos, born on overland march from Sonora. Married in 1805 at Santa Barbara, Rosaria Garcia. Mayordomo of Santa Cruz mission in 1812 and of Santa Clara mission in 1820.

CAYUELAS (also spelled Canuelas), Francisco
Spaniard. Catalonian Volunteer. Remained at Monterey in 1770. Recorded as *Natural de Ciudad de Lorca en el Reyna de Murcia*. Married Maria Dolores, neophyte of San Luis Obispo. He died at San Luis Obispo in 1830.

CERVANTES, Pablo Victoriano
Soldier in Portola. In records at Monterey in 1776. Killed in Yuma massacre on Colorado river in 1781.

CHACON, Juan
Skilled workman who remained at Monterey in 1770 but apparently returned to Mexico on the *San Antonio* in 1771.

CHAMORRO, Fernando Hernandez
Born in City of Mexico. Left at Monterey by the *Santiago* in 1774. Brought wife, Ana Maria Hurtado, and two daughters, Cypriana and Maria del Carmen The latter married Marcelino Bravo at San Carlos in 1774.

CLUA, Domingo
Catalonian Volunteer, left at Monterey in 1770. Married in 1773 at San Carlos, Carmel neophyte Maria Rosa.

CONTRERAS, Luis
Muleteer with Portola. Probably an Indian.

CORDERO, Cristobal
With Portola, says Eldredge.

CORDERO, Francisco
Soldier at Monterey in March, 1773.

CORDERO, Mariano Antonio
Born 1750 at Loreto. Soldier with Portola. Married January 7, 1777, at Mission Dolores, Juana Francisca Pinto, daughter of Pablo Pinto. Corporal of the Santa Clara mission guard in 1785. Tailor at Santa Barbara in 1790.

CORONEL, Juan Antonio (Mulatto)
Muleteer who by poultices cured Fr. Serra's leg May 18, 1769, on way from Vellicata to San Diego. He was at Monterey at its founding in 1770; at San Antonio in 1773. He is listed as a soldier February 21, 1773, when he was a godparent at Carmel.

CORTARA, Jose
Mexican soldier on *Fragata San Felipe* who had completed his term of enlistment on the China run; put ashore at Monterey in 1784. Buried January 15, 1786, at San Carlos.

CORTES, Alejo
Ex-sailor, servant or unskilled worker, left at Monterey by the *San Antonio* in 1771. There is a *Pedro* Cortes listed as a sailor-servant at Carmel in 1773.

COTA, Andres
In 1769 Portola expedition, says Eldredge.

COTA, Antonio
Soldier in Portola party. Born in 1732 at Fuerte, Sinaloa. God-father at San Gabriel in November, 1774, and at San Diego 1782–90.

COTA, Pablo Antonio
Soldier in Portola party who remained at Monterey in 1770. His wife was Rosa Maria Lugo, a native of Sinaloa. He was sergeant in command of the guard at San Buenaventura in 1782–87 and then at Purisima. His wife died in 1797 at San Buenaventura. Pablo, then alferez, died in 1800, Santa Barbara. Nine children were born 1779–1800.

CRUZ, Juan de la
In the Carmel and San Antonio missions' guards in 1773.

CRUZ, Tomas de la
Workman at San Francisco presidio in 1777.

⟋⟍

DAVILA, Jose Joaquin
Surgeon left at Monterey by the *Santiago* in 1774. He brought his wife, Josefa Carbajal, who died in San Francisco in 1780. Davila married at Santa Clara in 1782, Encarnacion Castro, daughter of Joaquin Isidro Castro. They left for Mexico before the end of 1783 and were in Mexico City in 1800.

DAVILA, Manuel
Master carpenter left at Monterey by the *Santiago* in 1774. He brought his wife, Geronima Montana, native of Guadalajara.

DOMINGUEZ, Juan Jose
Born in 1747 at Tepic. Soldier who arrived at Monterey in 1770 with a pack train from San Diego. He was corporal at San Luis Obispo and San Antonio in 1780 and in 1785 went to Santa Barbara as a settler and was given San Pedro rancho.

DUARTE, Alexo Antonio
Soldier, born in El Real del Rio Chico, son of Francisco Duarte and Ygnacia Espinosa. He appeared as godfather at San Gabriel in November, 1772; was at Monterey early in 1773 and married in June, 1773, at San Antonio, Maria Gertrudis, neophyte. He died in 1779 at Monterey. His widow married Francisco Villa-Gomez.

DUARTE, Juan Pasqual

Lower California Indian, born at Loreto. He remained at Monterey in 1770 and was sent to San Antonio mission on its founding in 1771.

ESPINOSA, Cayetano

With wife, Seraphina Lugo, and six sons came with Rivera in October, 1774. Both parents and all six sons were natives of Villa Sinaloa. A seventh son was born at Soledad in 1796. The sons were:

Antonio. Bachelor, soldier of Monterey presidio, buried September 5, 1779, at San Carlos.

Salvador Manuel. Married 1779 at Santa Clara, Gertrudis Valencia, daughter of Manuel Valencia.

Jose Joaquin. In 1770 soldier at San Diego. Married in 1780 at San Carlos, Catalina Maria, neophyte. Killed in the Yuma massacre of July 18, 1781, on the Colorado river.

Jose Tomas. Soldier at Monterey presidio, married 1785 at San Antonio, Maria Metilde.

Jose Gabriel, at Santa Barbara in 1785. Married, 1790 at San Gabriel, Maria Josefa Osuna, native of Loreto. He died before his son, Jose Gabriel Simeon, was born February 19, 1791, at San Gabriel.

Jose Cayetano. Soldier, married in 1793 at San Carlos, Maria Rose Tapia, widow of Sebastian Antonio Lopez, daughter of Felipe Santiago Tapia.

Salvador. Born March 28, 1796, at Soledad. Married in 1814 at Santa Clara, Josefa Lugarda Castro, daughter of Macario Castro.

ESPINOSA, Jose Miguel

Born in Rosario, Sinaloa. Soldier in 1781 Sonora Party to San Gabriel. Married in 1795 at Santa Clara, Maria Higuera, daughter of Jose Manuel Higuera.

ESTEVAN, Antonio

Ex-sailor left at Monterey by the *San Antonio* in 1771. Unskilled worker at San Antonio mission in 1773. He was a native of Guanaclatan, Soplotlan, Mexico.

ESTEVANEL, Ignacio
Catalonian Volunteer, probably came from Guaymas with Fages in December, 1771.

ESTRADA, Jose Bonifacio
Soldier. Godfather at San Gabriel in November, 1774. At Monterey presidio in 1783.

⊸≣⊷

FAGES, Pedro
Native of Catalonia. Lieutenant of Volunteers in 1769 Portola party. Remained at Monterey in 1770; military commander at Monterey in 1774; returned as governor of California in 1782–86.

FELIZ, Claudio
Soldier in Carmel in 1773, probably came with Fages in 1771.

FELIZ, Jose Vicente
Born in 1741 at Real de los Alamos, Sonora. Recruit soldier with Anza. His wife, Manuela Pincuelar, died in childbirth the first night out from Tubac. He brought seven children: Jose Francisco, Jose Doroteo, Jose de Jesus, Jose Antonio Capistrano, Maria Loreta, Maria Antonia, Maria Manuela. Jose Vicente was transferred to the San Diego company before 1782 and in 1802 or earlier was given Feliz rancho, now Griffith Park in Los Angeles.

Jose Doroteo, the second son, married Juana Josefa Villalobo at Santa Barbara in 1787.

FERRER, Pablo
Catalonian Volunteer, probably came with Fages in 1771. Godfather at San Carlos in 1773.

FIGUEROA, Jose Maria
At Monterey before 1776; probably servant.

FLORES, Antonio Cayetano
Sailor left at Monterey by the *San Antonio* in 1770. Buried September 20, 1770, at San Carlos.

FLORES (alias Fuentes), Jose Maria
Lower California Indian; servant. Soldier of same name at Santa Barbara, aged 24 in 1790, probably the same person.

FLORES, Hermenegildo
Soldier with Rivera in 1770.

FUENTE, Andres

Lower California Indian; remained at Monterey in 1770. Married Atanasia Maria, Carmel neophyte.

⊸≣⊷

GALINDO, Nicolas

Born in 1743 in Real de Santa Eulalia, Chihuahua. Brought wife, Maria Teresa Pinto, daughter of Pablo Pinto, and one son, Juan Venancio, in Anza party. They baptised in 1778 at Mission Dolores, Francisco Alexandro, who died in 1801, and in 1796 at Santa Clara, Pantaleon, who died the following year. Nicolas Galindo died in 1803 at San Jose and Teresa, his widow, in 1804, married Pedro Amador.

Venancio, by 1795 a soldier, married in that year at Mission Dolores, Ramona Lorenza Sanchez, daughter of Jose Antonio Sanchez.

GALLEGOS, Carlos

Veteran soldier with Anza. Brought wife, Maria Josefa Espinosa. Gallegos was killed by Yumas on the Colorado river in 1781.

GARCIA, Jose Antonio

Born in Culiacan, Sinaloa. Soldier with Anza Brought wife, Maria Josefa de Acuna, and five children. He was sent to the Santa Clara mission guard in 1777. He died the following year and his widow married Juan Antonio Amezquita.

The children who came from Sinaloa were: Maria Graciana, Maria Josefa, Jose Vicente, Jose Francisco, Juan Guillermo.

GARCIA, Felipe Santiago

Born in Villa de Sinaloa. Soldier with Rivera from Sonora in October, 1774. Brought wife, Petra Alcantara de Lugo. A son, Juan Jose, born November 11, 1774, at San Luis Obispo, was said the first all-white child born in California. The couple baptised at least fifteen children. Garcia, a blacksmith, died in 1822 at Monterey.

GONGORA, Jose Maria

Soldier who remained at Monterey in 1770. Born in Loreto. He married in 1776 at San Diego, Rosalia Verdugo, daughter of Diego Verdugo and Jacinta Carrillo. Gongora was corporal of the San Gabriel mission guard in 1772 and at San Diego in 1774.

GONZALES, Rafael Gerardo

Born in Sinaloa; soldier who came before Rivera He married in 1785 at San Buenaventura, Tomasa Quintero, daughter of Luis Quintero. He was poisoned by Indians at Santa Barbara February 14, 1797.

GONZALES, Diego

Lieutenant in command at Monterey 1781–85 and at San Francisco 1785–87, when he was sent back to the Mexican frontier.

GONZALES, Jose Maria

Soldier who remained at Monterey in 1770. Married Antonia Josefa, Carmel neophyte.

GONZALES, Alejo Antonio

Soldier at Monterey in 1773 or before. Corporal at San Luis Obispo in 1772. Transferred to San Diego in 1775.

GONZALES, Jose Manuel

Born in Valle de San Bartolome, Sonora. Soldier recruit with Anza. Brought wife, Maria Micaela Bojorgues, who was also referred to in records as Micaela Ruiz.

Children who came with them were: Juan Jose, Ramon, Francisco (Faustino?), Maria Gregoria.

Micaela died in 1780 at San Jose and Gonzales married in 1784, at Santa Clara, Maria Gertrudis Azeves, daughter of Antonio Azeves. Manuel Gonzales died in 1804 at San Jose.

GONZALES, Inocencio

Unskilled workman at Monterey before Rivera

GRIJALVA, Juan Pablo

Born in 1742 at la Valle de San Luis, Sonora. Enlisted January 1, 1763, at Presidio de Terenate, Sonora. Sergeant in Anza party. Brought wife, Maria Dolores Valencia, and three children:

Maria Josefa, aged 9 in 1776, married in 1782 at Mission Dolores, Antonio Yorba, Catalonian Volunteer of 1769 Portola party.

Maria del Carmen, aged 4 in 1776, married in 1785 at Mission Dolores, Pedro Regalado Peralta.

Claudio, few months old in 1776, died in 1806 at San Diego.

GUERRERO, Jose Maria

Native of Guadalajara Soldier of Monterey presidio, buried October 9, 1779, at San Carlos.

GUTIERREZ, Ignacio Maria

Recruit soldier with Anza. Brought wife, Ana Maria Osuna, and three children:

Maria Petronia, aged 10 in 1776, who married in 1782 at Mission Dolores, Juan Francisco Bernal. Two later husbands were Cornelio Valderrama and Francisco Gonzales.

Maria de los Santos, aged 7 in 1776, who married in 1780 at Mission Dolores, Alexo Feliciano Miranda.

Diego, born at the Gila river on the trip from Sonora.

GUTIERREZ, Tomasa and Eustaquia (see Arballo)

GUTIERREZ, Juan Nepomuceno

Lower California Indian. Remained at Monterey in 1770. Married in 1779 at San Antonio, Eulalia Vargas, neophyte of that mission.

HEREDIA, Bernardo de

Soldier who came with Rivera. He brought his wife, Nicolasa de Elisalde; both natives of Villa Sinaloa. Their daughter, Maria Josefa de la Luz, was the first white birth at Monterey on February 13, 1775.

HIGUERA, Jose Manuel

Head of one of twelve families who came from San Blas to Loreto and overland to San Diego in 1774. He brought his wife, Antonia Redondo, and two sons, Juan Jose, 3, and Juan Faustino, less than a year old. Jose Manuel was at Monterey in 1776 and at San Jose in 1778.

HIGUERA, Ignacio Antonio Anastacio

Born in 1753 at Sinaloa. Came in Anza party with his wife, 13-year-old Micaela Bojorgues, daughter of Jose Ramon Bojorgues. They baptised a son, Jose Loreto, at Mission Dolores in 1778.

HUGUET, Andres

Catalonian Volunteer who came probably with Fages in December, 1771. Godparent at San Carlos in 1773.

IBARRA, Francisco

Unskilled worker; at Monterey before 1776.

IBARRA, Ramon

Born in 1763 at Real de los Alamos, Sonora, son of Antonio

Ibarra. Soldier; married in 1785 at Monterey, Maria del Carmen, Yuma Indian from the Colorado.

INSUA (see LOPEZ Insua)

ISLAS, Miguel

Soldier in 1769 Portola party, who later accompanied Fr. Crespi with Rivera to San Diego.

◄■►

JUAREZ, Francisco

Soldier of the 1781 Sonora party to San Gabriel. His wife was Vicenta de Leon. Francisco died March 1, 1782, at San Gabriel and Vicenta married August 11, 1782, at San Gabriel, Jose Antonio Rodriguez and went with him to Monterey soon after. Francisco and Vicenta had two sons:

Jose Joaquin baptised at San Gabriel July 28, 1782. He settled at Santa Cruz after serving in mission guards at San Luis Obispo and San Carlos. His wife was Pasquala Lorenzana.

Francisco, an older brother of Jose Joaquin was born in Cosala, Sinaloa. In 1802 he married at Santa Barbara, Maria Dolores Cota, widow of Manuel Sepulveda. Francisco was in the Santa Cruz mission guard in 1803–14 and later at Monterey.

◄■►

LABRA, Juan Antonio

Soldier who came before Rivera. Executed by firing squad at Monterey; no reason given in burial record. Buried October 14, 1781, at San Carlos.

LARA, Jose Fernando de Velasco

Came from Sonora 1780 or 1781; died in 1782 at Santa Barbara. His widow, Maria Antonia Campos, married in 1782, Luis Gonzaga Lugo, member of the 1769 Portola party.

LINARES, Ignacio

Born in 1745 at San Miguel de Horcasitas. Veteran soldier in Anza party. Died June 5, 1805, at San Jose. Brought wife, Maria Gertrudis Rivas, and four children: Maria Gertrudis, 7; Juan Jose, 3; Maria Juliana, 4; Salvador, 1.

LOPEZ, Cosmo

Lower California Indian. Remained at Monterey in 1770. Married Escolastica, Carmel neophyte.

LOPEZ, Joaquin

Native of Villa de Fuerte, Sinaloa. Soldier of Monterey presidio when he died, unmarried, in 1779.

LOPEZ, Jose (see Arballo)

LOPEZ Insua, Manuel

Native Juy in the *Reyna de Galicia,* sailor. Buried 1774 at San Carlos.

LOPEZ, Sebastian Antonio

Recruit soldier in Anza party. Brought wife, Felipa Neri (some records said Felipa Xermana) and three children, all born in Sinaloa: Maria Tomasa, Maria Justa, and *Sebastian,* who married in 1780, at Santa Clara, Rosa Tapia, daughter of Santiago Tapia.

LUGO, Luis Gonzaga de

Native of Palo Blanco. Member of 1769 Portola party. God-father at San Gabriel in November, 1772. At San Antonio mission in 1773, probably skilled worker. Married in 1782 at Santa Barbara, Maria Antonia Campos, Indian, widow of Jose Fernando de Velasco y Lara. As widower in 1792 at Santa Barbara he married Perseverancia Cortes, widow of Tomas Gonzales.

LUGO, Francisco Salvador de

Came soon after 1769. His wife was Juana Maria Rita Martinez, alias Villanasur, Villanaques. They baptised a son, *Jose Ignacio,* at San Luis Obispo, in January, 1781. A daughter, *Tomasa Ignacia,* who at San Carlos in 1781 married Raimundo Carrillo, was undoubtedly born before her parents came to California.

LUGO, Zeferino de

Spaniard. Head of one of twelve families who came from San Blas to Loreto and overland to San Diego in 1774. He was brother of the wife of Xavier Beltran. He was in the 1778 San Jose census, aged 40; wife, Gertrudis Pacheco, 36. Zeferino was buried December 18, 1804, at Santa Cruz.

▪◼▪

MALARET, Domingo

Catalonian Volunteer who remained at Monterey in 1770.

MANIGUEZ, Sebastian

Invalido soldier who arrived at Monterey in 1770 with a pack train from San Diego.

MARCHA, Carlos de la

Catalonian Volunteer who probably came with Fages in December, 1771.

MARQUINA, Juan Tomas

Native of Pueblo de Huirivis, Sonora. Mariner of the Paquebot *El Principe*. One of five sailors put ashore with scurvy who died at Monterey in 1770.

MARTINEZ, Jose Maria

Native of Topahue, Sonora. In Rivera's 1781 recruits from Sinaloa and Sonora. Joined the Monterey company. Married February 7, 1785, at Santa Clara, Maria Josefa Garcia, daughter of Jose Antonio Garcia. He died in 1819 at San Jose.

MARTINEZ y GUZMAN, Toribio

Native of Guadalajara. Soldier who brought his wife, Ysabel Talamantes, native of El Real del Rosario, near Guadalajara.

MARTINEZ, Antonio Estevan

Native of Pueblo de Ahuacatlan, Zapotlan el Grande. Married to Juana Petrona Curial of that place. Sailor buried at San Carlos September 1, 1775.

MESA, Jose Valerio

Born in 1734 at Opodepe, Sonora. Veteran soldier, corporal, in Anza party. Brought wife, Leonor Barboa, and six children, all born at the Presidio of Altar: Jose Joaquin, 12; Jose Ignacio, 9; Ignacio Dolores, 8; Maria Manuela, 7; Jose Antonio, ?; Juan, 3.

MIRANDEZ, Alexo Feliciano

Servant or unskilled workman. Came to Monterey before 1776.

MOLES, Jose

Catalonian Volunteer who came from Guaymas 1771–72.

MONTANA, Antonio

Catalonian Volunteer. Native of Ossio in Cataluna, Obispado de Tortosa. In San Carlos records as early as August, 1771. At San Luis Obispo in 1773. When a widower of Maria del Pilar, a San Luis Obispo neophyte, he married in 1801 at San Carlos, Maria Isidora Rosalio, native of Monterey presidio. He was buried in 1802 at San Carlos.

MONMANY, Luis

Catalonian Volunteer. In records at San Antonio in 1772; at San Carlos in 1773.

MORAGA, Joaquin

Born in 1741. Soldier in Anza party. In 1781 he brought to San Francisco his wife, Maria del Pilar de Leon y Barcelo, who had been sick in 1776. With her came their son, *Gabriel*, born in 1765 at Presidio de Fronteras, Sonora. Joaquin was buried in 1785 at San Francisco. His widow died in October, 1808, at San Francisco Gabriel was buried in 1823 at Santa Barbara.

MUNOZ, Tomas Maria

Laborer left at Monterey by the *Santiago* in 1774.

MUNOZ, Francisco

Bachelor settler in 1776 Anza party.

MURILLO, Julian

Soldier at Monterey and San Antonio in 1773.

◆

NEVE, Felipe de

Spanish major of cavalry; governor at Loreto in 1775; at Monterey 1777 to 1782.

NIETO, (see Perez Nieto)

NORIEGA, Jose Ramon

Soldier at Monterey before Rivera in May, 1774. Corporal of the San Luis Obispo mission guard 1772-73. Godfather at San Gabriel in January, 1773.

◆

OCHOA, Maria Teresa

Native of Tepic, daughter of Maria Teresa Ochoa, married July 25, 1774, at San Carlos, Lorenzo de Resa. She had come to Monterey as servant for Don Rafael de Pedro Gil.

OLIVERA, Diego Jose

Native of Villa de Cadareita. Laborer who remained at Monterey in 1770; went to San Francisco in 1777. When in 1804 at Santa Clara he married Felipa Saens, he was widower of a neophyte.

OLIVERA, Juan Maria

Soldier. Godfather at San Gabriel in December, 1772; in the mission guard at San Antonio 1773-4; corporal at San Diego 1791-95. His wife was Guadalupe Briones.

ONTIVEROS, Jose Antonio

Soldier at Monterey 1773 or earlier. Perhaps the same Jose Antonio Ontiveros, soldier, with the 1780 Sonora expedition to Los Angeles, native of Chametla, Sonora.

ORTEGA, Jose Francisco

Born in 1734 at Celaya, Guanajuato. Corporal at Loreto presidio from 1756. Pathfinder in 1769 Portola party. Returned from San Diego to Monterey with a pack train in 1770. Died in 1798 at Santa Barbara. His son,

Ignacio, born in El Real de Santa Cruz, was perhaps also in Portola party. Ignacio was at San Juan Bautista in 1795 and settler near there from 1797.

◄Ξ►

PATRON, Francisco

Lower California Indian who remained at Monterey in 1770.

PACHECO, Juan Salvio

Recruit soldier in 1776 Anza party. Brought wife, Maria del Carmen del Valle, and five children: Miguel, 20; Ignacia Gertrudis, 15; Ignacio, 15; Bartolome Ignacio, 10; Maria Barbara, 10.

PATRON, Francisco

Lower California Indian who remained at Monterey in 1770.

PENA, Francisco Maria

Apparently laborer at Monterey before Rivera. Probably same as:

PENA, Francisco

Soldier at San Antonio in 1773, at San Juan Capistrano before 1775; killed in Yuma massacre on the Colorado River July 18, 1781.

PENA, Jose Antonio

Soldier at San Gabriel in 1772, at San Antonio in 1773. Married Gertrudis Lorenzana. Died in 1852 at San Jose.

PENA, Luis

Soldier in Portola party who remained at Monterey or returned there from San Diego in 1770–71. Married in 1780 at San Buenaventura, Maria Paula Segunda Cortes, a native of Cosala, Sinaloa.

PERALTA, Gabriel

Corporal in Anza party. Born in 1731 in Presidio de Terenate, Sonora. Died October 22, 1807, at Santa Clara. Brought wife,

Francisca Xaviera Valenzuela, and four children: Juan Jose, 18; Luis Maria, 17; Pedro Regalado, 11; Maria Gertrudis, ——.

PEREZ NIETO, Manuel

In Anza party. Retired, living at Santa Barbara in 1785.

PERIQUES (also spelled Pericas), Miguel Sobrevia

Corporal of Catalonian Volunteers. Remained at Monterey in 1770. Went with Serra in 1771 to command the guard at the founding of San Antonio mission. Probably went back to Mexico about 1773.

PICO, Santiago

Recruit soldier in Anza party. Brought wife, Maria Jacinta Vastida, and seven children, all born in San Xavier le Cabazan on Rio Piastla, Sinaloa: Jose Dolores, 12; Jose Dario, 11; Jose Miguel, 7; Francisco Xavier, ——; Patricio, 5; Maria Antonia Tomasa,——; Maria Josefa, ——.

PINTO, Pablo

Born in 1732 at Villa de Sinaloa. Recruit soldier with Anza. Brought wife, Francisca Xaviera Ruelas, and four children: Juan Maria, 17; Juana Santos, (wife of Casimiro Varela); Juana Francisca; Jose Marcelo.

PLANELLS, Valentin

Catalonian Volunteer, from Guaymas in 1771–72. Mentioned at San Antonio mission in 1772 as Ramon Planells.

PLANES, Geronimo

Catalonian Volunteer who remained at Monterey in 1770; godfather at San Gabriel in February, 1772.

PORTELLA, Francisco

Native of Ciudad de Tarragona, Cataluna. Catalonian Volunteer from Guaymas in 1771–72. Died on sentinel duty and buried April 26, 1774, at San Carlos.

PRAT, Pedro

Physician. Arrived at Monterey May 24, 1770, on the *San Antonio*. Was sent back, insane, to Mexico on *El Principe* July 1, 1771.

PUIG, Juan

Native of Figueroa, Cataluna. Sergeant of Volunteers who remained at Monterey in 1770. Godfather at San Gabriel in November, 1772, and at Carmel in February, 1773.

RAMIREZ ARRELLANO (see Arrellano)

RAMIREZ, Ignacio

Native of Compostela, Jalisco. One of five sailors with scurvy put ashore from *El Principe*. He died July 26, 1770, at Monterey. His was the first burial at Carmel mission. He was a mulatto slave who had saved enough money to buy his freedom.

RAMIREZ, Jose Basilio

Unskilled mission worker; arrived at Monterey before 1776.

RESA, Lorenzo de

Native of Ciudad de Xeres de la Frontera in Andalusia. Unskilled worker left by *Santiago* in 1774; departed in 1776. Married July 25, 1774, at San Carlos, Maria Teresa Ochoa.

REYES y DIAZ, Juan Francisco

Soldier in 1769 Portola party. At San Antonio mission in 1772–73. Soldier of Monterey company when, on January 1, 1782, at San Gabriel, he married Maria Lusia del Carmen Dominguez, daughter of Ildefonso Dominguez. He baptised two children at San Carlos in 1785 and 1786; in 1787 retired from the army, going to Los Angeles where two more children were born. He was alcalde of Los Angeles in 1793-95.

REYES, Martin (Sometimes Miguel)

Soldier in San Antonio mission guard 1772-73. Married August 26, 1795, at San Gabriel, Celia Martin, and settled at Los Angeles where he died before 1816.

RIERA, Cipriano

Lower California Indian who remained at Monterey in 1770.

ROBLES, Juan Jose

Soldier at San Antonio in 1772. Killed in 1781 Yuma massacre on the Colorado river.

ROBLES, Manuel

Soldier at Monterey before Rivera. Corporal of the San Gabriel mission guard in May, 1773.

RODRIGUEZ, Jose Antonio

Native of Compostela, Jalisco. Soldier at San Gabriel when, August 11, 1782, he married Vicenta de Leon, widow of Francisco Juarez. Sent to the northern mission guards he baptised eight children at San Carlos, San Luis Obispo and San Antonio. He settled at Branciforte as a retired soldier in 1798. He was buried in 1820 at San Carlos.

RODRIGUEZ, Manuel
Native of Guadalajara, where his parents were Jose Rodriguez and Antonia Estrada. He was a master carpenter. He married November 11, 1781, at San Carlos, Maria Valvanera Antuna, daughter of Jose Manuel Antuna. They baptised thirteen children at San Carlos, Santa Clara and Soledad.

ROMERO, Jose Antonio
Native of Guadalajara. Married January 12, 1778, at Santa Clara, Maria Petra Aceves. Settler at San Jose in 1778; land grantee in 1783. He was buried in 1802 at Santa Clara.

ROSALES, Jose Bernardo
A native of Parras, presidio muleteer at Monterey, 1773.

ROSALIO, Eugenio
Soldier who came with Rivera in May, 1774.

RUBIO, Carlos Maria
Catalonian Volunteer who remained at Monterey in 1770. He was married but his wife was not in California.

RUBIO, Juan Antonio
Soldier who came to Monterey before Rivera.

RUIZ, Diego
Soldier who came to Monterey before Rivera.

RUIZ, Jose Alexandro
Soldier who came to Monterey before Rivera.

RUIZ, Gervasio Antonio
Probably laborer; at Monterey before 1776.

RUIZ, Juan Maria
Sergeant of Catalonian Volunteers who remained at Monterey in 1770. He married Margarita Cortona, a neophyte of the San Antonio mission, who died at Santa Clara in 1823. They baptised at least six children 1783–1813 at San Antonio, San Carlos, and Santa Clara.

SAENS (or Saez), Justo Nazario
Born in Villa de Sinaloa; came with the Rivera recruits in October, 1774. Brought wife, Micaela Sotelo, also a native of Sinaloa. They brought no children with them but baptised *Juana Maria* on May 30, 1775, at San Carlos, and at least five more prior to Justo's death at San Jose in 1796.

SAL, Hermenegildo

Native of Valdomero, Toledo, Spain. Came as soldier with Rivera in October, 1774. Married May 16, 1777, at Mission Dolores, Maria Josefa Amezquita, daughter of Juan Antonio Amezquita. She had been born at the Presidio de Terenate, Sonora, and come to California with her parents in 1776.

SALAZAR, Jose Bonifacio

Probably laborer; at Monterey before Rivera.

SANCHEZ, Jose Antonio

Born in 1751 at Villa de Sinaloa. Recruit soldier in Anza party. Brought wife, Maria Dolores Morales, and two children, Maria Josefa, 7; Jose Antonio, 2; and an adopted son, Ignacio Cardenas. At least five more daughters were born by 1782.

SANCHEZ, Manuel

Sailor who remained at Monterey in 1770.

SANCHEZ, Jose Tadeo

Native of Sinaloa who came, aged 25, with the Rivera party from Sonora which arrived at San Gabriel July 14, 1781. He brought his wife, Petra Montiel, and a daughter, Maria Antonia. Sanchez and his wife were at San Antonio in 1781 and at Santa Barbara from 1785.

SANTIAGO, Feliciano

Skilled worker who came with Rivera in October, 1774.

SEGURA, Jose Gregorio

Blacksmith, from Guadalajara, left at Monterey by the *San Antonio* in 1771.

SERRA, (spelled also Sierra, q.v.)

SERRANO, Francisco

Native of Spain. At Monterey about 1780. In 1784, soldier of the San Diego Company, with wife, Valvanera Silva, baptised daughter Maria Rafaela Antonia at San Gabriel.

SEVILLA, Francisco

Married in 1778 at Santa Clara, Maria Petra Aceves, daughter of Antonio Quitario of the Anza party. He was undoubtedly the Indian boy servant who came with the family of Joaquin Isidro Castro.

SIERRA, (also spelled Serra) Jose

Catalonian Volunteer, from Guaymas in 1771–72. Mentioned at was godfather at San Carlos in 1773.

SINOVA, Francisco

Soldier with Rivera recruits in October, 1774. *Vaquero* at San Jose in 1777. Married January 7, 1777, at Mission Dolores, Maria Gertrudis Bojorgues, daughter of Ramon Bojorgues. He went in 1784 to Los Angeles, where he was alcalde in 1789.

SIRERA, Miguel

Catalonian Volunteer. At San Antonio in 1772, at Monterey in 1773.

SOBERANES, Jose Maria

Born in 1753 in Villa de Sinaloa. Soldier in 1769 Portola party. Married May 29, 1776, at San Carlos, Ana Josefa Castro, 16, daughter of Joaquin Isidro Castro. Buried at San Carlos September 23, 1803.

SOBERANO, Augustin Geronimo

Ex-sailor; laborer; came to Monterey before 1776.

SOBREVIA Periques (see Periques)

SOLER, Juan

Spaniard; storekeeper; left at Monterey by the *Santiago* in 1774. Died in Monterey in 1781.

SORDER, Jose

Catalonian Volunteer who came from Guaymas in 1771–72.

SOTELO, Jose Antonio

Recruit soldier in 1776 Anza party. Brought wife, either Gertrudis Peralta or Manuela Gertrudis Buelna (both are mentioned in various records), and one son, Ramon.

SOTO, Alejandro

Soldier at Monterey in 1770.

SOTO, Ignacio

Born in 1749 in Sinaloa. Recruit soldier with Anza. Brought wife, Maria Barbara Espinosa de Lugo, sister of Francisco Lugo, and two children, Maria Antonia, 2, and Jose Antonio, 1. Ignacio was buried at Santa Clara in 1807.

SOTO, Juan Antonio

Mission worker; skilled laborer; remained at Monterey in 1770.

SOTO, Mateo

Soldier who came before Rivera; at Monterey in 1773.

SOTO-MAYOR, Antonio de la Cruz

Soldier who remained at Monterey in 1770; at San Antonio in 1771.

TAPIA, Felipe Santiago

Born in 1745 in Culiacan. Recruit soldier with Anza. Brought wife, Juana Maria Cardenas, and nine children: Jose Bartolome, Juan Jose, Jose Christoval, Jose Francisco, Jose Victor, Maria Rosa, 15, Maria Antonia, 13, Maria Manuela, 10, Maria Ysidora. They baptised five more children at Santa Clara 1778–86.

TOLEDO, Conrado de

Mexican Indian; Sierra Gorda neophyte; left at Monterey by the *Santiago* in 1774.

◄═►

URCELINO, Jose

Carpenter; left at Monterey by the *San Antonio* in 1771. In San Carlos mission record in 1773. He was killed in the Indian attack on San Diego, November 4, 1775.

◄═►

VALLEJO, Ignacio Vicente Ferrer

Born at Hacienda de las Canadas, Guadalajara. His father, Geronimo Vallejo, had been sent by the Spanish government as an official to Mexico. Ignacio enlisted at Compostela; arrived at San Diego with Ortega in September, 1774. He died in 1832 at Monterey.

VALDEZ, Juan Bautista

In 1769 Portola party; later on 1774 trip with Anza to Monterey. Acted as courier for Anza.

VALENCIA, Jose Manuel

Born in 1749 at Guadalupe, Zacatecas. Recruit soldier with Anza. Brought wife, Maria de la Luz Munoz, and three children: Maria Gertrudis, 15; Francisco Maria, 8; Ignacio Maria, 3. A daughter, Maria de la Luz, was born at Monterey in 1776 while the parents were on the way to San Francisco. Valencia was buried in 1788 at Santa Clara.

VARELA, Casimiro

Came with Anza; husband of Juana Santos Pinto. They baptised a daughter, Marta, in 1778 at San Carlos.

VARGAS, Manuel

Soldier at San Francisco who in 1784 married at Mission Dolores, Maria Gertrudis Linares, native of Sinaloa, daughter of Ignacio Linares.

VASQUEZ, Juan Antonio

Born in 1735 in Ahualulco, Sonora. Recruit in Anza party; brought wife, Gertrudis Castelo, and three children, Jose Tiburcio, 20, Jose Antonio, 10, and Pedro Jose.

VELASQUEZ, Jose

In 1769 Portola party. First overland courier from Monterey to Loreto, leaving Monterey June 14, 1770.

VERDUGO, Juan Maria

Soldier who remained at Monterey in 1770. Brother of Mariano Verdugo. Retired at Santa Barbara after 1785.

VERDUGO, Mariano de la Luz

Soldier with Anza. Born in 1746 at San Xavier, Lower California. Married November 26, 1788, at Santa Barbara, Maria Loreto Gregoria Espinosa, native of Los Alamos, Sonora, widow of Jose Pedro Loreto Salazar. Mariano was alcalde of Los Angeles 1790–93, 1802. The corporal of the guard at San Antonio, May 15, 1722, was Mariano Verdugo, and in 1773 he is listed at Carmel as Mariano de la Luz Berdugo.

VERDUSCO, Anatasio Xavier

Soldier who married at Monterey in 1770.

VERMELL (Bermejo), Ramon

Catalonian Volunteer from Guaymas in 1771–72. Married May 29, 1773, at San Carlos, the neophyte Luisa Francisca.

VILLA-GOMEZ, Francisco

Soldier who came with Rivera in October, 1774. Married Gertrudis Maria, San Antonio mission neophyte, and Miliciana, San Carlos neophyte. Buried December 12, 1783, at San Carlos.

VILLAVICENCIO (also called simply Villa), Rafael

Native of the Presidio of Loreto. Soldier at Monterey before Rivera. Godfather at San Gabriel in October, 1772. Married June 23, 1773, at San Antonio mission, Ildefonsa, neophyte. Rafael, said aged 81, buried in 1831 at Santa Clara.

VILLELA, Juan Manuel

Soldier of the San Jose escolta in 1778. Probably same as:

VILLELA, Marcos

Soltero in 1776 Anza party. Native of El Real de Tetuache. Married April 25, 1786, at San Carlos, Viridiana Maria Carrillo, neophyte of San Carlos. Buried, retired soldier, at Santa Cruz in 1805.

~∋═∈~

YORBA, Antonio

Corporal of Catalonian Volunteers who remained at Monterey in 1770. Married November 3, 1782, at Mission Dolores, Maria Josefa Grijalva. An earlier wife had been Maria Gracia, San Carlos neophyte; their son, Pedro Antonio, first birth of a white father at Monterey, had died at the age of six years.

PAGE

5. *1787*: More likely 1789; it is improbable that the letter took two years to arrive. Torchiana and Bancroft date the letter October 31, 1789.

5. *1840 earthquake*: May not have happened. In *Annals*, p. 98, Rowland mentions only heavy rains in 1840. See *Santa Cruz Mission* by Phyllis Patten, p. 16.

9. *mission replica*: Work was begun in 1931, according to the plaque on the building.

17. *Juzgado*: It was apparently still standing in the early 90's according to the *Santa Cruz Sentinel* and the County Sanborn maps. It is sometimes known as the Golden Eagle Hotel.

39. *land grants*: The dates and acreages given here differ in some cases from those listed in the *Annals*, p. 101–2. Whether these differences represent corrections, misprints or approximations is unclear. The figures may be compared with those in Robert G. Cowan's *Ranchos of California*.

43. *Roman Rodriguez*: Given as Ramon Rodriguez in some histories.

64. *Bowman house*: South side of Soquel drive, 1½ miles toward Aptos.

64. *Izant place*: North side of Soquel drive, across from Bowman house.

64. *Averon house*: Still standing on west side of Capitola avenue near Highway One.

65. *Martina Castro adobe*: North side of east end of Hill street; torn down.

66. *flour mill*: Just NE of Soquel and Porter.

67. *Daubenbiss and Hames houses*: The Daubenbiss home has been restored. The Hames house, located near the intersection of Papermill road and Old San Jose road, no longer stands.

68. *Starkie's gas station*: NE corner Soquel and N. Main.

68. *Porter's store*: SE corner Porter and Soquel.

71. *apple dryer*: Between Daubenbiss and Porter.

71. *Angell's store*: SE corner Porter and Soquel; followed Porter's store.

72. *Cunnison's garage*: NE corner Soquel and Porter.

72. *Kasseroller's corner*: South side of Soquel drive at Main street.

73. *Fletcher's garage*: Just north of main intersection on west side.

75. *SRA camp*: State Relief Agency, west side of Old San Jose road several miles north of town.

76. *Soquel Inn*: NW corner W. Walnut and Porter.

76. *I.O.O.F.*: SW corner Soquel and Porter; twice rebuilt; now a theater and bakery.

82. *Heath*: Followed in 1940 by T. Davis Preston.

82. *7th Day Adventist*: Still standing, 2501 Porter.

82. *Christian Science*: Now the Soquel Grange, just north of the elementary school.

82. *iron bridge*: Near intersection of Olive Springs and Old San Jose road.
86. *Daubenbis*: Generally spelled with two "s's," although Rowland's copy of the voting list shows only one.
98. *Chapman's mission*: Chapman's view (and all others) was modeled on an 1876 painting by the French artist Leon Trousset.
100. *June 24*: Given as July 24 in *Villa de Branciforte* and July 27 in other sources.
103. *vestige of the villa*: The Lorenzana adobe on N. Branciforte still stands and is the last building of the Villa days.
107. *Pescadero 1857*: This date is most often given as 1868.
121. *Bolcoff*: According to Santa Cruz deed records (Book 3, p. 36), Bolcoff sold the mill to Fleck October 29, 1855. It later passed to Louis Miller, A. Miller and W. A. Mathie before R. C. Kirby took possession.
131. *Rancho del Oso*: About two thirds of the land is now part of Big Basin State Park. The remainder is owned by Hoover's daughters.
143. *adobes*: According to the Santa Cruz deed records (Book 13, p. 240), James and Martin Neary bought the adobe from Patrick Nolan in October, 1870. Nolan bought it October 9, 1865 (Book 7, p. 716).
151. *London Nelson*: Mr. Nelson's first name is variously spelled. Rowland's notes show "Loudon" in typescript and "London" in pencil notation. An article by Jeannette Rowland in *News and Notes of the Santa Cruz Historical Society* for April, 1955, says that the handwritten legal material with Nelson's name can be read either "u" or "n" and that the legal notices in the papers opted for "n." The sign in front of the community center named after Nelson has it "Louden," thus introducing doubt about the last syllable as well as the first.
174. *chalk rock caves*: According to the *Santa Cruz Sentinel*, September 12, 1887, the caves were dug by Santa Cruz Mountain Wine Company and purchased later by Ben Lomond Winery.
197. *East side church*: Was located at 175 Soquel drive.
198. *Methodist Parsonage*: No longer standing, was at 207 Church.
198. *Seventh Day Adventist*: 429 Pennsylvania.
199. *Unitarian*: 517 Center; now Progressive Baptist.
199. *Hackley Hall*: 513 Center; now a vacant lot.
205. *Car barn*: No longer standing.
207. *54 Pacific*: Now 1521 Pacific.
208. *42 Pacific*: Now 1535 Pacific.
210. *1863*: This date is out of sequence, but it is unclear what date is meant.
211. *Park street*: Now Union street.
247. *Planes*: After this entry should come, "Porta, Nicolas, Corporal of Catalonian Volunteers, from Guaymas in 1771–72."

Thanks to Edna Kimbro for her assistance on the notes.

⇥ LOS FUNDADORES INDEX

Aceves, (Azebes)
  Antonio, 240
  Antonio Quitario, 250;
    family, 223
  María Gertrudis, 240
  María Petra, 249, 250
Acuña, María Josefa, 239
Aguilar (Aguiar)
  Cecilia, 229
  Francisco, 224
  José, 226
Alegre, Antonio, 224
Alsaldo, Francisco, 224
Altamirano
  José Antonio, 226
  Justo & family, 224
  Tiburcio, 224
Alvarado
  Bernardo, 225
  José, 225
  Juan, 225
Alvarez
  Ascencio, 225
  Luis & family, 225
Alvirez, Manuel, 225
Alviso
  Domingo, 230; family, 225
  Francisco, 230
Alvitre, see Arbite
Amadór
  Antonia, 234
  Pedro, 226, 234, 239
Amarillas, Juan, 226
Amezquita
  Gertrudis, 224
  Juan Antonio, 239, 250;
    family, 226
  Manuel, 226
  María Agustina, 224
  María Josefa, 250
  Salvador, 226
  (Buena) Ventura, 234
Antuna
  José, 227, 249
  María, 227, 249
Aquezon, Francisco, 224
Arballo, María, 227

Arbitre (Alvitre)
  Juan, 227
  Sebastián, 227
Arce (Arze)
  Joaquín, 228
  José, 227
Archuleta, Ignacio, 227
Arias, Miguel, 227
Arrellano, Ramirez & family, 227–8
Arroya, Manuel, 228
Aruz, Domingo, 228
Arze, see Arce
Avila, Francisco, 228
Ayala, Francisco, 228
Azevedo, Francisco, 228
Azeves, see Aceves

Badiola, Manuel, 228
Barboa, Leonor, 244
Basiola, Marian, 228
Beltrán
  Francisco, 243; family, 228
  Joaquín, 229
  Nicolas, 229
Berdugo, see Verdugo
Bernal
  Francisco, 229
  Juan, 226, 241; family, 229
  Manuel, 230
  Margarita, 226
  María, 230
Berryessa
  Cayetano, 230
  Gabriela, 234
  Isabel, 230
  Nicolás, 230, 234; family, 230
Bojorques
  José, 241; family, 230
  María Agustina, 225
  María Gertrudis, 249
  María Micaela, 240
  Micaela, 241
  Pedro, 225; family, 230
  Ramón, 249
Bonbau, Francisco, 230

General Index ⇥